HISTORY

OF

TENNESSEE

From the Earliest Time to the Present; Together with an Historical and a Biographical Sketch of Cannon, Coffee, Dekale, Warren, White Counties, Besides a Valuable Fund of Notes, Original Observations, Reminiscences, Etc., Etc.

ILLUSTRATED.

Nashville:
THE GOODSPEED PUBLISHING CO.,
1887.

This volume was reproduced from
An 1887 edition located in the
Knoxville Public Library,
Knoxville, Tennessee

All rights reserved. No part of this publication
may be reproduced, stored in a retrieval system,
transmitted in any form, posted on to the web
in any form or by any means without the
prior written permission of the publisher.

Please direct all correspondence and orders to:

www.southernhistoricalpress.com
or
**SOUTHERN HISTORICAL PRESS, Inc.
PO BOX 1267
375 West Broad Street
Greenville, SC   29601**
southernhistoricalpress@gmail.com

Originally published: Nashville, 1882
Reprinted with New Material by:
Southern Historical Press, Inc.
Greenville, SC 2017
New Material Copyright 1979 by
The Rev. Silas Emmett Lucas, Jr.
Easley, SC
ISBN #0-89308-118-3
All rights Reserved.
Printed in the United States of America

PREFACE.

THIS volume has been prepared in response to the prevailing and popular demand for the preservation of local history and biography. The method of preparation followed is the most successful and the most satisfactory yet devised—the most successful in the enormous number of volumes circulated, and the most satisfactory in the general preservation of personal biography and family record conjointly with local history. The number of volumes now being distributed appears fabulous. Within the last four years not less than 20,000 volumes of this class of works have been distributed in Kentucky, and the demand is not half satisfied. Careful estimates place the number circulated in Ohio at 50,000; Pennsylvania, 60,000; New York, 75,000; Indiana, 35,000; Illinois, 40,000; Iowa, 35,000, and every other Northern State at the same proportionate rate. The Southern States, with the exception of Kentucky, Virginia and Georgia, owing mainly to the disorganization succeeding the civil war, yet retain, ready for the publisher, their stories of history and biography. Within the next five years the vast and valuable fund of perishing event in all the Southern States will be rescued from decay, and be recorded and preserved—to be reviewed, studied and compared by future generations. The design of the present extensive historical and biographical research is more to gather and preserve in attractive form while fresh with the evidences of truth, the enormous fund of perishing occurrence, than to abstract from insufficient contemporaneous data remote, doubtful or incorrect conclusions. The true perspective of the landscape of life can only be seen from the distance that lends enchantment to the view. It is asserted that no person is competent to write a philosophical history of his own time—that, owing to conflicting circumstantial evidence that yet conceals the truth, he can not take that luminous, correct, comprehensive, logical and unprejudiced view of passing events that will enable him to draw accurate and enduring conclusions. The duty, then, of a historian of his own time is to collect, classify and preserve the material for the final historian of the future. The present historian deals in fact, the future historian, in conclusion; the work of the former is statistical, of the latter, philosophical.

To him who has not attempted the collection of historical data, the obstacles to be surmounted are unknown. Doubtful traditions, conflicting statements, imperfect records, inaccurate private correspondence, the bias or untruthfulness of informers, and the general obscurity which envelops all events combine to bewilder and mislead. On the contrary, the preparation of statistical history by experienced, unprejudiced and competent workers in specialties; the accomplishment by a union of labor of a vast result that would cost one person the best years of his life and transfer the collection of perishing event beyond the hope of research; the judicious selection of important matter from the general rubbish; and the careful and intelligent revision of all final manuscript by an editor-in-chief, yield a degree of celerity, system, accuracy, comprehensiveness and value unattainable by any other method. The publishers of this volume, fully aware of their inability to furnish a perfect history, an accomplishment vouchsafed only to the dreamer or the theorist, make no pretension of having prepared a work devoid of blemish. They feel assured that all thoughtful people, at present and in future, will recognize and appreciate the importance of their undertaking and the great public benefit that has been accomplished.

In the preparation of this volume the publishers have met with nothing but courtesy and assistance. They acknowledge their indebtedness for valuable favors to the Governor, the State Librarian, the Secretary of the State Historical Society and to more than a hundred of other prominent citizens of Nashville, Memphis, Knoxville, Chattanooga, Jackson, Clarksville and the smaller cities of the State. It is the design of the publishers to compile and issue, in connection with the State history, a brief yet comprehensive historical account of every county in the State, copies of which will be placed in the State Library. In the prosecution of this work they hope to meet with the same cordial assistance extended to them during the compilation of this volume.

THE PUBLISHERS.

NASHVILLE, May, 1887.

CONTENTS.

CANNON COUNTY.

CANNON COUNTY	854
County and Other Courts	857
Churches	856
Early Settlers	855
Formation	854
Lawyers	858
Officers, County	858
Organization and Boundary	856
Population	857
Rivers and Creeks	854
Schools, Early	855
Valuation	857
War Record	859
Woodbury	859

COFFEE COUNTY.

COFFEE COUNTY	827
County Officers, List of	833
Churches	838
Lawyers	835
Manchester	840
Merchants	840
Mills	830
Newspapers	841
Organization	831
Population and Assessment	832
Schools	837
Settlers, Early	828
Surface Formation	828
Tullahoma	841
War Record	835

DE KALB COUNTY.

DE KALB COUNTY	845
Alexandria	852
Boundary	847
County Court	849
Lawyers	849
Liberty	853
Officials, County	849
Population	848
Settlements, Early	846
Smithville	851
Topography	845
War Record	850

WARREN COUNTY.

	PAGE.
WARREN COUNTY	812
County Court and Officers	818
Churches	823
Geological Formation	812
Lawyers	819
Location	812
Merchants	824
McMinnville	824
Mills	815
Newspapers	826
Organization	816
Physicians	826
Schools	821
Secret Societies	826
Settlers, The First	814
Taxes	817
War Record	820

WHITE COUNTY.

WHITE COUNTY	797
Area	801
Boundary	801
Coal and Other Deposits	798
County Court, When Organized	803
Courts and Officers	804
Clerks, List of	803
Judges	804
Lawyers	805
Merchants, The First	810
Mills and Factories	800
Names of Early Settlers	799
Newspapers	811
Population and Valuation	802
Religious Denominations	808
Schools	807
War, Record in	806

BIOGRAPHICAL APPENDIX.

Coffee	827
Cannon	854
DeKalb	845
Warren	812
White	860

tical history by experienced, unprejudiced and competent workers in specialties; the accomplishment by a union of labor of a vast result that would cost one person the best years of his life and transfer the collection of perishing event beyond the hope of research; the judicious selection of important matter from the general rubbish; and the careful and intelligent revision of all final manuscript by an editor-in-chief, yield a degree of celerity, system, accuracy, comprehensiveness and value unattainable by any other method. The publishers of this volume, fully aware of their inability to furnish a perfect history, an accomplishment vouchsafed only to the dreamer or the theorist, make no pretension of having prepared a work devoid of blemish. They feel assured that all thoughtful people, at present and in future, will recognize and appreciate the importance of their undertaking and the great public benefit that has been accomplished.

In the preparation of this volume the publishers have met with nothing but courtesy and assistance. They acknowledge their indebtedness for valuable favors to the Governor, the State Librarian, the Secretary of the State Historical Society and to more than a hundred of other prominent citizens of Nashville, Memphis, Knoxville, Chattanooga, Jackson, Clarksville and the smaller cities of the State. It is the design of the publishers to compile and issue, in connection with the State history, a brief yet comprehensive historical account of every county in the State, copies of which will be placed in the State Library. In the prosecution of this work they hope to meet with the same cordial assistance extended to them during the compilation of this volume.

THE PUBLISHERS.

NASHVILLE, May, 1887.

WHITE COUNTY.

TOPOGRAPHICALLY White County is divided into three parts, i. e., the table-land or mountains, the valleys and caves and the barrens. The eastern side of the county lies on the Cumberland table-land with a level or gently rolling surface, cut in places into gorges or gulches. The mountain slopes on the face of the table land and its spurs and ridges, with a broken surface, occupy a large part of the county. The escarpment of the table-land is marked by a line of hard sandstone and conglomerate cliffs in places towering above the tall trees on the slopes below. A range of small mountains extends southwest entirely across the county, terminating near Rock Island, in Warren County. The valley of Calf Killer River occupies a wide belt across the county. Beginning in Putnam County, where it is narrow, this valley gradually widens as it extends toward the southwest, and is on an average four miles wide through White County. Hickory Valley lies in the northern part of the county between Pine and Milk Sick Mountains, and is five miles long with an average width of one mile. Cherry Creek Valley opens into that of Calf Killer, above Yankeetown, in the northern part of the county, is seven miles long and from three-quarters to a mile in width. The valley of Lost Creek is cut off and completely encompassed by Pine Mountain, and is on a level with the terrace. The soil of these valleys is rich, and corn, wheat, potatoes, oats, tobacco and the grasses grow well. The soil on the table-land is light and sandy, and adapted to the growth of wild grasses, vegetables and fruit. The barrens are beyond the range of mountains which bounds Calf Killer Valley on the west. Most of the surface is level or gently undulating, the soil thin, much of which is unfit for cultivation. The table-land or mountain part of the county belongs to the great Cumberland coal fields, and three distinct strata, and in some places four are found. The coal is of superior quality, but up to the present only sufficient to supply the local demand has been mined. As early as 1836 Bryce Little began mining coal a few miles east from Sparta, and continues at the present, and a number of other mines have been in operation, as demand requires, by Kinzie & Butler, near Little's mine, and by M. C. Dibrell, seven miles east of Sparta. The Bon Air, Coal, Land & Lumber Company, of which Samuel J. Keith, of Sparta, is president, W. C. Dibrell, of Sparta, is secretary and treasurer, and E. W. Cole, of Nashville, is chairman of the executive committee, own 11,000 acres of coal, iron and timber land, and have perfected arrangements for mining coal on an extensive scale at Bon Air, five miles east of Sparta. A vein of coal-three and a half feet thick has been worked at the above mine for the past fifteen years by Gen. G. G. Dibrell, and within a few yards of the same are two other veins, one being two and a half feet and the other eighteen inches in thickness. The company have obligated themselves to ship 5,000 bushels of coal per day over the extension of the Bon Air Railroad for fifteen years, beginning with the completion of said road. A number of large coke ovens will also be erected by this company. Iron ore is found in various places in the county, and in about 1815 or 1820 T. B. Rice had an iron forge one mile south from Sparta, on Calf Killer River, on the present site of the cotton factory, and later one Brown erected a forge on Falling Water Creek, twelve miles north from Sparta, and A. C. Rodgers erected one on Rocky Creek, all of which, however, were abandoned many years before the civil war. Salt was also mined in large quantities at an early date. Several wells were worked on Calf Killer River, one of which yielded as many as fifty bushels per day.

Rich deposits of variegated marble are supposed to exist in the mountains, and specimens of lead ore have been picked up in the mountain streams, which lead many to suppose, and some to claim, that there is an abundance of that mineral hidden in the mountains, while others go farther and claim silver will yet be developed. The completion of the Bon Air extension of the railroad is looked forward to by the owners of mineral lands with bright hopes and expectations. The water courses of the county are as follows: Caney Fork and Calf Killer Rivers, and Fallingwater, Town, Cherry, Plum, Wild Cat, Post Oak and Fancher Creeks, besides their numerous small tributaries. Splendid water power is afforded by the two rivers and the larger of the creeks.

White County was settled, though sparsely, as early as 1800, seven years prior to its organization as a county. At that time, however, the country was nothing more than a wilderness of canebrake and forest. The hardy pioneers coming across Cumberland Mountains were struck with the beauty and promise of the land, as viewed from the mountain tops, and at once began the work of civilization. A single tribe of Cherokee Indians was found here, the English name of whose chief was Calf Killer, and it was for, or by him, Calf Killer River was probably named, though there are many unreasonable traditions to the contrary. So far as can now he learned, these Indians were of a peaceful and friendly disposition, and the relations between them and the few white settlers were of a cordial nature.

WHITE COUNTY.   799

Much of the land embraced in White County had been granted by the State of North Carolina to the survivors, or their assignees, of the Revolutionary war, for military services in the line, but very few of the original owners ever became settlers of the county. Among those to whom land was thus granted, in tracts of from 640 to 1,000 acres, were Robert King, James Comer, James Cummin, William Forester, James Gains, Robert King, Thomas Wade, Rhea & Tynell, James Cowan, John Rutledge, Elijah Robertson, Elijah Williams, Elijah Chisem, Edward Harris, Joshua Davis, Richard Barbour and John Williams.

The Calf Killer Valley was the scene of the first settlements in the county, the neighborhood of what is now Sparta being in all probability the first, though Thomas Simpson settled on Calf Killer River four miles below Sparta, and Joseph Terry at Rock Island, on Caney Fork, now in Warren County, at about the same time. Among those who settled in the Sparta neighborhood during the years between 1800 and 1815, were Benjamin Lampton, William Anderson, Matthis Anderson, Lewis Fletcher, John Hancock, ——— Dibrell, T. B. Rice, Thomas Bounds, Alexander Lowrey, Anthony Dibrell, Joseph Terry, Jacob A. Lane, Thomas Eastland, George W. Gibbs, Jesse Lincoln, Wm. Glenn, Nathaniel Davis, William Burton, Joseph Collins and Montgomery Carrick. Other settlers of the county of that period, were Thomas Matthews, Moses Guest, David May, Wm. Ledbetter, Thomas May, Wm. Phillips, Thomas K. Harris, James Simpson, Caleb Fraley, John Gabe, Wm. Tyrell, Thomas Wilcher, Andrew Bryan, John White, Elijah Lewis, John Turner, Richard Hill, Thomas Dillon, Isaac and John Anderson, David Nicholson, Wm. Lewis, Philip Kirby, August Gunter, Charles H. Nelson, John Sharp, George Lane, Peter Huston, Wm. Madding, Benjamin Cooper, Wm. Rowland, Elijah Cameron, Thomas Vining, Alexander Brown, Joseph McDaniel, Samuel Harpole, Abraham Mayes, John Seratt, Jacob Harty, Joseph Flemming, David Hauks, Mannering Brookstein, Elijah Bates, John Knowles, John Jenkins, David Connelly, James Winter, B. H. Henderson, N. W. Williams, Wm. McGuire, James Whitehead, David Thompson, J. H. Bowen, Benjamin Pollock, Wm. Mackay, John Vaughn, T. H. Payne, James Laxon, Jacob Drake, Thomas Laxon, John Howard, Hard Sugg, Isaac Sharon, Hercules, Ogle, Joben Fitzgerald, Arthur Markum, Aaron English, Benjamin Weaver, James Fulkerson, Nicholas Gillentine, Archibald Overton, Wm. Phillips, Isaac Taylor, John Dergan and Joseph Roberts. Probably the first mill in the county was the water-power corn-mill erected on Caney Fork River, in the Thirteenth District, by Wm. Scarborough, in about 1810 or 1812. Wm. Glenn erected a similar mill on the Calf Killer in about 1815, and Thomas Simpson one on the same stream four miles below Sparta, at about the same time. From that date up to about 1820, mills were erected by Samuel Denton, six miles from Sparta, on the Calf Killer, Thomas Sperry and Jacob A. Lane on Town Creek, Wm. Basson on Caney Fork, Clark Swindler, Sr., on Cedar Creek, T. B. Rice and J. W. Taylor, on the Calf Killer, all of which were corn-mills, and were operated by water power. A number of years before the late war, a large brick cotton factory was erected on the Calf Killer, one mile below Sparta, which was in successful operation up to the war, when the machinery was removed farther south for protection and safety, and never returned. The building is a large three-story house, with a basement, and cost not less than $15,000 or $20,000. The water power is one of the best in the State, and several attempts have been made to utilize the property, and while idle at present, was used for awhile as a handle factory, for the manufacture of which article it is supplied with machinery; at present the property belongs to the Bon Air Coal, Land & Lumber Company, and is for sale. Besides the numerous portable saw-mills, the manufactories of the county are as follows: First District: C. L. Sperry's corn-mill; Pearson & Co.'s steam saw-mill; Williams & Co.'s steam planing and grist-mill; S. D. Wallace's steam saw and planing-mill and O. F. Young's saw, corn and wheat-mills, on Calf Killer; M. L. Clark's, Matthias Anderson's and A. L. Potts' flour, corn and saw-mills on Town Creek. Second District: T. L. & J. M. Mitchell's and James Williams' corn, flour and saw-mills on Caney Fork. Third District: Taylor & Co.'s and J. W. Taylor's mills on Calf Killer; H. B. Ward's and G. W. Bickford's saw and corn-mills on Caney Fork. Fourth District: G. W. Blankenship's, Wm. Bassom's and Cooper & Green's saw and corn-mills on Caney Fork and Wm. Cooper's steam saw and planing-mills. Fifth District: Wm. Frank's, J. A. McWhister's, Edward Pollard's —— Swindler's and C. Sander's corn and saw-mills on Cedar Creek. Sixth District: J. A. P. Faucher's wheat and corn-mill on Taylor Creek; H. L. Jones' and R. A. Swift's corn-mills on Cedar Creek and Joel Hess' corn-mill. Seventh District: W. S. Burgis' corn-mill on Fallingwater Creek. Ninth District: James Robertson's steam corn and wheat-mill and woolen-carder, on Post Oak Creek. Tenth District; Mumford Wilson's, Felix Dodson's and J. A. Hayes' corn-mills on Caney Fork. Eleventh District: Samuel Johnson's, H. C. Snodgrass' and G. W. Gillins' corn and wheat-mills on Calf Killer River. Twelfth District: George Gillins' corn and wheat-mill on the Calf Killer and Stephen Wilhite's, S. M. Snodgrass' and James Wilhite's corn and saw-mills on Cherry Creek. A large distillery, of 140 gallons daily capacity, is operated by Messrs. Wakeman & Hodges, one and a half miles southwest from Sparta.

WHITE COUNTY.

White County was erected out of Smith County by an "act entitled an act to form a new county south of the counties of Wilson, Smith, Jackson and Overton," passed by the General Assembly on September 11, 1806, with the following boundaries: "Beginning at the late Indian boundary line at the southwest corner of said Wilson County; thence eastwardly with the said counties of Wilson, Smith, Jackson and Overton to the west boundary of Roane County; thence southwardly with the line of said Roane County to the south boundary line of this State; thence with the said south boundary line to the southeast corner of Rutherford County; thence north with the east boundary line of Rutherford County to the beginning aforesaid." Thus it will be seen that at its formation White County embraced all the territory east of Smith County to Walden's Ridge and extended to the southern boundary of the State. Yet, possessed as it was of such vast domain at its organization, this county is at present below the average of Tennessee counties in size, having been reduced in 1807 by the erection of Warren County on the south, on the west by DeKalb County in 1837, again on the south by Van Buren County in 1840, and on the north by Putnam in 1854, and Cumberland on the east in 1856. At present the county has an area of 440 square miles, or 281,600 acres, and is bounded on the north by Putnam County, on the east by Cumberland County, on the south by the counties of Warren and Van Buren, and on the west by De Kalb County. The above act designated the house of Joseph Terry, at what is now Rock Island, in Warren County, mention of which is made in the history of that county, as the place of holding the courts of White County until a permanent seat of justice should be located, and it was there the county was organized in 1807. A temporary log courthouse was erected, in which the courts were held for three years. The General Assembly, on October 18, 1809, passed an "act entitled to establish the permanent seat of justice for White County," which act provided for the calling and holding of an election for the selection of seven commissioners whose duties would be the locating of a county seat, which town should be called Sparta, the surveying and laying off into lots of said town, the selling of such lots, and the erection of the necessary county buildings, the expenses to be met with the moneys accruing from the sales of the lots. The election was held on the first Monday and Tuesday in January, 1810, and resulted in the election, as such commissioners, of Thomas Bounds, Aaron England, Benjamin Weaver, Turner Lane, James Fulkerson, Alexander Lowrey and Nicholas Gillentine. A site on the Calf Killer River was immediately chosen, but being unable to agree upon which side of the river the location should be made, the commissioners called an election and submitted the question to the people, who chose the east side, though the west side was more suitable, for the reason that the owner of the west side, Alexander Lowrey, one of the commissioners, donated forty acres to the county, while the owner of the east side, thinking of course his land would be selected, placed too high, and at that time an exorbitant, value on his land. The town was at once surveyed and laid off into lots, the same sold, and in the course of a few months a log courthouse and jail were erected, and the courts removed from Rock Island to Sparta. The log courthouse stood until about 1815, when the present brick building was erected at a cost of not over $5,000. The building is a small, square-shaped, two-story structure, which when erected answered fully the requirements of a courthouse, but at the present is inadequate, and two of the most important county officials find quarters elsewhere. The building bears ample evidence of its extreme old age, being probably one of the oldest public buildings in the State, and should be replaced with a structure more in keeping with the advancement of the town, county and times. The log jail was but little more than a pen, yet answered all purposes until about 1820, when a brick jail was erected. This building has been damaged by fire on several occasions, but was each time repaired, the last time in about 1869, and is now a substantial building, valued at about $2,000.

In 1810 White County had a population of 4,028, of 8,701 in 1820, of 9,967 in 1830, of 10,747 in 1840, of 11,444 in 1850, of 9,381 in 1860, of 9,375 in 1870, of 11,143 in 1880, and of 12,500 in 1886. The rating population in 1870 was 1,900, and at the August election, 1886, the county polled 2,183, of which 1,811 were Democratic and 372 Republican. In 1870 there were 217,101 acres assessed for taxation in the county, valued at $1,140,836, and the total valuation of taxable property was $1,320,610. In 1886 there were 220,228 acres assessed, valued at $936,960, and the total valuation of taxable property, including real, personal and all other property, amounted to $1,132,844. The tax aggregate for 1886 shows the following tax assessment: poll, $1,618; State, $3,395.43; county, $3,803.02; school, $4,528.41; special, $1,132.81; railroad, $1,699.23; highway, $906.23; total $15,465.13.

The cereal products of the county in 1860 were, of wheat, 55,181 bushels; corn, 347,944 bushels; oats, 22,129 bushels; rye, 1,158 bushels; potatoes, 15,500 bushels; tobacco, 21,180 pounds, and of wool, 15,000 pounds. In 1886 the products were, of wheat, 45,653 bushels; corn, 650,000 bushels; oats, 25,900 bushels; rye, 2,837 bushels; tobacco, 30,000 pounds; potatoes, 17,000 bushels and of wool, 16,000 pounds.

The live stock of the county in 1870 amounted to 2,694 head of horses and mules, 2,988 head of cattle, 8,144 head of sheep, and 17,340 head of hogs. In 1886 the live stock amounted to 3,625 head of horses and mules, 8,208 head of cattle, 5,000 head of sheep, and 25,000 head of hogs.

The McMinnville branch of the Nashville, Chattanooga & St. Louis Railway, was extended to Sparta in 1884. There are thirteen miles of track in White County, and Sparta is the terminus. Work, however, is in progress on an extension of the railroad from Sparta to the Bon Air Coal Mines, which, when complete, will be about six and one-half miles in length. The work is being pushed with a large force of hands, and is to be completed and cars running during the year 1887.

The county has erected but three bridges of consequence in the county, they all spanning Calf Killer River, one of which is at Sparta, one at Simpson's mills, in the First District, and one at Gillin's mills, in the Twelfth District.

There are no turnpikes in White County, but numerous highways lead out from Sparta to all parts of the county. These, during the late spring, summer and fall months are in splendid condition, but in winter are all but impassable for vehicles. The county is subdivided into thirteen Districts, though originally there were but eight.

The county court of White County was organized at the house of Joseph Terry, near Rock Island, on Caney Fork River, in February, 1807. Joseph Terry was chosen clerk; William Phillips sheriff, and John Dergan register. The records of this court, prior to 1814, have been destroyed, hence the proceedings of the first session cannot be given. The court continued to meet at the log courthouse at Mr. Terry's place until the location of the permanent seat of justice at Sparta and the completion of the log courthouse at that place, when the records were removed thereto.

The following is a list of the clerks, sheriffs and registers from the organization of the county to and including those now in office:

Clerks—Joseph Terry, 1807–08; John M. Carrick, 1808–14; Jacob A. Lane, 1814–35; Nicholas Oldham, 1835–44; Wm. Little, 1844–48; G. G. Dibrell, 1848–60; John Voss, 1860–64; J. A. Pettit, 1865–69; F. A. Williams, 1869–73; F. M. Simms, 1873–77; Wm. Dinges, 1877–81; Gardner Green, 1881–86; J. D. Goff, 1886, and present incumbent.

Sheriffs—Wm. Phillips, 1807–12; Isaac Taylor, 1812–14; Isaac Taylor, Jr., 1814–16; Thomas Taylor, 1816–20; John Jett, 1820–35; D. L. Mitchell, 1835–40; Jonathan T. Bradley, 1840–44; Smith J. Walling, 1844–46; Joseph Herd, 1846–52; Charles Meeks, 1852–58; Andrew J. Gamble, 1858–64; Wm. F. Carter, 1865–66; F. S. Coatney, 1866–70; Samuel Snodgrass, 1870–74; S. V. McManus, 1874–76; Charles Smith, 1876–78; George M. Hill, 1878–82; T. L. Lewis, 1882–86; J. M. Montgomery, 1886, and present incumbent.

Registers—John Dergan, 1807-15; Turner Lane, 1815-35; Joseph W. Robertson, 1835-39; Charles McGuire, 1839-43; Robert H. Officer, 1843-45; Wm. H. Boyd, 1845-65; Thomas H. Fancher, 1865-69; Wm. Holter, 1869-73; Wm. G. Simms, 1873-86; John S. Cope, 1886 and present incumbent.

The circuit court of White County was organized also at Joseph Terry's house in 1807, by Judge Nathaniel Williams, who appointed as clerk of the court Archibald W. Overton. The early records of this court are also missing, having been destroyed during the late war.

The judges and clerks of the court from its organization to the present have been as follows:

Judges—Nathaniel Williams, Jacob C. Isaacs, Abraham Caruthers, Wm. B. Campbell, John L. Goodall, Samuel M. Fite, W. W. Goodpasture, W. W. McConnell and M. D. Smallman, the present incumbent.

Clerks—Archibald W. Overton, 1807-14; Anthony Dibrell, 1814-35; Wm. G. Simms, 1835-47; Joseph Brown, 1847-55; H. L. Carrick, 1855-58; John J. Duncan, 1858-64; Anthony Dibrell, 1865-67; Wm. M. Russell, 1861-71; Waymond L. Woods, 1871-75; M. C. Dibrell, 1875-81; W. C. Smith, 1881-86; J. O. Snodgrass, 1886 and present incumbent.

The chancery court was organized at Sparta in 1842, under the provisions of the new constitution, by Judge B. L. Ridley, chancellor, who appointed B. S. Rhea clerk and master of the court. The chancellors and clerks and masters of this court have been as follows:

Chancellors—B. L. Ridley, 1842-54; T. Nixon Van Dyke, 1854-60; B. L. Ridley, 1860-62; John P. Steele, 1865-67; B. M. Tillman, 1867-71; W. W. Goodpasture, 1871-72; W. G. Crowley, 1872-86; W. W. Wade 1886 and present incumbent.

Clerks and masters—B. S. Rhea, 1842-45: W. E. Nelson, 1845-57; M. C. Dibrell, 1857-62; Peter Turney, 1865-71; W. L. Dibrell, 1871-76; John S. Rhea, 1876-82; A. E. Rhea, 1882-87 and present incumbent.

The supreme court of this State met at Rock Island, and later at Sparta, for several years, one of the presiding judges being Andrew Jackson. At the bar of this court all the leading attorneys of Tennessee would practice, and the old log courthouse was the scene of many able and eloquent discussions.

The early lawyers of Sparta were George W. Gibbs, John Catron, Nathaniel Haggard, Richard Nelson, David Ames, Alexander Lane, Samuel Turney, John H. Anderson and Hopkins L. Turney, all of whom practiced from the organization of the courts to about 1855. For several years after the close of the war the attorneys were John L. Goodall, S. H. Combs, Thomas B. Murray and D. L. Snodgrass. The lawyers of the present are C. Marchbanks, H. C. Snodgrass, M. A. Cummings, W. G. Smith, W. T. Smith, W. F. Story, E. Story, E. Jarvis, L. D. Hill, T. J. Bradford, S. E. Cunningham and James Cope. Of the above George W. Gibbs was a State senator and general in the war of 1812, was the first president of the Union Bank of Tennessee at Nashville and later founded Union City, Tenn. John Catron was appointed United States circuit judge by President Jackson and died in office; Hopkins L. Turney was a State senator and the father of Judge Peter Turney, of the supreme court of Tennessee; John L. Goodall occupied the circuit court bench; D. L. Snodgrass is a member of the present supreme court bench; L. D. Hill is State senator, and W. F. Story is county judge of the White County Court. Besides the above, White County has furnished the following public men: Thomas K. Harris was the first representative in Congress from White County and the district. In a subsequent canvass for the same office Harris was killed in a duel with Gen. John W. Simpson, also of White County, his opponent. The two met at Shell's Ford, on Caney Fork River. Both rode into the stream from opposite sides and stopped, facing each other, while their horses quenched their thirst. One of them, after a few words had been exchanged, proposed they settle their differences then and there. The proposition was accepted, and riding out together they dismounted, drew their pistols and began firing. Harris was mortally wounded, and his death served to defeat Simpson for the office he sought. Anthony Dibrell, father of Gen. G. G. Dibrell, was for years receiver of the land office at Sparta, was a director of the Bank of Tennessee, was for ten years State treasurer and for twenty-two years clerk of the White County Circuit Court. Gen. George G. Dibrell was clerk of White County for a number of years, was a member of the State Convention in 1861, being elected as a Union man; was a general of cavalry in the Confederate Army; was a member of the constitutional convention in 1869; represented his district in Congress from 1874 to 1884 continuously, retiring voluntarily from that body, and was one of the leading Democratic candidates for governor of Tennessee in 1886. Gov. Throckmorton, of Texas, was once a citizen of Sparta.

When the war department made a requisition on the State of Tennessee for 2,500 men to serve in the war of 1812, White County contributed two full companies, which were commanded by Capts. John W. Simpson and George W. Gibbs. Capt. Simpson was promoted to the rank of lieutenant-colonel and distinguished himself for bravery at the battle of New Orleans, and Capt. Gibbs, who was serving as State senator at Knoxville but resigned his position to join the war, arose to a generalship.

White County was also represented in the bloody war against the Creek Indians, she responding to Gov. Blount's call for volunteers by raising two companies, which were commanded by Capts. Ratan and Randals.

Again, when the United States and Mexico became involved in war and volunteers were called for, White County organized and furnished one company, which was commanded by Capt. Anthony.

White County furnished nine full companies to the Confederacy and one to the Federal Government during the late civil war, besides portions of other companies organized in adjoining counties. The first organized was Capt. D. T. Brown's company, in the early part of 1861, which joined the Sixteenth Regiment of Tennessee Infantry, at the organization of which Capt. Brown was elected lieutenant-colonel. Over half of Capt. P. C. Shield's company in the same regiment was made up from White County. In July, 1861, three companies were organized in White County and reported to Camp Zollicoffer, in Overton County. When the Twenty-fifth Regiment of Tennessee Infantry organized at that place the following month, George G. Dibrell was elected lieutenant-colonel of the same, he having entered the service as a private. The White County companies in this regiment were commanded by Capts. D. M. Southern, W. G. Smith and J. H. Snodgrass. At least one-half of Capt. Abraham Ford's company, of the above regiment, organized in Putnam County, was composed of White County citizens. In October, 1861, Capt. E. P. Simms organized a company in White County and joined the Twenty-eighth Regiment of Tennessee Infantry, and in December of the same year Capts. David Snodgrass and Wm. M. Simpson organized a company each and joined Combs' battalion, and in the latter part of 1862 Capt. Thomas E. Taylor organized a company and joined Murry's battalion of cavalry.

At the reorganization of the Twenty-fifth Regiment at Corinth, Miss., in May, 1862, Col. Dibrell failed to secure a re-election and returned home. His sterling worth was appreciated, however, and he was at once given authority to raise a full regiment of cavalry. This he succeeded in more than doing, raising twelve companies in all, though the country in which he raised the same was inside the enemy's lines. The regiment organized at Yankeetown, White County, September 4, 1862, when George G. Dibrell was elected colonel; F. H. Daugherty, of Overton County, lieutenant-colonel; Jeffrey Forrest, major; while F. H. Smallman, now of McMinnville, and present circuit judge, was appointed adjutant to

Col. Dibrell. White County furnished two companies to this regiment, which were commanded by Capts. Jefferson Leftwick and J. M. Barnes. The regiment reported for duty at Murfreesboro, October 8, 1862, where it was given a place with Gen. N. B. Forrest's command. Col. Dibrell served with distinction and ability in the several trying positions he was assigned, and on July 24, 1864, he was commissioned a brigadier-general.

In 1862 Capt. Edmund Pennington organized a full company in the northwest part of the county and joined Col. Jarrett's Fourth Regiment of Tennessee Mounted Infantry (United States), which comprised the sum total of White County's assistance and contribution to the Federal Army. Several skirmishes occurred during 1862 in White County, the first of which took place at Simpson's mills on the Calf Killer, four miles below Sparta, between Col. Whorton's Texas troops and the Federal advance under Gen. Nelson, in which several were killed and the advance of the Federals checked. In August, of the above year, Gen. Dibrell's cavalry, 400 strong, had a lively skirmish with the Federals, 4,000 strong, under Col. Mintor, at Wildcat Creek, near the Calf Killer, about three and a half miles above Sparta, in which twelve men and twenty-four horses were killed on the Federal side, and one killed and several wounded on the Confederate side. The above occurred before dinner, and in the afternoon the Federals, having been reinforced by three additional regiments, returned to the attack. Gen. Dibrell had been reinforced by two companies from Col. Starnes' regiment, and again the Federals were driven back with considerable loss.

The first school of any consequence established in White County was Priestly Academy, in about 1815, at Sparta, for which a small log house was erected by the united efforts of the citizens on the hill west of town, where now stands the Christian Church. The school was taught for a number of years by the Rev. Memucan Wade, whose strict mode of imparting education can be remembered and testified to by several citizens now living. In 1831 the log building was replaced by a substantial brick, and the school became the county academy. David Ames, one of the leading attorneys of Sparta, was the first teacher to hold forth in the new building. The old building stands at the present, being owned and occupied by the congregation of the Christian Church. A second log school building was erected on the hill east of town in about 1823, but it soon passed out of existence, the school being eclipsed by its rival on the west side. In 1850, by permission of the Legislature, the county academy building was sold, and with the proceeds applied to the purchase of H. L. Carrick's brick residence, about three blocks from the courthouse, and Nourse Academy was established. A frame additional schoolroom was erected in 1852, and such is the school of Sparta at the present.

In about 1825 an excellent school was established at Zion Church, in the Sixth District, which is in operation at the present; is chartered, and known as Zion Academy. At about the same time Cumberland Institute was established in a frame building erected for that purpose in the Eleventh District, and is in operation at present, and working under a charter. Onward Seminary, a chartered school, was established in the Third District in about 1840. A good two-story frame building was erected in which the school has since been taught. Pealed Chestnut Academy, in the Sixth District, was established in about 1845, is chartered, and is one of the schools of the county. At Doyle Station, on the McMinnville Branch Railway, in the Third District, is one of the best schools and buildings to be found outside of the cities in the State. The building is a two-story brick, handsome and substantial, and was erected in 1883 at a cost of about $9,000. The school is working under a charter, and is the leading school of this mountainous country. The above embraces the leading schools of White County. The common schools are to be found in numbers all over the country, but they are only taught from three to five months in the year, and of an inferior quality. The scholastic population of White County in 1838 was 2,886, and the county's share of the school fund for the same year amounted to $1,798.41, In 1868 the scholastic population of the county, by race and sex, was as follows: White—male, 1,639; female, 1,490. Colored—male, 202; female, 186. Total, white and colored, male and female, 3,517. In 1885 the scholastic population was as follows: White—male, 2,470; female, 2,164. Colored—male, 206; female, 206. Total white and colored, male and female, 5,046. In the school fund apportionment of 1885, the county received $1,108.38. During the above year teachers were employed in the county as follows: White—male, 57; females, 8. Colored—male, 5; females, 5. Total white and colored, 75; and there was in the county at that time fifty-six white and eight colored schools.

The various religious denominations had organizations in White County at a very early date in its history, but few if any church or meeting-houses were erected in the county, however, prior to 1820, services being conducted in schoolhouses and at the houses of the settlers. In Sparta, the court-house was used as a place of worship by the different denominations. Upon the completion of the County Academy building, that was used as a church. The first building erected in Sparta exclusively for church purposes was the Methodist, which was completed in about 1852. The building is in use at the present, and is a substantial brick. During the late war the Federal soldiers tore up the floor in this building, and used the same in which to stable their horses. In about 1853, the Cumberland

Presbyterians, Baptists and Christians combined, purchased the County Academy and converted it into a Union Church, which, at the present, belongs to the Christian congregation. In 1880 the Cumberland Presbyterians erected a frame church, and the above three, together with two frame colored churches, represent the religious institutions of the county seat.

The early and present churches of the county are as follows, by districts: First District—Lowrey's Chapel and Clark's Schoolhouse, Union; Gracey's Chapel and Mt. Gilead, Methodist Episcopal South; Rose's Chapel, Methodist Episcopal and Union, Missionary Baptist. Second District—Davis' Chapel, Rogers' Chapel and Frazier's Chapel, Methodist Episcopal South; Union, Cumberland Presbyterian, and Possum Trot, Missionary Baptist. Third District—Greenwood, Missionary Baptist; Bethel, Free-Will Baptist: Eden, Union; Bethlehem, Christian, and Doyle's Chapel, Methodist Episcopal. Fourth District—Joppa, Methodist Episcopal South; Jericho and Walnut Grove, Christian. Fifth District—Shady Grove, Mt. Pisgah, Methodist Episcopal South; Philadelphia, Primitive Baptist; Dogwood Grove, Christian, and Spring Hill, Missionary and Free-Will Baptist. Sixth District—Old Zion and Mt. Union, Cumberland Presbyterian; New Hope, Free-Will Baptist; Liberty, Pleasant Hill and Lewis' Schoolhouse, Missionary Baptist; Gracy's Chapel, Methodist Episcopal; and Wesley Chapel, Methodist Episcopal South. Seventh District—New Macedonia and Pistol's, Free-Will Baptist. Eighth District—Mt. Zion and Cave Chapel, Methodist Episcopal South and Old Macedonia, Union. Ninth District—Mt. Carmel, Methodist Episcopal South, and Sugar Chapel, Cumberland Presbyterian. Tenth District—Dodson's Chapel, Methodist Episcopal South, and Lost Creek, Missionary Baptist. Eleventh District—Board Valley, Missionary Baptist. Twelfth District—Bowles' Chapel, Christian, and Cherry Creek, Cumberland Presbyterian.

Sparta, the county seat and principal town and commercial point of White County, is situated on the left bank of Calf Killer River, in a beautiful valley at the foot of and about five miles distant from the Cumberland Mountains, and at the terminus of the Sparta & McMinnville Branch of the Nashville, Chattanooga & St. Louis Railway, about 140 miles from the first named city, and has a population of about 800. The town was founded in 1810 by the commissioners elected to locate a permanent seat of justice for the county, and was incorporated in 1813. Under its charter, when received, the town continued to work until 1879, when the same was surrendered in order to give its citizens the benefit of the "four mile" temperance law, since which time intoxicants have been excluded from sale. In 1820, by permission of the Legislature, an addition of six acres was made to the town, the land for the same being purchased from Jacob A. Lane. A turnpike road was surveyed and constructed from Nashville to Knoxville, running through Lebanon, Sparta and Kingston in about 1815, and Sparta at once sprang into prominence, as the road became the great thoroughfare from east to west, and all passenger and freight vehicles would stop at the town for rest and feed. Over this road goods were transported from Knoxville to Nashville; long wagon trains of emigrants passed over it daily seeking homes in the West, and four and six-horse stage coaches loaded with passengers passed each way uninterruptedly. A train of from fifty to one hundred emigrant wagons, winding down the side of the mountain, was a common sight in those days, and Sparta being one of the stopping places and relays, her merchants and hotel proprietors flourished as they have not since.

The first mercantile establishment in Sparta was opened in 1809 by Keys & Clemmons. Other early merchants and tradesmen, from that time up to about 1820, were Wm. Glenn, Jesse Lincoln (cousin to President Lincoln), Fletcher & Lumpton, Jubal Hancock, T. B. Rice, and Simpson & Allen; W. C. Brittan operated a large hattery, working from six to eight hands; Thomas Sperry and Wm. Musgrove and Nathan Starkley were tailors; Wm. Mitchell, Nat Davis and Wm. Glenn were the tavern-keepers; Joseph Copher and Wm. Burton were the blacksmiths, and Wm. Anderson operated an extensive tanyard, the first sunk in the town or county. Between 1830 and 1840, the merchants were Jesse Lincoln, Warren & Dibrell, Wm. Glenn, James H. Jenkins, Wm. Simpson, T. B. Rice, Waymond Leftwick, S. & H. Carrick, and James & Wm. Young. Between 1840 and 1850: Wm. Simpson, Wm. Glenn, Waymond Leftwick, S. & H. Carrick, James Snodgrass & Sons, R. G. Smith, I. N. Wright, M. & C. Dibrell, Warren & Dibrell, Sevier & Evans, Wm. Little, and White & Young. Between 1850 and 1860: Leftwick & Dibrell, Snodgrass Bros., T. L. Sperry, W. M. Young, S. & H. Carrick, John W. Floyd, Warren & White, and W. M. Moore. Between 1865 and 1870: T. L. Sperry, J. C. Officer, G. G. Dibrell, J. J. Cummings, J. P. Franklin, Turney & Carrick, and J. T. & J. L. Quarles. Between 1870 and 1880: T. L. Sperry, J. T. & J. L. Quarles, J. J. Cummings, Dibrell & Officer, J. P. Franklin, J. P. England, W. H. Magness, and T. B. Biles. Of the present: Quarles Bros., C. C. Young, England Bros., W. H. Magness, E. D. Austin, R. N. Crawford and G. J. Spurlock, general merchandise; T. L. Sperry, dry goods; J. Cram, fancy groceries and confections; Gist & Marchbanks and J. P. Franklin, drugs; J. W. Norwood and R. P. Biles, hardware and groceries; Lyles & Co., undertaking establishment; Anderson & Bronson and Hill & Womack, livery stables; hotels, Rhea House, Mrs. A. J. Rhea, proprietress; Sparta House, Mrs. T. J. R. Swofford, proprietress, and Depot House, H. L. C. Moore, proprietor. A branch of the Bank of Tennessee was established at Sparta, in March, 1840, and remained until the breaking out of the civil war, when the funds were removed for safety. The house now occupied as the Rhea House, was erected as a bank building. Of the bank, John Jett was the first president; A. L. Davis, cashier; G. G. Dibrell, clerk; the following year President Jett was succeeded by W. M. Young, Jett dying. Afterward James Snodgrass, John Warren, J. G. Mitchell, and Wm. Goodbar served as presidents in the order given, and John Warren, W. M. Young, John B. Anderson and Joseph G. Mitchell, served as cashiers. The bank of Sparta was established in March, 1885, with W. M. Cameron as president, and J. N. Walling as cashier. The institution was converted into the Sparta National Bank, on January 1, 1887, of which Richard Hill is president, W. M. Cameron is vice-president, and J. N. Walling, cashier; the capital stock is $50,-000. The practicing physicians of Sparta, from the earliest to the present, have been as follows, in about the order given: Drs. Fisk, Nourse, Cox, Farmer, Lawson, Throckmorton, Hall, Madison, Brockett, Renshaw, Thomas Snodgrass, J. H. Snodgrass and Smith, the present being Drs. J. H. Snodgrass, W. S. Findley, D. R. Gist, M. Anderson.

The first newspaper published in Sparta was the *Sparta Gazette*, which was established by John W. Ford, on May 28, 1820. The writer examined a copy of the *Gazette* of date of August 24, 1820; it is a four-column* folio, the body type of pica and small pica, and the advertisement and foreign news in great primer. The subscription price of the *Gazette* was $2 per year in cash, and $3 on credit. Since the publication of the *Gazette* several newspaper enterprises were put on foot only to collapse after a short life. The papers of the present are the *Expositor*, established in 1877, by the Hill Bros., and purchased in 1881 by R. P. Baker, the present editor and publisher, and the *State and Farm*, F. M. Morrison, editor and publisher, established August, 1886. Both papers are weekly, well edited, and organs of the Democratic party, the *State and Farm*, however, as its name would indicate, having a tendency toward agricultural matters. Bon Air, on the Cumberland Mountains, five miles east from Sparta, was, before the late war, a celebrated watering and summer resort, and contributed not a little to Sparta's bygone prosperity. A large hotel was erected some time during the forties by Christopher Hoffman, who sold the property to John B. Rodgers, and later it passed into the hands of a Northern man whose name can not be obtained. The site was one of the most beautiful and healthy in the South, the view from the hotel being unsurpassed in grandeur, and offered fine inducements to the health and pleasure seekers of *ante bellum* days, from 400 to 500 of whom would throng the hotel during a single season. The buildings were destroyed by Scott's Confederate Cavalry during the late war, and have not been rebuilt, though another hotel is among the probabilities of the near future, as the property belongs to the Bon Air Coal Land and Lumber Company.

Doyle Station, Yankeetown, Onward and Pealed Chestnut, are hamlets, with one exception having not over 50 inhabitants. Doyle has about 150 inhabitants, and a splendid college which gives it prominence.

WARREN COUNTY.

WARREN COUNTY occupies a position nearly midway between the northern and southern boundaries of the State, and lies for the most part at the western base of the Cumberland table-land. Portions of the county have a high elevation, but most of it is from 900 to 1,000 feet above sea level. Ben Lomond, within about two miles of McMinnville, is the end of one of the spurs included within the county. Most of the county is based on the lithostrotion bed of the Lower Carboniferous. On the slopes of the table-land, including its spurs and outliers, the mountain limestone outcrops in full force, and at points, especially on the northern slopes, it is covered with a rich soil. Capping the table-land and its flat-topped spurs are found the coal measures, which include two or three thin strata of coal, but which are of little value. In the lithostrotion bed are a number of layers of impure limestones, which, when burned, yield a hydraulic lime or cement. Quite a number of wells have been bored in the county for petroleum, but with poor success, very little of that article of commercial importance being met with. Excluding the mountain portion, the county may be said to be flat highland, sufficiently cut by streams, with deep valleys, to give contrast and variety to the surface. The eastern portion is made rough by the spurs and outliers of the table-land, and it supplies many mountain valleys, coves, and picturesque gorges, precipices and waterfalls. The southeastern part of the county lies on the Cumberland plateau, and has the elevation, soil and physical features which pertain to that region. Over thirty varieties of stone are found in the county, varying from the grayish limestone to coarse sandstone. Near Collins River, seven miles from McMinnville, running into Forest Peak, is Higginbotham Cave, which consists of numerous halls and grottoes, adorned and beautified with incrustations. Some of the chambers are magnificent in their proportions, one extending over an area of seven acres. The cave is a point of much interest to pleasure seekers.

The lands situated on the lithostrotion bed have the characteristic chocolate color, and are naturally very fertile, being in some respects preferable to the rich, black lands of the central basin. The depth of the clay sub-soil enables the land to retain an amount of moisture which the underlying limestone in the central basin renders impossible. Three-fourths of the county are red or chocolate lands, and the remainder are mountainous, but some of the best soils in the county are to be found in coves on the mountain sides. By cove lands are meant those lands which run up on the sides of the mountains. They are generally very productive. The north sides of the mountains are of unusual fertility. Corn, wheat, rye, oats, the grasses, and all fruits grow well in the county, particularly the latter, of which the apple grows in extreme abundance.

The timber of the county includes yellow poplar, ash, linn, chestnut, buckeye, sugar, hickory, oak, black walnut, locust, dogwood and the many other unimportant species.

Collins River is the main stream of the county. This stream rises in Grundy County, passes near McMinnville, just below the town receives the waters of Barren Fork, and empties into Caney Fork. Hickory Creek is a branch of Barren Fork, and Charles Creek empties into Collins River, they, with the two named and Mountain Creek composing the principal streams of the county.

When the pioneers came to what is now the territory of Warren County, they found the valleys and coves covered with an almost impenetrable growth of tall cane and the mountains and hills with heavy timber. Game was plentiful and many are the stories of exciting bear and deer hunts handed down and now told with keen relish by the sons of the hardy pioneers. The Indians had all been removed prior to that time, yet ample evidence of their presence here at one day remains; the ruins of an Indian village on Woodley Creek in the Seventh District, near John Woodley's old mill site, and an Indian mound of large dimensions on Collins River, in the Sixth District, and numerous other mounds and old burying-grounds remaining at present. Among those who secured grants from North Carolina calling for lands in Warren County were Wm. Banton, P. W. Anderson, Richard Butcher, Jeremiah Bolin, Joseph Colville, John Doak, Jesse Dodson, Sarah Elam, Joseph Franks, Robert Gordon, James Hubbard, Edward Hogan, Edward Hopkins, John Jones, Enoch Tobe, David Johnston, Wm. Johnston, Thomas Lowery, Isaiah Lowe, Luthrell Lott, John Looney, Samuel McGee, Wm. Richardson, John McGee, Daniel Cherry, Wm. C. Smartt, James Kane, John Woodley, Henry J. A. Hill and Aaron Higginbotham. So far as known, the first man to settle in the county was Elisha Pepper, who came to what is now the neighborhood of McMinnville from Virginia in about 1800, and lived to be one hundred years of age, during which time he never saw a train of cars. When the question of voting money to aid in building the McMinnville Branch Railroad, Mr. Pepper vigorously and bitterly opposed the scheme, and upon the success of the proposition, declared he would have none of the railroad in his, and although living for years in sound of the passing trains, persisted in his opposition and declaration, and never could be induced to look at the cars. Other settlers of the same neighborhood were Andrew Gambill, Lyon Mitchell, Joseph Colville, Drs. John Wilson and Wm. P. Lawrence, Edward Hogue, Wm. North, John Davis and Wm. Lisk, all of whom came between 1800 and 1810. The different settlements over the county made at the above time were as follows: John Smith, James Elkins, Thomas Russ, John Russ, Wm. Collier, James Collier, Wm. Lusk, in the Second District; Rock Martin, Jeremiah Jaco, Thomas Gribble and Joseph Campaign, in the Third District; Wm. Neals and the Hillises, in the Fourth District; Jacob Martin, Jacob A. Kome, W. J. Stubblefield, Wm. Smith, George Edwards, Jesse Safley, David Safley, Ezekial McGregor, Wylie Ware and John Meyers, in the Fifth District; Henry J. A. Hill, John Rogers, Isham Dikes, John Gross, John Bass, James Kane and Charles Sullivan, in the Sixth District; Joseph Cope, Robert Tate, Levi Rogers, John Woodley and Joshua Cartwright, in the Seventh District; Elisha Reynolds, Dr. Archibald Faulkner, Asa Faulkner, Leroy Hammond, Jesse R. Edwards, Stephen Tipton and Ransom Gynn, in the Eighth District; W. C. N. King, Miles Bonner, Wm. Smartt, John A. and James Northcup, George Matthewson and H. J. King, in the Ninth District; Maj. Rains, Silas Alexander, Dr. Turner, Thomas Wilson, Isaac Wilson, Thomas Hopkins, Mason French, John, James and Brown Spurlock and Jesse Crisp, in the Tenth District; Michael DeBerry, George Spangler, Allen Youngblood, James Lanse, Russell Brewer, Richard Ware, Britain Snipes, Isaac Starkley, Reuben Davenport, Archibald Prater, Robert Biles and James Whitlock, in the Eleventh District; John Kirby, Wm. Kirby, the Hoppes, the Edges, the Stockstills and the Womacks, in the Thirteenth District; Jesse Gibbs, Thomas Borin, Samuel Honn, Clement Sullivan, Absalom Clark, Chesley

Webb, Pleasant Blackman, James Durham and Samuel Hooster, in the Fourteenth District; Wm. Womack, James Webb, Sr., Solomon Mulligan, Anderson Mulligan, James Green, Biras Webb, Abner Womack and Harrel Byers, in the Fifteenth District. Among the settlers of various parts of the county from 1810 to 1815 were James Cope, James Forest, John England, Alexander Brown, Stephen Jones, Wm. Miller, Joseph Mitchell, Elihu Sanders, John Campbell, Joshua Adkins, John Dodson, Jesse Dunlap, Reuben Elan, Micajah Estes, Ralph Elkins, John Flemming, Hughes French, Elijah Fletcher, John Fortner, Jesse Gibbs, Lewis Howell, Joshua Hickerson, Howell Harris, Gillam Hurst, Nicholas Hughes, Irwin Hill, Lewis Jarvis, Reuben Hampton, Thomas Allen, Andrew Buchanan, John Barclay, Jeremiah Coombs, James Kane, Oliver Charles, Wm. Cummings, Elijah Drake, Martin Johnson, John Lucas, Jonathan McMahan, Wm. Jacobs, Geo. Lane and Joel Mayberry.

Among the early mills of the county were the water-power gristmills of Archibald Porter, on the head waters of Barren Fork of Collins River, near the Cannon County line; ——— Perry and James Whitrock, on Barren Fork, all in the Eleventh District; W. A. Hancock, on the southwest prong of Barren Fork, in the Tenth District; James Martin, on Barnes Creek, in the Fifteenth District; John Woodley, on Woodley Creek, and Joshua Cartright, on Henry Creek, in the Seventh District; Henry Hill, on Hill Creek, in the Sixth District; James Shell, on Collins River, John Drake, at Buck Springs, and John Schrader, on Hickory Creek, in the Fifth District; Harry Macon, on Hickory Creek, George Savage, on Barren Fork, and ——— Tillford, on Little Hickory Creek, in the Ninth District; ——— Wilson, on Barren Fork near McMinnville, in the First District; Dr. Archibald Faulkner had a gristmill, and the first woolen-mill and cotton-gin on Hickory Creek, in the Eighth District; Henry Bridleman built and operated a cotton factory, on Charley Creek, in about 1812. In 1846 Asa Faulkner erected a large cotton-mill on Charley Creek, two miles north from McMinnville, which was operated successfully until the late war, after which time it was converted into a cotton-gin, and run as such for a number of years. In 1861 Mr. Faulkner and S. B. Spurlock erected a second cotton factory on Barren Fork of Collins River, within 100 yards of the railroad, which went into operation the following year with 2,000 spindles, and had a daily capacity of 2,500 yards of cotton domestics. The mill was destroyed by the Federal Army in 1863, and rebuilt on the same foundation in 1866, and has 2,016 spindles, 60 looms, employs 54 hands and has a daily capacity of 2,400 yards. Since Mr. Faulkner's death, in the latter part of 1886, the mills have been idle, the property being in litigation. The mills of the present, outside of McMinnville, are as follows: First District, Meed & Debard's planing-mill, saw, flour and grist, on Collins River, at Shell ford; Marshall & Mason's, J. C. Ramsey's, and C. M. Fingers' saw and corn-mills, on Charley Creek; W. T. Chasteen's saw and corn-mill on Collins River; J. Grizzle's and Wisley Wilson's saw and grist-mills on Barren Fork, Third District; T. H. and Clay Faulkner's saw-mill on Caney Fork, Fourth District; Jacob Stype's flour and corn-mill on Rocky River, Fifth District; George Mead's corn and saw-mill on Collins River, Sixth District; H. L. W. Hill's gristmill on Hill Creek, T. J. Mansfield's grist-mill on Woodley Creek, and Fitts & Faulkner's saw-mill on Dry Branch of Hill Creek, Seventh District; John Woodley's corn and saw-mill on Woodley Creek, Eighth District; Garrison McCullough's saw, flour and corn-mill at Viola, and Thomas Pea's grist-mill on Little Hickory Creek, Ninth District; W. T. Swan's corn-mill on Hickory Creek, and Widow Davis' corn-mill on Barren Fork, Tenth District; Dave Darnell's saw-mill on Barren Fork, Eleventh District; B. F. Youngblood's woolen and corn-mill on Barren Fork, and J. B. Justice's corn-mill on same stream, Twelfth District; ———— Bundrant's saw and grist-mill on Mountain Creek, Thirteenth District; C. Finger's and Adam Title's corn-mills on Charley Creek, Fourteenth District; Cleve Williams', William Houston's and Dr. Parker's saw and grist-mills on Charley Creek, Fifteenth District; S. W. D. Green's corn-mill and A. J. Goodson's corn-mill on Caney Fork.

On November 22, 1807, the General Assembly passed an act entitled "An act to divide the County of White into two separate and distinct counties," thereby establishing Warren County, and in February, 1808, the new county was organized with following boundaries: "Beginning on Cumberland Mountains where the line of White County strikes the same; thence northwesterly with the said mountain to the Indian boundary line; thence along said line to the most eastwardly branch of Duck River; thence north to the east boundary of Rutherford County; thence with lines of Rutherford, Wilson, Smith and White Counties to the beginning." The territory of Warren was subsequently materially reduced by the formation of Franklin and Grundy Counties on the south in 1809 and 1844 respectively; Coffee and Cannon Counties in 1836, and De Kalb in 1837, leaving an area of only 440 square miles, and with boundaries as follows: "North by the Counties of De Kalb and White, east by Van Buren County, south by the Counties of Grundy and Coffee, and west by the Counties of Coffee and Cannon. During the first two years of the county's existence the courts were held at the house of

Joseph Westmoreland, and in a log courthouse erected near there, on the east side of Barren Fork of Collins River, only a short distance from the present county site. In March, 1809, the county court appointed James Taylor, Thomas Matthews, Benjamin Lockhart, John Armstrong and James English as commissioners to locate a site for the permanent seat of justice, purchase the same, lay it off into town lots, and after selling them at public auction, let contracts for the erection of a courthouse and jail. The commissioners selected a site on the lands of Robert Cowan, Joseph Colville and John A. Wilson on the north side of Barren Fork of Collins River, which land is described as follows: "Beginning at a stake near Dr. Wilson's improvement and running thence west $99\frac{1}{2}$ poles to a stake; thence south 66 poles to a stake; thence east $99\frac{1}{2}$ poles; thence north 66 poles to the beginning, containing 41 acres." The land was deeded to the commissioners August 4, 1810, for the consideration of $100, and later in that month McMinnville was laid off and the lots sold. Contracts were at once let for the erection of a brick courthouse and jail, both of which were completed the following year. The courthouse was a two-story building and stood in the center of the public square. It was torn down and the present building erected in 1858 at a cost of about $12,000. The building is a large, roomy structure, two stories in height, and stands to the left of the public square, the latter having been neatly fenced and converted into a park. A log jail was built near the log courthouse in 1808, and a brick one was built at McMinnville in 1810 upon the removal of the county site. A third jail was erected in 1839, and the present substantial stone and brick was erected in 1876, costing about $4,000.

Warren County is divided into fifteen civil districts and has a total area of 281,600 acres of land. In 1870 there were 247,070 acres assessed for taxation, which were valued at $1,800,862, and the total value of taxable property was $2,535,768; in 1886 the number of acres assessed was 231,888, valued at $1,135,563, and the total value of taxable property was $1,617,171. The tax aggregate for 1886 shows taxes assessed in the county as follows: State, $1,976; county, $3,234.34; school, $4,042.92; poll, $494. In 1870 the cereal and fruit products of the county amounted to 73,391 bushels of wheat, 339,250 bushels of corn, 56,348 bushels of oats, 1,072 bushels of rye and $27,539 worth of fruit, while 12,328 gallons of brandy was distilled from the latter. The live stock for the same year amounted to 3,884 horses and mules, 3,687 cattle, 12,495 sheep and 18,814 hogs. In 1886 the products amounted to 66,200 bushels of wheat, 680,850 bushels of corn, 52,500 bushels of oats, 2,173 bushels of rye and $60,000 worth of fruit, from which there were distilled 50,000 gallons of brandy, and the live stock amounted to 4,500 horses and mules, 6,815 cattle, 8,100 sheep and 22,000 hogs.

The county had a population of 5,725 in 1810, of 10,348 in 1820, of 15,210 in 1830, of 10,803 in 1840, of 10,179 in 1850, of 11,147 in 1860, of 12,714 in 1870, of 14,092 in 1880 and of 15,050 in 1886. There were 2,431 votes cast in the county at the August election, 1886, of which 1,885 were for the Democratic nominees and 546 for the Republican.

While the county is watered by numerous streams, several of which become at times too high for fording, there is not a single bridge of any consequence in the county and not one built by the county. The county roads are improved to a certain extent, but not sufficient to prevent their becoming almost impassable during a few of the winter months. There is but one railroad in the county—the McMinnville branch of the Nashville, Chattanooga & St. Louis Railway—which enters the county near the Warren, Grundy and Coffee lines, passes in a northeast direction almost through the center of the county and out near where the Warren, White and Van Buren County lines come together, the length of the road in the county being thirty-four miles. The road was completed from Tullahoma to McMinnville in 1858 and to Sparta, in White County, in 1886.

The county court of Warren County was organized in March, 1808, at the house of Joseph Westmoreland, half a mile south of Barren Fork, where a log courthouse was afterward erected. Upon the location of the county seat at McMinnville, the court was removed thereto. The early records of this court were destroyed during the late war, and but little or nothing can be learned of the proceedings or of the officers of the same. The same is true of the other courts. The following is an incomplete list of the officers of this court:

Chairmen—Since 1850 the chairmen of the county court have been in the order given, Philip Hoodenpyle, Thomas Mabry, John Smith, Philip Hoodenpyle, Thomas S. Meyers, S. D. Walling, John Smith, John S. Meyers, W. B. Smartt, S. C. Norwood, John Smith, John W. Ford, J. L. Miller, J. W. Gales, I. B. Neal, S. J. Walling, John R. Parker and J. C. Meyers, the present incumbent.

Clerks—Joseph Colville, from 1808 to 1835; then in the order given: Wm. Edmondson, Wm. Armstrong, Wm. Lusk, Richard McGregor, J. F. Morford, A. R. Hammer, Samuel Henderson, J. H. Roberson, S. Henderson, J. H. Roberson, A. H. Gross and W. L. Swann, the present incumbent.

The circuit court was organized with the county, but as to the early officers nothing can be learned, save that Pleasant Henderson was probably the first clerk. Since 1865 the clerks have been S. C. Norwood, John J. Lowery and A. J. Curl, the present incumbent.

Sheriffs—Wm. Smartt, from 1808 to 1816, Isham Perkins succeeding him. Since 1848 the sheriffs have been J. E. Higgenbotham, Chas. M. Forrest, R. P. Burks, Wm. Grove, G. W. Hennegan. Wm. Grove, R. P. Burks, W. L. Lust, R. P. Burks, John M. Drake, W. L. Steakley, H. P. Maxwell and Ulysses Vanhooser, the present incumbent.

The chancery court was organized in 1836 with Wm. Anderson presiding as chancellor, who appointed J. F. Morford clerk and master.

Since the organization the chancellors have been Wm. Anderson, B. L. Ridley, John P. Steele, B. M. Tillman, A. S. Marks, John W. Burton, E. D. Hancock and Walter S. Beardon, present incumbent.

Clerks and masters—J. F. Morford, R. H. Mason, P. H. Coffee and J. C. Biles, the present incumbent.

Among the early lawyers of Warren County were Thomas K. Harris, Commodore Rogers, Stokley D. Rowan, B. L. Ridley, Andrew J. Marchbanks, Napoleon Baird and William Armstrong. Other lawyers of a later date and up to the beginning of the civil war, were Archibald Hicks, John B. Forrester, George Stubblefield, Joseph Carter, Washington Britain, Horace H. Harrison, Wright S. Hackett, John L. Spurlock and Thomas V. Murry. For several years after the close of the war the practicing attorneys were T. V. Murry, J. F. Thompson, John H. Savage, F. M. Smith, C. J. Spurlock, W. J. Clift and M. D. Smallman. The lawyers of the present are John H. Savage, F. M. Smith, E. W. Munford, M. B. Smallman, James S. Barton, C. C. Smith, Thomas Lynd, W. V. Whitson, W. E. B. Jones, Samuel T. O. Neal, W. W. Fairbanks, W. T. Murry and Frank Spurlock.

Several of the above were men of profound learning and of more than ordinary ability, while all of them enjoy reputations of successful lawyers and practitioners. B. L. Ridley was judge of the chancery division from 1840 until 1861; Andrew J. Marchbanks was circuit judge from 1836 until 1861; John H. Savage represented the district in Congress from 1849 to 1857 and was chairman of the Tennessee Railroad Commission from April, 1883, to December, 1884, and is, at present, member of the House of Representatives of Tennessee; M. B. Smallman is at present, circuit judge; W. V. Whitson is the present attorney-general, and W. W. Fairbanks is a member of the present Tennessee Senate. Col. H. L. W. Hill, now a resident of the Sixth Civil District, represented the district in Congress in 1847–48.

When a call for volunteers to defend Texas in her struggle for independence was made, a company was quickly raised in Warren County, at the head of which, as captain, was Gen. John B. Rogers. Later, when a call was made for volunteers to enlist in the Florida war another company was organized, but from some cause was not received. Again, in 1846, Warren County responded to the call for volunteers, and organized and sent a company to the war between the United States and Mexico. The company was commanded by Capt. Northcup, and belonged to the First Regiment of Tennessee Volunteer Infantry.

When the war between the North and South broke out Warren County, with her usual promptness, arrayed herself on the side of and espoused the cause of the South, and in answer to Gov. Harris' call for volunteers raised four companies. The men rendezvoused at Estill Springs, Coffee County, and from there, on May 24, 1861, went to Camp Trousdale, where they were organized into the Sixteenth Regiment of Tennessee Volunteer Infantry, of which John H. Savage, of McMinnville, was unanimously elected colonel, and Thomas B. Murray lieutenant-colonel. The Warren County companies were as follows: Company 1, Thomas B. Murray, captain; A. P. Smartt, first lieutenant; James Hill, second lieutenant; Thomas York, third lieutenant. Company 2, D. M. Donnell, captain; W. S. Hackett, first lieutenant; E. C. Read, second lieutenant; J. M. Castleman, third lieutenant. Company 3, P. H. Coffee, captain; George Marchbanks, first lieutenant; W. W. Mooney, second lieutenant; J. G. Rains, third lieutenant. Company 4, L. H. Meadows, captain; H. L. Simms, first lieutenant; W. G. Etter, second lieutenant; B. J. Solomon, third lieutenant. At the reorganization of the regiment at Corinth, Miss., in 1862, Col. Savage was re-elected, and of the Warren County companies the following officers were chosen: Company C, D. C. Spurlock, captain; E. C. Read, first lieutenant; Cicero Spurlock, second lieutenant; J. L. Thompson, third lieutenant. Company D, J. G. Lamberth, captain; Wm. White, first lieutenant; F. M. York, second lieutenant; H. L. Brown, third lieutenant. Company E, J. J. Womack, captain; J. K. P. Webb, first lieutenant; B. B. Green, second lieutenant; Jesse Walling, third lieutenant. Company H, James M. Parks, captain; W. G. Etter, first lieutenant; H. L. Hayes, second lieutenant; John Akeman, third lieutenant.

The Fifth Regiment of Tennessee Volunteer Infantry, subsequently known as the Thirty-fifth Regiment, was organized at Camp Smartt, near McMinnville, September 6, 1861, and of which Benjamin J. Hill, of McMinnville, was elected colonel. Five companies of this regiment were raised in Warren County, as follows: Company B, Capt. John W. Towles; Company C, Capt. Charles W. Forrest; Company D, Capt. W. T. Christian;

Company F, Capt. Ed. J. Wood; Company H, Capt. John Macon. From Camp Smartt the regiment went to Camp Trousdale, and from that place went to Bowling Green, Ky., and was placed in Gen. P. R. Cleburne's brigade of Albert Sidney Johnston's army. Later in the war Col. Hill was made a brigadier-general of cavalry. Warren County was visited at periods throughout the occupation of Tennessee, by detachments from both armies, and considerable damage resulted to both the county and McMinnville from such visits.

The first school of any consequence established in Warren County was Quincy Academy at McMinnville, which was chartered by the Legislature in 1809, and of which John A. Wilson, W. C. Smartt, Alexander Perryman, Leroy Hammond, John Armstrong and Joseph Colville were appointed trustees. The following year a log school building was erected on Jail Street, and that fall the school was opened with Prof. R. McEwin as teacher. The school was attended by both males and females, and was taught for about fifteen years, being considered one of the best institutes of learning in this part of the country. In 1820 the Edmondson Female Academy was established at McMinnville, a two-story brick building having been secured for that purpose, continued in operation until the civil war. During the occupation of this section of country by soldiers the school building was used as a hospital, and later was destroyed. In 1830 a brick building was erected at McMinnville and Carroll Academy established, a charter for the same having been secured from the Legislature. The school was successfully conducted until the civil war, when the building was destroyed and the school broken up. Irving College, nine miles south from McMinnville, was established in about 1835, and in 1845 was rebuilt and chartered by the Legislature, Prof. M. Owen being at the head of the same. The school passed through different hands and changes, but was successfully conducted up to May, 1861, when it was suspended, and remained so until 1882, when it was rechartered. The buildings consist of a main school building and four dormitory buildings, all of brick. The Cumberland Female College at McMinnville was founded in 1850 by the Middle Tennessee Synod of the Cumberland Presbyterian Church, under a charter from the Legislature, and has continued to the present in successful operation. The main building is a substantial brick structure, 125 feet in length and three stories in height. The east wing was added in 1885, and is a beautiful building, two stories in height and seventy-five feet long. The present faculty is as follows: N. J. Finney, A. M., president, and professor of languages, and mental and moral sciences; J. M. Paschal, A. B., mathematics and physics; Thomas Black, M. D., lecturer on natural science; Miss Tommie Buchanan, M. A., English intermediate branches; Miss Fanny Mashen, primary department; Mrs. Juanita B. Ewing, elocution and special vocalization; Miss Annie Wendel, instrumental music; Miss Nannie G. Halsell, piano, guitar and vocalization; Miss Laura Howell, M. A., principal of art department; Mrs. Tennie Tannatt, embroidery and general needlework; Miss Annie Clift, governess. In 1856 a brick building was erected at the hamlet of Vervilla, nine miles from McMinnville, and Hanner Highland Male and Female College established. With the exception of the suspension during the civil war this school has been in continuous operation. A private school was taught by Prof. J. P. Clark in McMinnville during the last year of the civil war, which was probably the only one in existence in the county at that time. A scheme was put on foot at the close of the war to establish a large college at McMinnville, to be known as Ben Lomond College, but the plan failed to materialize.

The first school of importance established in McMinnville after the war was Waters and Walling College, for which a substantial brick building was erected. The name of the school was that of its founders, L. B. Waters and H. L. Walling, one of whom donated the ground and the other the building. This was the public school of McMinnville until 1886, when the property was exchanged for the building occupied and owned by the colored Methodist Episcopal congregation, since when the latter has been used as a public school building and the former as a colored church and schoolhouse. Prof. W. E. Bell is the present superintendent of the city schools and principal of the white school.

At Viola, a hamlet on Hickory Creek, eleven miles from McMinnville, is a male and female college, which was established in 1883, at which time a handsome brick college building was completed. The above schools are the educational establishments of Warren County in addition to the common or public schools, which are distributed throughout the county. The terms of the public schools last from four to five months each year, and are, on the whole, an advancement over those of the surrounding counties, with a promising future. In 1839 Warren County had a scholastic population of 2,970, and received as her apportionment of school money that year $1,850.75. In 1867 the scholastic population was: White—male, 1,172; female, 1,214. Colored: male, 312; female, 296; total, white and colored, 2,994. The scholastic population in 1885 was: White—male, 2,301; female, 2,232. Colored: male, 416; female, 447; total, white and colored, 5,396. The county, for the above year, received $1,367.18 as her share of the school fund. There were, in 1886, eighty schoolhouses in the county, of which four were brick, thirty frame, and forty-six log. The estimated value of school property, including buildings, sites, desks, seats and apparatus was $16,200.

It was impossible to learn which were the pioneer churches of Warren County. All the denominations had organizations at an early date, and a number of churches were erected as early as 1804 and 1805, before the county was organized. The following, however, is a list of those of which information could be gleaned: The Primitive Baptists and Methodists erected Shiloh, a union church, in the Sixth District, as early as 1809 or 1810, and Sulphur Springs Meeting-house was a union church, erected by various denominations in the Seventh District as early as 1815, while Hickory Grove, Methodist, was erected in the Thirteenth District several years before. Mt. Zion, also Methodist, was erected in the Fifth District as early as 1820, and Caney Branch, Baptist, in the Tenth District, as early or before 1825. Ivey Bluff Meeting-house, in the Eleventh District, was erected in about 1835 by the Christians or Campbellites.

There were no churches erected in McMinnville prior to 1837, the several school buildings and the courthouse being used in which to hold religious services by the various denominations, all of which had organizations. The first church erected in the town was the Primitive Baptist, a one-story brick, in 1837, at a cost of about $1,200. The old building stands at present. The Methodist Episcopal Church South was erected in 1838, costing about $1,200. The house is still in use but the congregation is building a handsome brick structure, which is nearing completion and which will cost upward of $15,000. The Cumberland Presbyterians erected a brick church in 1840 which was destroyed in 1850, and the present handsome brick edifice was completed in 1871 at a cost of about $14,000. In about 1848 the Christian congregation erected a church, and in 1871 erected their present brick house of worship, which cost about $6,000. The Methodist Episcopal Church North, a brick, costing about $3,000, was erected in 1867, and, the congregation disbanding, the building became the property of the colored Methodist Episcopal congregation and by them was used until 1886, when it became the property of the public schools by exchange. In 1876 the Presbyterian congregation erected a handsome frame church at a cost of $1,500. The churches of the county by districts are as follows: First District, Faulkner's Chapel Methodist Episcopal South and Baptist, and Liberty Cumberland Presbyterian; Second District, New Union Methodist Episcopal South; Third District, Friendship Baptist, Shiloh Cumberland Presbyterian, and Pine Bluff Methodist Episcopal South; Fourth District, Rocky River Primitive Baptist, Rocky River Christian, and Neal Schoolhouse Methodist Episcopal South; Fifth District, Bucks Springs Separate

Baptist, New Smyrna Christian, and Centre Union, and Dark Hollow Union; Sixth District, Shiloh Methodist Episcopal South, St. Mary and Sinai, both Union; Seventh District, Sulphur Springs and Hebron, both Union; Eighth District, Mt. Zion Methodist Episcopal, Blue Springs Primitive Baptist, and White Hall Cumberland Presbyterian; Ninth District, Bascoms' Chapel Methodist Episcopal, and Philadelphia Christian; Tenth District, Caney Branch Primitive Baptist, Dripping Springs Baptist, Hollow Springs Baptist, and Wilson's Chapel Union; Eleventh District, Ivy Bluff Christian, Big Springs Separate Baptist, Oak Grove Methodist Episcopal South and Missionary Baptist, and Clearmont Presbyterian; Twelfth District, Hawkins' Chapel and Chapel Hill, both Methodist Episcopal South; Thirteenth District, Hickory Grove Methodist Episcopal, Mt. Zion Christian, and Bethlehem Presbyterian; Fourteenth District, Concord Separate Baptist, and Salem Christian; Fifteenth District, Caney Ford Separate Baptist, and Bybee's Chapel and Mason's Meeting-house, both Methodist Episcopal South.

McMinnville, the county seat, is situated about 100 miles east from Nashville, on the McMinnville branch of the Nashville, Chattanooga & St. Louis Railway, and has a population of about 2,500. The town is situated on an elevation, about 1,000 feet above sea level, on Barren Fork of Collins River, and is encircled on two sides by mountain peaks and spurs that rise at least 1,000 feet above the town. The nearest and most prominent of the peaks or spurs is Ben Lomond, which is south about two and one-half miles. To the east five miles distant is Cardwell Mountain, and between the two are a succession of peaks and spurs of no particular name.

The town was founded in 1810, by the commissioners appointed by the county court to locate the permanent seat of justice, and the following year the courts were removed thereto from across the creek where they had been held for two years. Probably the first merchant of McMinnville was John A. Wilson, who opened a general merchandise store in 1811. From that time up to 1820, the principal merchants were Cane & Coffee and Joel Mabry. Since that time, the merchants up to and including the present have been as follows: Between 1820 and 1830, Thomas Caldwell, John Black & Bros., Alexander and William Shields, S. Colville and James A. Jenkins & Co. Between 1830 and 1840, Black & Mabry, William Black & Co., Black & Mercer, John Black & Bros., Thomas Caldwell, Alexander and William Shields, H. C. Coffee, S. Colville, John J. & R. B. Cane, L. A. Kincannon & Co., Kincannon, Bell & Pendleton, Payne & Lust, and M. T. Cox. Between 1840 and 1850, the same with but few exceptions as the preceding ten years. Between 1850 and 1860, Kincannon, Bell & Pendleton, Cane & Lust, D. G. Stone & Co., Morford & Coffee, S. L. Colville & Co., J. F. Colville & Co., Read & Glasscock, Cane & French, Spurlock, Henderson & Spurlock, B. J. Hill & Co., Colville & Brown, Colville & Ross and M. T. Cox. There was no business transacted during the civil war. Between 1865 and 1870, Mercer & Coffee, R. Martin, Colville & Ross, C. Coffee & Co., Morford & Womack, W. P. & H. H. Faulkner, W. J. Jones, Milton Woodley, J. M. Cane, Gillis & Graves, Chapman & McCall, Hughes & Ritchey, Jesse Walling, Morford & Biles, B. J. Hill & Co., D. L. Brown, H. L. Walling and Parker & Hurbert. Between 1870 and 1880, Womack & Colville, D. L. Brown, W. D. & H. H. Faulkner, Morford & Co., H. L. Walling, Ross & Son, J. B. Ritchey, O. M. Thurman, J. C. Martin, Joseph Brown, R. H. Mason, Burroughs & Co., and Gross & Walling. At present, Womack & Colville, C. G. Black, Potter Bros., H. L. Walling, Hoodenpyle Bros., Webb & Brown, general merchandise; D. L. Brown, F. M. Smartt & Co., D. O. Jinkens, groceries; J. C. M. Ross & Son, O. M. Thurman, dry goods, boots and shoes; J. B. Ritchey, W. H. Flemming, drugs and books; W. H. Meadows, L. F. Jeanmire, jewelry; Mrs. Joseph Livingston, dry goods and notions; A. P. Seitz, hardware; Lively Bros., furniture; Mrs. W. C. Womack & Co., milliners; Houckins & Biles, livery stable; Warren Hotel, C. McClarty, proprietor. The McMinnville National Bank, P. W. H. Magness, president, C. Jesse Walling, cashier, was established in 1875, and has a cash capital of $70,000, with a surplus of $28,700. The People's National Bank, Sam. T. Colville, president, C. Coffee, cashier, was established in 1882, has a cash capital of $55,000, and surplus of $13,000. Both are first-class institutions, and do a general banking business.

The manufactories of McMinnville are as follows: Stave and barrel factory, Mead & Co., proprietors, was established in 1884, has a daily capacity of 3,000 staves and 1,500 sets of heading, with $12,000 capital invested; stave and handle factory, Burroughs & Co., proprietors, was established in 1874, has a daily capacity of 100 sets of spokes and 100 dozen handles, employs from fifty to sixty hands, and has invested $50,000; flour-mills, Faulkner & Walling, proprietors, was established in 1879, has a daily capacity of fifty barrels, with a capital of $7,000—the mill will in a few weeks be fitted out with a plant of the roller or patent process, which will cost about $7,000; M. B. Harwell, manufacturer of furniture, has $5,000 capital, and manufactures about $5,000 worth of furniture annually—factory was established in 1869, and improved in 1876; leather manufactory, Carson & Bass, proprietors, was established in 1886, manufactures leather annually to the amount of $3,000.

Situated two miles from town are the woolen-mills of Cantrell & Faulkner and Clay Faulkner. The former was established in 1877 by Faulkner Bros. & Co. and has a capacity of 1,000 yards of cloth per day, employs sixty-two hands, and has $75,000 capital invested. The latter was established in 1873 by T. H. & Clay Faulkner, and in 1877 Clay Faulkner became sole proprietor. The mill has annual capacity of 150,000 yards of cloth, employs twenty hands, and has capital invested to the amount of $15,000. Wagon and buggy manufactory, J. P. Gardner, proprietor, established in 1867—capacity about fifty wagons and buggies annually, and general repairing; capital, $3,000. All the above are in active operation. (Notice of the cotton-mills, near the town, may be found elsewhere in the history of the county.)

The *Mountain Echo* was the first paper published in Warren County, and was established in about 1815, by Henry Bridleman. In about 1830 Wm. Ford founded the *McMinnville Gazett*. Both papers suspended years ago. The papers of the present are the *New Era*, established in 1855 by D. F. Wallace, and now published by his sons, Wallace and Perry S., and the *Southern Standard* established in 1879 by R. P. Baker and John R. Paine, the former, publisher, and the latter, editor. In 1880 A. M. Burney became a partner in the *Standard*, and later became sole proprietor. For a few weeks in January, 1882, the paper suspended, and was revived by J. B. Ritchey and W. C. Womack, and conducted until the fall of 1882, when H. P. Neal and R. M. Reams purchased the outfit. R. M. Reams became, proprietor, and, editor of the *Standard* in March, 1884, and occupies that position at present. Both the *New Era* and *Southern Standard* are Democratic in politics, are well edited, and successfully published. The *Standard* offices is fitted out with a Campbell cylinder press.

Warren Lodge, No. 125, F. & A. M., was instituted in 1847; McMinnville Chapter, No. 99, was instituted in 1871; McMinnville Lodge, No. 146, I. O. O. F., was established in 1869; Coleman Encampment, No. 41, was instituted in 1885; Eureka Lodge, No. 6, Daughters of Rebecca, was instituted in 1876; Mountain City Lodge, No. 140, K. of H., was instituted in 1871; Tulip Lodge, No. 138, K. & L. of H., was instituted in 1880. One of the first physicians to practice medicine in McMinnville was Dr. J. P. Lawrence. Among the other physicians who practiced as late as the civil war were Drs. Sloan & Le Grand, Jesse Barnes, Dr. A. C. Rogers, Dr. Thomas Black, Drs. Alford and Bird Paine, Dr. Wilson, Dr. Smartt, Dr. John S. Young and Dr. M. Hill. Those practicing since the war and of the present are Drs. Sparks, Smith, Smartt, Black, Burger and Harrison.

Rock Island, on Caney Fork, at the mouth of Rocky River, was the first town of what is now Warren County, it having been the old county seat of White County at the time when that county embraced this county. It was quite a flourishing village at one time, and several sessions of the supreme court were held there, Gen. Andrew Jackson presiding. For years, however, there has been no town there, and but few people are aware of the fact of it having been the county seat. The site is in the Second District, twelve and a half miles east from McMinnville.

The villages of the county, all of which have populations ranging from 50 to 150, are as follows: Viola, on Hickory Creek, eleven miles from the county seat, in the Eighth District; Vervilla, on a branch of Hickory Creek, nine miles from the county seat, in the Ninth District; Morrison, 10 miles from the county seat, on the McMinnville Branch Railroad, in the Tenth District; Increase, in the Third District; Clearmont, in the Twelfth District; Meadville, in the Sixth District; Dibrell, in the Thirteenth District, and Jacksboro in the Tenth District.

COFFEE COUNTY.

COFFEE COUNTY is situated partly on the Highland Rim and at the base of the Cumberland. The rocks are the same as found everywhere in the basin. Near Manchester, the county seat, a bluish or dove-colored marble appears in abundance, forming the bed of Bark Camp Fork of Duck River, which is admired by geologists for its subdued beauty and fine quality. Near the above town a conglomerate is met with that answers a very good purpose for millstones. Some of it has all the characteristics of buhrstone, being hard and gritty. Wherever exposed, it has a cellular structure. A short distance from Manchester, on the Bark Camp Fork, is a copperas cave, so called, being a great opening under a huge, shelving rock. The copperas found in this cave is used by the people for domestic purposes, such as dyeing, etc. The cave is semi-circular and lies beneath a precipice over which a stream of water falls fifty feet. The projecting rock above is a mixture of flint and limestone, and below is a bed of black shale. The late Dr. Troost, State geologist, made a report on the minerals of Coffee County in 1837 in which he mentioned the existence of iron ore in more than one place, notably near the mouth of Compton Creek, where he reported were ore banks sufficient to warrant the erection of furnaces.

The surface of the country is beautifully diversified with hill and valley, abounding in springs of pure water, and traversed by numerous streams which furnish splendid water-power for milling purposes. The water-power near Manchester is probably unsurpassed in the State, both Barren and Bark Camp Forks of Duck River having several waterfalls each of from twenty-five to thirty-five feet. The site of the present paper-mills was surveyed in 1847 by Government civil engineers with a view to locating a United States armory at that point, and had the locality been accessible then, as now, the armory would have been established, as the report was favorable.

The soils of the valleys are very fertile, and adapted to the raising of all kinds of grain and the grasses, and grapes, apples, peaches, pears and other fruits grow in abundance.

The timber is beech, sugar, maple, elm, ash, black and white walnut, cherry, mulberry, yellow poplar, locust, linn, buckeye and other varieties.

Barren and Bark Camp Forks unite and form Duck River near Manchester, and the other streams of the county are Dowdy, Riley, Cat, Spring, Compton, Gatewood, Woolen, Gage, Norman and Noah Creeks, all emptying into Duck River, and Berry Fork, Garrison Fork, Bean and Pond Springs Creeks. Elk River touches Coffee County at Call's mill, in the Twelfth District.

Coffee County, or rather the territory now embraced within the boundaries of the county, was probably settled as early as 1800, at which time, so say traditions, the face of the country was covered with a thick growth of tall cane. However, if such was the case, there remain few if any indications of that fact at the present. Probably the first settlement was made on Noah Fork of Duck River, in the neighborhood of the site of the present hamlet of Needmore, in the Second District, by Daniel, John and Neeley Patton, brothers, while at or near the same time one Eastland settled in the neighborhood of the old stone fort, near the site of Manchester, in the Sixth District. Just when and from where those pioneers came is not definitely known, though the date is supposed to be about 1800, as other settlers coming seven and eight years later found them here with surroundings indicating a domicile of several years' duration. During the year 1809 Joseph Hickerson, John J. Smith and William Roberts came to the county, the former from North Carolina and the two latter from South Carolina. Mr. Hickerson settled on Duck River, two miles southwest from Manchester, in the Sixth District; Mr. Smith on Dowdy Creek, in the Fourth District; and Mr. Roberts in Adam Bend of Duck River, in the Fifth District.

The other early settlers of the county were as follows: Hunley and Herald Wiggins, William Murry, Timothy Carroll, James Nelson, Andrew Ervin, James Berry, Lecil Bobo, R. E. Lasater, William S. Watterson, Jesse Wooton, George Arrington, H. Morgan, Samuel Murry, Claiborne Harper, William Howard, D. S. Wright, John and David Hickerson, Louis Carden, Henry Rivers, John L. Taylor, Thomas Allison, Reuben Carden and Joseph Brown, in the neighborhood of Manchester and the Sixth District; Reuben George, Robert S. and Adam Rayburn, William Hodge, William Cross, Norman Norton, Thomas Douglass, Whitley Herald and Robert McCreary in the First District; William Watterson, Sr., Andrew Maxwell, William McFaddin and James Moore in the Second District; Thomas Patton, John Keel, Alexander, James and William McMirtle, Andrew Irwin, Thomas Bell, Jonathan Webster, William Farren and James Cunnegan in the Third District; Smith and Willis Burke, John Blythe, James Prier, William Holland and Henry Wilson in the Fourth District; Duncan Neal, William Bowden, Hugh Davidson, Sr., Hugh Davidson, Jr., William Smith, Harvard Blackman, Benjamin Jenkins and William Barton in the Fifth District; Walter Brixey, S. J. and J. T. Crockett, G. W. Roberts, Abraham Howard, James F. Phillips, Samuel Austell and William Howard in the Seventh District; John Charles, William L. Carden, E. Good, M. C. Phillips, W. C. Charles and James Winton in the Eighth District; Charles Colston, Richard Cunningham, Stephen Winton, Hiram Harpole, David Simpson and David Banks in the Ninth District; William Lackey, John Adcock, Charles Roach, Hugh O'Neal, James Darnell, John Brandon and Daniel Epley in the Tenth District; Robert Bean, James Cunningham, Isham Womack, James Sheid, John Crockett, Sr., Stewart Cowan and P. T. Stephenson in the Eleventh District; William J. Howard, Amos Austell, Peter Willis, H. M. Rutledge and Robert Lackey, in the Twelfth District; William Moore, Benjamin Deckerd, Thomas Anderson Robert Ragon, —— Montgomery, —— Ferrill, B. S. Stephenson and the Gunn family in the Thirteenth District; James Timmons, Arthur Rutledge, Coleman Blanton and John Childress in the Fourteenth District; William Heathcock, John Nelson, Hamilton Duncan, Ambrose Duncan, Douglas Duncan, William Lunley and John Sherrill in the Fifteenth District. Among the citizens of the county at the time of its organization, living in various localities, were Randolph Gibson, William Richardson, Walter Stroud, Ephram Cate, Alfred Bradley, Jesse Reynolds, Rush N. Wallace, R. R. Price, Larkin Burnham, John G. Walker, Westley Sutton, Henry Powers, Isaac Rains, Gabriel Jones, James Zell, Johnson Gossett, Wade Stroud, Alexander Downey, Josiah

Berry, John Lusk, William Montgomery, John Bragg, Charles and Joseph Gentry, Alexander Neal, John W. Camden, David Ewell, William Johnson, Thomas Blair, A. Stafford, Smith Carney, Moses Hart, C. Rainwater, David Butler, Henry Flipp, William Collins, Hiram Wyatt, Moses B. Childress, Samuel V. Simms, Sherill, Adam, Anderson and James Oliver, Daniel McLain, James Taylor, Travis Bowden, John and William Beard, Charles Oldfield, J. D. Robinson, William and Felix Carroll, G. W. Haggard, J. L. Keeling, G. W. McGrew, Michael Stevens, Levi Donnell, James A. Brantley, R. F. Ross, Moses F. White, H. S. Emmerson, Larkin Burnham, Johnson Garrett, Gabriel Jones, John Herriford and William Holmes.

So far as known, the first grist-mill erected in Coffee County was that of Josiah Berry on Barren Fork of Duck River, three miles northwest from Manchester, built in 1812, and the second one was built by Joseph Hickerson, on Brewer Creek, near Manchester, in 1815. Both were water power. Between 1820 and 1830 Joseph Hickerson erected a saw and corn-mill on Duck River in the Sixth District. Arthur Rutledge erected what was afterward known as the Childress mill, on Compton Creek, in the Fourteenth District. Thomas Busby built a corn, wheat and powder-mill on Spring Branch of Duck River, in the Fifth District, which was afterward bought by Lecil Bobo, and as such ran up to about 1850, and Wm. Williams built a corn-mill on Barren Fork of Collins River, all of which were water power. Between 1830 and 1840 Jonathan Webster built a corn-mill on Noah Fork, in the Third District; Howard Blackmore built one on Spring Branch of Duck River in the Fifth District; John Stevens built one on Gage Creek in the same district; Wm. Smith built one on Bradley Creek; all water power. In 1830 Wm. Bowden and Hugh Davidson erected cotton-gins on Duck River, in the Fifth District. At Blue Springs, two and a half miles north from Tullahoma, Messrs. Nash and Calley established a wagon manufactory, planing-mill and saw-mill in 1863, to which a branch of the Nashville, Chattanooga & St. Louis Railway was built during the same year, and for several years an immense business was transacted. The mills were removed a number of years ago and the railroad torn up. The minor industries of the county, located outside of Manchester and Tullahoma, are as follows: Third District—Samuel Brantley's saw and grist-mill and Beckman Bros.' flour and grist-mill on Noah Fork. Fourth District— James Drake's still-house. Fifth District—Sims, Davis & Hildebrand's flour, grist and still on Gage Creek. Sixth District—B. P. Bashan's and John Tolliver's grist-mills on Brewer Creek; L. D. Hickerson's (Jr.), saw-mill on Haggard's branch and James W. Stephen's grist-mill on

Goodman's branch. Seventh District—T. E. Jones' grist and saw-mill at Hillsboro; James Howard's corn-mill, and Call & Huffer's still-house on Bradley's Creek. Ninth District—John A. Bryant's two grist-mills on Barren Fork of Hickory Creek. Tenth District—George Schroeder's corn-mill and still on Hickory Creek, and James Fletcher's still on Barren Fork of Collins River. Eleventh District—O. H. Allen's grist-mill on McGowan Creek, and J. A. Lusk's corn-mill and T. S. Gunn's still on Bean Creek. Twelfth District—E. A. Call's flour and grist-mill, Ellis Davidson's grist-mill, E. A. Call's and W. W. Harris' stills; all on Bradley Creek.

On January 8, 1836, the General Assembly passed an act entitled "An act to establish the county of Coffee" out of territory to be cut off from the counties of Bedford, Warren and Franklin. The above act appointed Hugh Davidson, Alexander Blakely, John Hickerson, William Bradshaw, Thomas Powers and Lecil Bobo commissioners to run the boundary lines and locate a permanent seat of justice for the new county, and in February following the lines were run, leaving the county bounded on the north by the counties of Rutherford, Cannon and Warren, east by Warren and Grundy, south by Franklin and Moore and west by Bedford. The seat of justice was located upon the lands of James Evans and Andrew Haynes, the same being described as "situated on the south side of Bark Camp Fork of Duck River on both sides of the road leading from Winchester, Franklin County, to Nashville, being within four miles of the center of the county and supposed to contain 200 acres." Messrs. Evans and Haynes donated the above land to the county by deed registered March 1, 1836.

An election of county officers was held in March and the county formally organized in May, when William S. Watterson, John G. Walker, John O. Johnson, Joseph Hickerson and Jesse Wooten were appointed to survey and lay off the county site into town lots, sell the same and award contracts for building a courthouse and jail. The sale of lots took place soon afterward and the contracts awarded for a brick courthouse and jail. The courthouse was completed in 1837 and was destroyed by fire in December, 1870. The building was a two-story brick and cost about $10,000. The present courthouse was completed in 1871 and stands on the site of the one destroyed. It is a handsome brick two-story building of modern style. On the ground floor is the county court room and the quarters of the county officers, while the second floor is devoted to the circuit court and jury rooms. The building stands in the center of a large public square, inclosed with a combination iron and wood fence, and cost about $15,000. The first brick jail was completed in 1837 and was used as such up to about 1857, when it was destroyed by fire. The present brick and stone jail was completed in 1859, costing about $6,000.

At the organization of the county it was laid off into thirteen civil districts, but was subdivided at different times until there are now sixteen their territory belonging originally to counties as follows: First, Second, Third, Fourth, Sixteenth and part of the Fifteenth Districts to Bedford; Fifth, Sixth, Seventh, Eighth, Eleventh, Twelfth, Thirteenth and Fourteenth to Franklin; Ninth, Tenth and part of Fifteenth to Warren. The county had a population of 8,184 in 1840; of 8,354 in 1850; of 9,689 in 1860; of 10,237 in 1870; of 11,500 in 1880, and about 12,000 in 1886. At the August election, 1886, there were 2,249 votes polled in the county, of which the Democratic ticket received 1,833, and the Republican ticket 416, giving a Democratic majority of 1,387. In 1870 there were 253,816 acres of land assessed for taxation in Coffee County, the value of which was $1,520,201, and the total value of property assessed was $1,911,074. The number of acres assessed in 1886 was 261,610, valued at $986,599, and the total value of property assessed was $1,421,415. The tax aggregate for 1886, shows taxes assessed as follows: State, $4,264; county, $4,039; school, $6,695; roads, $888, with additional railroad and telegraph taxes as follows: Main stem of Nashville, Chattanooga & St. Louis Railroad, total tax of $1,262.02; McMinnville Branch of Nashville, Chattanooga & St. Louis Railway, total tax of $1,270.77. In 1870 the cereal products of the county were, wheat, 43,075 bushels; rye, 10,226 bushels; corn, 309,503 bushels; oats, 25,462 bushels. In 1886 the products were, wheat, 58,160 bushels; rye, 4,500 bushels; corn, 650,290 bushels; oats, 35,000 bushels.

In 1870 there were in the county, 3,009 head of horses and mules; 2,448 head of cattle; 8,107 head of sheep, and 17,226 head of hogs. In 1886 there were 4,100 head of horses and mules; 5,800 head of cattle; 7,300 head of sheep, and 20,800 head of hogs.

The Nashville, Chattanooga & St. Louis Railroad runs through the extreme southwest corner of Coffee County, and was completed in 1852, while the Sparta or McMinnville branch of the same runs in a northeast direction across the county, being completed to McMinnville in 1856, and to Sparta in 188 . The two roads furnish ample transportation facilities for the county.

Adam Rayburn, Alfred Ashley, Robert S. Rayburn, Alex Downey, John G. Walker, Larkin Burnham, Wm. Hodge, Johnson Garrett, James Zell, Wm. Montgomery, Gabriel Jones, Lecil Bobo, Josiah Berry, John W. Camden, John Herriford, John Charles, James W. Arnold, John

Lusk, Jesse Wooton, Wade Stroud and Wm. Holmes, all bearing commissions from the governor appointing them magistrates for Coffee County, met at the old log Baptist meeting-house which stood on the site of Manchester, the county seat, on Monday, May 2, 1836, and after taking the oath of office, organized the county court by electing John W. Camden, chairman. Daniel McLain, John Bell, James A. Brantly and Moses F. White, who had been chosen clerk, sheriff, register and trustee, respectively, at the March election, produced their certificates of election, qualified and assumed the duties of their offices. The sessions of the court were held in the meeting-house until the completion of the court-house in 1837.

The circuit court was organized in June, 1836, at the old Stone Fort Tavern, with Judge Samuel Anderson on the bench, and James Whitesides as attorney-general; George W. Richardson was the clerk, he having been elected to that office at the March election. The early records of this court were destroyed by fire, there being none now previous to 1854, and the writer secured the above information from the older citizens, among whom were Messers. Wylie Hickerson and R. E. Lasater, of Manchester, both of whom were residents of the county at its formation.

Like those of the circuit court, the records of the chancery court were destroyed to a great extent by fire, those of the year 1868 being the earliest, and the deficiency was filled by the memories of the citizens. The court was organized with the county, and Judge B. L. Ridley was probably the first chancellor presiding, George Arrington being appointed clerk and master.

Below is given a list of the judges, chancellors, attorney-generals and different county officers, together with the date of their service:

Samuel Anderson, 1836-44; A. J. Marchbanks, 1844-61; Wm. P. Hickerson, 1865-67; N. A. Patterson, 1867-69; Wm. P. Hickerson, 1869-77; J. J. Williams, 1877-86; M. B. Smallman, present incumbent.

Attorney-generals: James Whitesides, 1836-44; Joseph Carter, 1844-52; George Stubblefield, 1852-61; Fred A. Hanford, 1865-66; Newton I. Temple, 1866-68; W. J. Clift, 1868-69; J. G. Mohler, 1869-70; J. H. Holman, 1870-72; J. D. Tillman, 1872-78; A. B. Woodard, 1878-86; W. V. Whitson, present incumbent.

Chancellors: B. L. Ridley, 18——; B. M. Tillman, 1868-71; A. S. Marks, 1871-78; John W. Burton, 1878-84; E. D. Hancock, 1884-86; S. A. Key, present incumbent.

Clerks and Masters: George Arrington; J. L. Thompson; S. N. Burger; J. J. Pittman; James Price, 1868-71; T. J. Wilson, 1871-77; John S. Moore, 1877, and present incumbent.

Chairmen of county court: John W. Camden, 1836–37; Adam Rayburn, 1837–39; Robert S. Rayburn, 1839–41; Michael Stevens, 1841–42; Robert S. Rayburn, 1842–45; John G. Walker, 1845–46; Wm. B. Williams, 1846–47; John G. Walker, 1847–48; James L. Woods, 1848–49; L. W. Marbury, 1849–50; Michael Stevens, 1850–51; John G. Walker, 1851–52; James A. Brantley, 1852 until June, 1856; R. W. Casey, county judge from June, 1856, to January, 1858; James A. Brantley, chairman, 1858–60; R. W. Casey, 1860–61; M. A. Carden, 1861–62; R. W. Casey, 1862–66; Greenville Fletcher, 1866–68; H. W. Carroll, 1868–69; James Price, 1869–70; W. L. Carden, 1870–71; James K. P. Carroll, 1871–72; E. A. Rutherford, 1872–74; J. M. Sims, 1874–75; E. A. Rutherford, 1875–79; C. N. Townsend, 1879–82; J. W. Wagoner, 1882–83; H. F. Smartt, 1883–84; W. L. Carden, 1884–85; C. T. Wilson, 1885–86; Lewis B. Morgan, 1886–87, and present incumbent.

County court clerks: Daniel McLean, 1836–38; Levi Donnell, 1838–39; W. A. Hickerson, 1839–40; Lecil Bobo, 1840–44; John W. Anderson, 1844–48; James Darnell, 1848–52; A. M. Short, 1852–54; Hiram S. Emmerson, 1854–70; James Darnell, 1870–78; Simeon Ashley, 1878–86; Charles T. Wilson, August, 1886, to January, 1887, when court appointed J. W. Wagoner.

Circuit court clerks: George W. Richardson, 1836–38; Daniel McLain, 1838–42; Willis Blanton, 1842–50; Frank Ragsdale, 1850–54; C. C. Brewer, 1854–61; Daniel McLain, 1865–70; John A. Moore, 1870–74; W. T. Wilson, 1874–78; H. A. Phillips, 1878–86; Simeon Ashley, present incumbent.

Sheriffs: John Bell, 1836–42; Daniel McLain, 1842–48; Columbus Brawley, 1848–54; Francis M. Boyd, 1854–58; J. A. Carden, 1858–61; Burrell Ward, 1861–68; A. J. Usselton, 1868–72; H. W. Carroll, 1872–74; J. H. L. Duncan, 1874–78; F. H. Thomas, 1878–79; H. W. Carroll, 1879–80; E. Gray, 1880–82; H. W. Carroll, 1882–84; John H. Ashley, 1884–86, and present incumbent.

Registers: James A. Brantley, 1836–40; R. F. Ross, 1840–48; Charles Toliver, 1848–56; W. F. Gibson, 1856–58; Daniel McLain, 1858–65; Burr H. Emerson, 1865; R. R. Ferrill, 1865–66; Burr H. Emerson, 1866–79; B. S. Stroud, 1879–86, and present incumbent.

Trustees: Moses F. White, 1836–42; Uriah Sherrill, 1842–50; James N. Campbell, 1850–52; E. E. Thacker, 1852–61; H. Shackleford, 1861–65; J. A. Carden, 1865–66; H. Shackleford, 1866–68; Wm. P. McDonald, 1868–69; G. D. Emerson, 1869–72; John S. Moore, 1872–76; E. Gray, 1876–80; W. T. Wilson, 1880–82; J. H. Smith, 1882–86; B. P. Layne, 1886, and present incumbent.

H. S. Emerson was the first resident lawyer of the county, he beginning the practice of that profession in 1836. Following soon after and contemporaneous with Mr. Emerson, were W. P. Hickerson and Robert and Isaiah Richardson. Between 1850 and 1860 P. C. Isbell and Thomas C. Goodner were the attorneys; between 1865 and 1870 P. C. Isbell, W. P. Hickerson, R. M. Vannoy, I. C. Stone, C. A. Sheafe, and A. T. Seitz; between 1870 and 1880, P. C. Isbell, W. P. Hickerson, James G. Aydelott, G. W. Cross, I. C. Stone and R. M. Vannoy; of the present, P. C. Isbell, G. W. Cross, I. C. Stone, R. M. Vannoy, P. B. Bashaw of Manchester, George W. Davidson, James G. Aydelott, J. M. Travis, L. B. Morgan and T. H. Baker of Tullahoma.

While Coffee County did not furnish a company to the Florida war, the following citizens joined companies from adjoining counties: R. E. Lasater, Richard B. Lasater, Hinton Jones, S. G. Crockett, Stephen Winton, Gordon McCutcheon, Ransom Davidson and Daniel Marshall.

Under the first call for volunteers in 1846 to serve in the war of the United States with Mexico, Company B, of the Third Tennessee Regiment of Volunteers, was raised chiefly in Coffee County. The company rendezvoused at Manchester, and elected John W. Anderson, captain: John O. Brixey, first lieutenant; Mack Clark, second lieutenant, and James Buckaloo, third lieutenant. Among the members of Company B were Wm. Lowery, James Taylor, Mitchell Adams, Joshua Penn, James Butler, Wm. Flippo, living, and Wm. Bobo, F. M. Bobo, Ed. Scott, D. W. Duncan, John Stephens, Wm. Couch, Robt. Couch, Daniel Blackburn, John Blackman, Joshua Clark, John Owens, Aaron Carroll, Joseph Carroll, Samuel Anderson, W. G. Corey, Wm. McBee, Mathias McBee, dead. The following companies were organized in Coffee County for the Confederate Armies during the civil war.

Company B, First Regiment of Tennessee Infantry (Turney's) was organized at Tullahoma in April, 1861, and joined the regiment at Winchester, from there they went to Virginia. The officers were Pierce B. Anderson, captain; John Bennett, first lieutenant; George W. Edwards, second lieutenant; R. R. Enoch, third lieutenant. At the organization of the regiment Anderson was elected major of the same, and the officers of Company B were promoted according to rank at organization, Bennett being elected captain.

Company G, Twenty-fourth Regiment of Infantry, was organized in June, 1861, at Hillsboro, and Wm. May was elected captain; I. T. Roberts, first lieutenant; John Oliver, second lieutenant; David Hepp, third lieutenant. At the reorganization at Corinth, Miss., in 1862, I. T. Roberts was chosen captain; F. M. Womack, first lieutenant; John Arnold, second lieutenant; Wm. Meadows, third lieutenant.

Company A, Thirty-seventh Regiment of Infantry, was organized at Tullahoma in the summer of 1861, of which E. F. Hunt was elected captain; Carroll Blackwell, first lieutenant; Lewis Powell, second lieutenant; Arthur Edwards, third lieutenant. Hunt was elected major of the regiment at the reorganization of the same at Corinth.

Company K, Twenty-fourth Regiment of Infantry, was organized at Manchester in July, 1861, and officers were elected as follows: T. C. Goodner, captain; Wm. Seay, first lieutenant; Henry McBrown, second lieutenant: Frank H. Ragsdale, third lieutenant. At the reorganization at Corinth T. C. Goodner was re-elected captain; Frank H. Ragsdale, first lieutenant; C. Barton, second lieutenant; Robert McGuire, third lieutenant.

Company E, Sixteenth Regiment of Infantry, was organized at Manchester in the early part of 1861, electing officers as follows: C. C. Brewer, captain; S. G. Crocker, first lieutenant; G. W. Turner, second lieutenant; J. E. Bashaw, third lieutenant. At the reorganization at Corinth the letter of the company was changed to that of B, and J. H. L. Duncan was elected captain; E. W. Walker, first lieutenant; J. H. Ensey, second lieutenant; W. H. Fisher, third lieutenant.

Company A, Forty-fourth Regiment of Infantry, was organized at Needmore in September, 1861, of which W. P. Cherry was elected captain; Marion Chandler, first lieutenant; Carroll Haley, second lieutenant; Samuel Hart, third lieutenant. At Bowling Green, Ky., the letter of the company was changed to B, and the reorganization at Corinth the Forty-fourth and Forty-fifth Regiments were consolidated. Of the company David Buckner was elected captain; Thomas Goodlow, first lieutenant; Jack Chandler, second lieutenant; Jonathan Webster, third lieutenant. Buckner resigned the same year, and Chandler succeeded him as captain, and later in the same year Chandler resigned and was succeeded by Goodlow.

Company I, Fourth Regiment Infantry (Starnes') was organized at Manchester in 1862. P. H. McBride was elected captain; Hal. Mason, first lieutenant; Wm. Crocker, second lieutenant; George Morgan, third lieutenant.

Company D, Forty-fifth Regiment of Infantry, was organized at Winchester, and was composed of men from Coffee, Lincoln and Moore Counties. A. Walt of Lincoln County was elected captain; James Grant, of Moore County, first lieutenant; Joseph Baxter, of Coffee County, second lieutenant.

Company H, Eleventh Regiment of Cavalry, was organized at McMinnville in October, 1862, and was composed of about twenty men from Coffee and eighty from Warren County. The officers elected were

Chatham Coffee, of Warren County, captain; J. J. Lowery, of Warren County, first lieutenant; Robert Bruce, of Coffee County, second lieutenant;— Gurley, of Warren County, third lieutenant. In June, 1861, several of the prominent young men of Tullahoma, among whom were W. H. McLemore, Adam Grass, James and Ezekial Jones, joined Rutledge's battery, and served with distinction throughout the war.

But little can now be learned of the schools of Coffee County previous to 1820. That there were schools in the county before that date there can be no doubt, but as to their location and who taught them there is no record. In 1820 Timothy Carroll opened a school on Cat Creek, a small stream of the Sixth District, and taught several months in the year up to about 1823. James Nelson taught a school at the foot of the hill, on which is now located Manchester, for a number of years beginning in 1823, and in 1839 Daniel McLain, the first county clerk, and afterward sheriff, register and circuit clerk, taught a school on Duck River. In 1837 a school was established in the old Baptist Church at Manchester, and when the new Baptist Church was erected it was moved there too and taught there until the county academy was built in 1847. This school was chartered by the Legislature in 1846, and the year following a one-story brick schoolhouse was erected. The building was burned in 1858. From that time until 1867 the school was taught in the Methodist Church building. At the above date a large frame building was erected and the Manchester Male and Female College was established, and is in operation at the present. Probably the first school taught in Tullahoma was by Mrs. Witherby, mother of Mr. James G. Aydelott, now a leading citizen of the city, who opened a small school in 1853. From that time until the close of the late war nothing but free schools were taught in the town. A school was established by the Masonic Lodge in 1867, known as the Masonic Institute, and taught in the frame building erected by the soldiers. This school continued, and was the only one taught in Tullahoma up to 1871, when it was abandoned. The Tullahoma College, was established under the auspices of the Methodist Church in 1872, and taught in that church until 1876, when a large frame building was completed for the school. The school continued in active operation until 1886, when it was succeeded by the graded public school. For the accommodation of this school a large two-story brick building was erected at a cost of about $6,000. At present 350 students are in attendance and six teachers employed. The Tullahoma High School was established by a stock company in 1882, under the management of Profs. Carden and Farras, and is at present under the tutorship of Prof. Samuel J. Farras, assisted by a corps of three teachers. A substantial frame building, costing upward of $3,000, was completed in 1883 for this school. The important schools of this county in operation at present are Bell Springs Academy, at the hamlet of Noah, chartered in 1880; Beech Grove Academy, chartered in 1869; Hillsboro Academy, chartered in 1879, besides the above mentioned schools of Manchester and Tullahoma. Good free schools are taught in each school district from four to six months in the year. In 1839 the scholastic population of Coffee County was 2,224, and the amount of money received from the school fund apportionment was $1,385.88. In 1867 the scholastic population was as follows: White—male, 1,642; female, 1,555; colored—male, 272; female, 254; total, white and colored male, 1,914; white and colored female, 1,809; grand total, 3,723. In 1885 the scholastic population was as follows: White—male, 2,389; female, 2,328; colored—male, 337; female, 385; total, 5,439. During the latter year the county received by the semi-annual apportionment of school funds, $665.94 in April, and a similar sum in October. In 1885 teachers were employed in the county as follows: White—male, 38; female, 15; colored—male, 4; female, 5; total, 62; and teachers were licensed as follows: White—male, 38; female, 15; colored—male, 4; female, 5; total, 62.

The first church erected in what is now called Coffee County was the log meeting-house on Garrison Fork of Duck River, in the Second District, which was built as early as 1812 or 1814 by the Separate Baptists, and the second was the log meeting-house on the site of Manchester, erected by the Baptists in about 1815, and in which the magistrates met to organize the county in 1836. The former church was replaced with a frame building in 1859 and the latter also by a frame in about 1837, being used by all denominations up to that date. The other early churches of the county were Pond Spring, Baptist, in the Seventh District, erected in 1819; Carroll's meeting-house, Methodist Episcopal, in the Fifth District, erected in 1820, now gone; Riley Creek Baptist Church, in the Fourth District, built for a church and schoolhouse in 1820; Hillsboro Cumberland Presbyterian Church, in the Seventh District, erected in 1820; Goose Pond Methodist Episcopal Church, in the Fifteenth District; Bean Creek Separate Baptist, in the Eleventh District, and Mount Pleasant Methodist Episcopal, in the Eighth District, all built in 1830; Mount Carmel Methodist Episcopal, in the Ninth District; Mount Zion Methodist Episcopal, in the Fifth District; Fountain Grove Methodist Episcopal, in the Tenth District, and Noah Fork Baptist, in the Third District, all erected between 1830 and 1840; Hopewell Primitive Baptist, in the Eleventh District; Union Cumberland Presbyterian, in the First District; Hayter Camp Ground Methodist Episcopal, in the Twelfth District; Beech Grove Cumberland Presbyterian, in the Second District; Asbury Methodist Episcopal, in the Eighth District, and Mount Vernon and Spring Creek, both Methodist Episcopal, in the Fifth District, all erected between 1840 and 1850; Hurricane Grove Separate and Missionary Baptists, in the Third District, erected in 1853. Of the above Goose Pond Church was destroyed by fire in December, 1886, leaving the District without a church, and Fountain Grove, Hayter's Camp Ground, Hurricane Grove, Pond Spring, Mount Zion, Mount Vernon, Manchester Baptist, Carroll's Meeting House and Spring Creek Churches have all been abandoned some five, ten, fifteen and twenty years ago. The churches of the present are as follows: In the town of Manchester, Cumberland Presbyterian Church, frame, erected in 1850; Methodist Episcopal Church, erected first in 1852 and a new brick in 1883; Christian, frame, erected in 1870, and Missionary Baptist, brick, completed first part of 1887; Tullahoma Churches: Methodist Episcopal, frame, erected in 1855 and destroyed during the war. At the close of the war the military authorities stationed at the town caused a large frame building to be erected, and presented the same to the citizens to be used as a church, school and public building generally. Methodist Episcopal South, frame, erected in 1868; Methodist Episcopal North, frame, erected in 1872; Episcopal, frame, erected in 1875; Baptist, frame, erected in 1876; Cumberland Presbyterian, frame, erected in 1878; Christian, brick, erected in 1881, and Presbyterian, brick, erected in 1886. Beech Grove Churches: Cumberland Presbyterian, frame, erected in 1844; Christian, erected in 1878; Methodist Episcopal South, in course of erection; of the First District, Union Cumberland Presbyterian and Jarnigan's Schoolhouse, Baptist; Second District, Mount Ararat Methodist Episcopal school; Third District, Noah Fork Separate Baptist, Wiser's Bluff, Christian and Noah Methodist Episcopal South; Fourth District, Riley Creek Baptist and Holland Creek and Reden's Chapel, both Methodist Episcopal South; Fifth District, Neal's Chapel and Bethany, both Methodist Episcopal South; Sixth District, Blanton's Chapel, Union, Ragsdale and New Union Methodist Episcopal South, Bethel Separate Baptist, Hull's Chapel Methodist Episcopal North, and Busby Branch Separate Baptist; Seventh District, Hillsboro Cumberland Presbyterian and Union Churches and Pond Spring Baptist; Eight District, Mount Pleasant and Asbury Methodist Episcopal South; Ninth District, Mount Carmel and Hickory Grove Methodist Episcopal South and Antioch, Christian; Tenth District, Hopewell and Summitville Methodist Episcopal South, Pleasant Grove Separate Baptist and Mud Creek Missionary Baptist and Christian;

Eleventh District, Bean Creek Separate Baptist and Christian and Pleasant Hill Cumberland Presbyterian; Twelfth District, Pleasant Plains Christian; Fourteenth District, Concord Separate Baptist; Sixteenth District, Bacon's Chapel Separate Baptist and Philadelphia Christian.

Manchester, the county seat, lies on the south side of Bark Camp Fork of Duck River, on a high beautiful level, 1,050 feet above sea level, eighteen miles distant from, and in full view of the Cumberland Mountains, and on the McMinnville branch of the Nashville, Chattanooga & St. Louis Railway, twelve miles from Tullahoma, and has a population of about 600. The location upon which the town was founded in 1836, was for many years known as the Stone Fort, a diagram and sketch of which may be found in the state department of this book, and was a post hamlet on the old stage route from Winchester to Nashville. As early as 1815 — Eastland established a tavern or ordinary at the foot of the hill on which the town now stands, which was known as the Stone Fort Tavern. In later years the tavern was kept by the father of Col. A. S. Collier, editor of the Nashville *Union*. Among the pioneer merchants of Manchester were John Bell, James White, Joseph Brown, Grimer & Morgan, Blanton & Co., and Hickerson & Powers, all of whom engaged in business prior to 1840. Between 1840 and 1850 Wylie, William A. and Leander Hickerson, Harvard Morgan, Anderson Powers and George Arrington were the merchants; R. E. Lasater, Shacklefold & Co., James Neal, J. E. and G. W. Jackson, and L. Hickerson, from 1850 to the breaking out of the civil war, from which time to the close of the same there was no business transacted. Between 1865 and 1870 the merchants were Lasater & Rathbone, D. P. Rathbone, Wm. Blood, R. E. Lasater, Shackleford & Co., and Marcell & Bro. Between 1870 and 1880 D. P. Rathbone, C. McCrury, Marcell & Bro., Emmerson & Co., Burger & Kelton, Riggs & Son, Rutherford & Terrell, Moore & Timmons, G. T. Sain and Samuel Cross. The present business men are E. S. Hough and Price & LeCroy, drugs; Wooton & Winton, Bryant & Harmon, I. J. Green, I. N. Jones, J. P. Adams and Willis & Wilkerson, general merchandise; T. J. Scott, W. J. Taylor and Wm. Ferguson, family groceries; Burger & Allwood, livery stable; Wm. H. Clay, undertaker, and Turner & Thomas, meat market; hotels, W. M. Green and L. M. Robinson. Samuel Murry erected a rope factory at the little falls on Bark Camp Fork of Duck River at Manchester, in 1823, which was destroyed by fire, and in 1847 A. B. Robertson erected a flour, grist and saw-mill on the same site, which was also destroyed by fire in 1871. During the first named year Wm. Murry began the erection of a cotton factory on

Brewer Creek, three miles north of Manchester, which was completed and operated for a number of years by J. E. Bashaw. — Eastland operated a still-house under the hill at Manchester, as early as 1812, and in 1830 Joseph Hickerson erected a cotton-gin in the neighborhood. In 1852 W. S. Whiteman erected a paper-mill on Barren Fork of Duck River, at Manchester, which was burned in 1871. He also erected a powder-mill in 1862 near the same site, and manufactured powder for the Confederate Army until the destruction of the mill and magazines by the Federal soldiers in 1863. In 1878 Charles Ohlemacher erected a hub and spoke factory near the depot, and operated the same for about five years, and then removed the same to Shelbyville. In 1879 the Stone Fort Paper Company erected a large frame paper-mill on the site of the old paper-mill, which is now operated by Hickerson & Wooton. The mill has a daily capacity of 4,000 pounds of paper, and about thirty hands are employed. Writing, news and wrapping paper are manufactured. The pulp used is also manufactured at these mills. Capital to the amount of $40,000 is invested in the enterprise. The early and present physicians of Manchester are Drs. Williams, J. E. Rhoades, Jackson, Miller, A. F. Vincent, Burgie, Barnes, J. D. Wooton and C. E. Price.

The newspaper of the town is the *Manchester Times*, F. N. Miller, editor and proprietor. It was established in November, 1881, and is a live, progressive Democratic paper, and ably edited. Other newspaper adventures of the past were, in the order given, the *Gospel Herald*, founded in 1860 by Rees Jones; the *People's Paper*, established in 1860 by A. Butterworth; the *True Patriot*, established in 1862 by P. C. Isbell; the *Conservative*, established in 1868 by Hulfish Bros.; the *Coffee County Democrat*, established in 1871 by G. M. Emack; and the *Manchester Guardian*, established in 1874 by C. T. and T. J. Wilson, all of which were published for periods ranging from seven weeks to four years.

Harmony Lodge, No. 214, F. & A. M., was instituted in 1850. Stone Fort Chapter, No. 62, Royal Arch Masons, was instituted in 1851; Manchester Lodge, No. 207, I. O. O. F., instituted in 1878, and Stone Fort Lodge, No. 2146, K. of H., was instituted in 1881.

Manchester was incorporated January 6, 1838, and the charter was surrendered March 28, 1883, in order to permit the four-mile school temperance law to take effect, the Manchester College being a chartered institution.

Tullahoma, one of the most flourishing towns in Middle Tennessee, and a manufacturing center, is situated on the Nashville, Chattanooga & St. Louis Railway, and at the terminus of the McMinnville branch of the same, sixty-nine miles southeast from Nashville, eighty-two miles northwest from Chattanooga and twelve miles southwest from Manchester, and has a population of 3,000. Situated on the Highland Rim, 1,170 feet above sea level, being the highest point on the railroad between Nashville and Chattanooga, with the Cumberland Mountains in view, a climate unsurpassed in the South, surrounded by excellent mineral springs, with a moral and progressive class of citizens, Tullahoma is one of the most desirable locations in the South, and is also a summer resort of considerable note.

The town was founded in 1851 by a town company organized for that purpose, at the head of which were Thomas Anderson, Benjamin Deckerd, Wm. Moore, Volney S. Stephenson and Pierce B. Anderson. In February, 1858, a charter of incorporation was granted the town, which, as amended, is in force at present.

A grocery store was opened by James Grizzard, the pioneer merchant, in the year 1851, and later in the same year L. W. Ingle opened a dry goods store and the first hotel, the Lincoln House," was erected by Meredith P. Pearson. Following the above and up to the breaking out of the civil war, the merchants were Gowan & McLemore, J. B. Witherby, J. E. Pearson & Co., Jordan & Morgan, Hunt & Shaw, John B. Smith, James Daniels, Simpson Bros., Berry & Gowan, McLemore & Enoch, Geo. W. Walden, J. W. Marshall, Simpson & Co., J. E. Rosborough, Jones & Galloway, M. Hollander, Edwards & Norton, J. F. Thomas, A. Woods and J. R. Graham. Wm. Moore was the liveryman of that period, and during the latter part of the same the Veranda Hotel, was erected, of which J. E. Hogan was proprietor. Drs. J. E. Hogan, James Norton, Thomas Anderson, C. S. Harris, J. R. Blake, A. M. Holt and son Joseph, Street, Strong and Fain were the physicians of that period.

By March, 1862, business had been entirely suspended in the town, but upon the arrival of Federal troops in 1863 stores were opened by J. F. Thomas, Wm. Crane and Lasater & Rathbone. From 1865 to 1870 the merchants were Campbell & Genthner, W. Wait & Co., S. J. Leichleucher, Marshall & Norton, Lasater & Elkins, Crane & Witherby, Witherby & Aydelott, Hickerson & Powers, Collins & Co., Marbury & Freeman and Lasater & Hill. From 1870 to 1880 they were I. F. Maynard, Ward & Powers, S. W. French, R. Wilson, D. S. Monger, Witherby & Aydelott, Hickerson & Powers, Campbell & McLemore, M. P. Marbury, Aydelott, Davidson & Co., and C. F. Hickerson & Co.

The business of the present is as follows: Maynard & Sons, Carroll Bros. & Co., R. H. Richardson, Brainard & Smith, Moore & Hickerson, general merchandise; W. E. Russell, J. W. Yates, W. M. Ross, S. J. McLemore, Crowell Bros., M. N. Moore & Sons, family groceries; A. B. Conley, R. Wilson, dry goods and clothing; Rutledge Bros., clothing and furnishing goods; George R. Crane, Williams & Sewell, drugs; George N. Carter, G. W. Bowden, jewelry; W. A. Marshall, furniture; Baird & McCoy, agricultural implements; Jacob Graft, Lawson & Dean, stoves and tinware; J. L. Jones, produce; Frank Hodgkins, restaurant; W. H. Gilbert, bakery and meat market; R. M. Staley, photographer; Mrs. Blakemore, Misses Bailett, milliners; Ward Bros., Elan & Kirk, livery stables; Marcell & Dewey, undertakers; hotels, St. James, John B. Carroll, proprietor; Hurricane Hall, Miller Bros., proprietors; and De Corzelius, F. Corzelius, proprietor. The Tullahoma First National Bank was established in 1883, with L. D. Hickerson, Sr., president, and S. J. Walling, cashier. The present officers are L. D. Hickerson, Sr., president, and L. D. Hickerson, Jr., cashier, the latter having been elected in October, 1885. The cash capital of the bank is $50,000, with $6,000 surplus.

Since the close of the war up to the present time the following physicians have practiced in Tullahoma, in about the order named: Drs. W. T. Allen, Seth Hart, A. M., and Joseph Holt, W. M. Fariss, A. W. Booth, J. B. Cowan, J. W. Phillips and J. C. Smith, the last five being those of the present.

The manufacturing establishments are as follows: The Tullahoma woolen-mill, W. R. French, proprietor, was established in 1875, has 125 hands employed and capital to the extent of $100,000 invested; Tullahoma hub, spoke and rim factory, M. R. Campbell, proprietor, was established in 1874, employs forty hands, and has invested $45,000; Tullahoma file works, M. R. Campbell, proprietor, established in 1882, employs twenty-five hands, and has $30,000 invested; Tullahoma planing and saw-mill, George W. Steagall, proprietor, established in 1883, employs thirty hands, and has $20,000 capital invested; Tullahoma flour-mills, Hawkins & Co., proprietors, established in 1871, has a capacity of forty barrels per day, and capital to the extent of $10,000 invested; Tullahoma distillery (registered No. 533) established in 1882, has a daily capacity of three barrels, and capital invested $5,000; Tullahoma shirt factory, G. A. Moulton, proprietor, established in 1885, capital invested $800. Tullahoma Lodge, No. 262, F. & A. M., was instituted in 1853; Grizzard Chapter, No. 122, was instituted in 1869, and reorganized as Tullahoma Chapter, No. 122, in 1886; Tullahoma Lodge, No. 101, I. O. O. F., was instituted June 17, 1857, and reorganized March 21, 1866; Tullahoma Encampment, No. 34, I. O. O. F., was instituted originally at Lynchburg, and removed to Tullahoma, May 28, 1886; Tullahoma Lodge, No. 75, A.

O. U. W., was instituted January 28, 1882; Tullahoma Lodge, No. 1,210, K. of H., was instituted in 1878.

The *Tullahoma Courier* was the first newspaper published in the town, it being established in 1856 by Martin Van Buren Hale, and published for about two years. Preparations were made a year or two later by Dr. Fain to publish a paper, but the same never made its appearance. In 1867 the *Tullahoma Appalachian* was established by a party of gentlemen, and of which George W. Davidson was editor-in-chief and John W. Davidson and James G. Aydelott were local editors. Following this was the *Independent*, which was owned by W. R. French and edited by John Bateman Smith. In 1874 the material of the *Manchester Guardian* was removed to Tullahoma and the *Tullahoma Guardian* established by T. J. Wilson, and is at the present the Democratic organ of the town. The *Guardian* is ably edited, and has a good advertising and subscription patronage. The *Tullahoma Messenger*, an independent journal, was established in 1884 as the *Enterprise* by J. D. Alexander. Subsequently the name was changed to that of the *Republican*, and in January, 1887, the paper made its appearance as the *Messenger*, with T. S. Givan as editor and proprietor. Like its contemporary, the *Messenger* is meeting with success, being well edited and conducted. Tullahoma has been visited by three damaging conflagrations. The first fire occurred in 1861, the second in 1867 and the last in 1883. At the breaking out of the civil war Tullahoma had a population of about 500, with a good number of substantial business houses, but at the close of the conflict but little if anything remained of the once flourishing village, all the churches, schools and a majority of the business houses and residences having been destroyed. But to-day the town has seven churches, two schools and business and dwelling-houses that will compare favorably with those of any town in the South. The surface of the town is level, and the streets broad and regular, and, together with the principal business houses, are lighted with electricity, a first-class dynamo and full electrical apparatus having been purchased and put in operation in January, 1887. Rock Creek, a shallow tributary of Elk River, divides the town east and west and supplies ample water to the various manufactories located on or near the stream.

Tullahoma was considered an important point by both armies during the civil war, and when the Confederates fell back in 1862 the town was occupied by the Federals. During the same year the Federals evacuated the town, and after the battle of Murfreesboro Gen. Bragg and army occupied the town until the summer of 1863. While in possession of the place this time the Confederates erected Fort Raines on an eminence in the northern part of the town and dug rifle pits around the entire town. The earthworks, enclosing about four acres of ground, can be traced at the present. In the latter part of the summer of 1863 Gen. Bragg evacuated the town, which was at once occupied by the Federal forces, who held it until Hood's raid, when they temporarily evacuated, but occupied it after Hood's retreat from Franklin and held it until the close of the war.

Beech Grove, in the northwest part of the county; Hillsboro, in the southeast part; Summittville, on the McMinnville Railroad, eight miles from the county seat and Noah (Needmore) eight and a half miles north of Manchester are villages of from fifty to one hundred inhabitants each.

DE KALB COUNTY.

THE greater portion of De Kalb County lies on the Highland Rim, the remainder in the central basin and the valleys. The highlands occupy the eastern and northern parts of the county, and the surface is gently undulating. The western part of the county lies in the central basin, and embraces several valleys of considerable size and of great agricultural value, separated from each other by ranges of hills. The Valley of Caney Fork begins below the falls between White and Warren Counties, near the southeast corner of De Kalb, is very narrow at the upper end, but gradually widens to the average width of three-quarters of a mile. Its length is about thirty miles. The valley of Smith Fork extends through the western part of the county, from north to south, and has an average width of one mile and is about fifteen miles in length. Each of the tributaries of Smith Fork have valleys of their own. The lands of these valleys are rich, and produce large crops of wheat, corn, oats, hay, potatoes and other cereals. The cap rock of the highlands is siliceous and calcareous. Layers of flinty chert are found in many places, resting on beds of yellow clay. The underlying strata are hard siliceous limestone, and the soils found here are not fertile, the best highland lands being found on the hillsides and along the streams. Underlying the valleys and extending about half-way up the hills is found the limestone common to all parts of the central basin. On the east side of Caney Fork, near the White County line, are found beds of rich iron ore, extending over a space of several miles. The same ore exists on the west side of the stream, though not as extensive. Magnetic iron ore is also supposed to exist in various parts of the county. The black shale underlies the siliceous rocks of the highlands, cropping out on the sides of the hills facing Caney Fork Valley and the basin, but is not valuable. In caves and rock houses are found copperas and alum. The shale also yields mineral oils, in some instances amounting to forty gallons to the ton. The black shale is the source of sulphur springs, of which there are several on the table-land. Caney Fork, Smith Fork and Pine, Fall, Hurricane, Eagle, Holmes, Dry and Mine Lick Creeks are the principal streams of the county, some of which afford splendid water power. Caney Fork is navigable for small steamboats at certain seasons of the year. Two miles below the county seat, on Fall Creek, is a fall of over ninety feet, which presents a rare bit of natural scenery, a view of which may be found in the state department of this work. The timber of the county is abundant, and embraces hickory, walnut, poplar, oak, gum, maple, and other valuable species.

The settlement of De Kalb County dates back to the year 1797, at which time Adam Dale settled on Smith Fork, in the immediate neighborhood of the present town of Liberty. Dale was a Marylander in search of a home, and was attracted to Tennessee by the abundance of cheap land, and to the above locality by the fertile land and healthy climate. Being satisfied with the outlook he at once sent word back to his friends in the East, and two years later a colony of forty families, composed of his relatives, friends and acquaintances, left Maryland to join the pioneer in his frontier home. The colony came down the Ohio River, up the Cumberland to Nashville, and from that point made their way overland to the Dale settlement in wagons. There were no roads in those days and the journey from Nashville required several weeks' time, passages for the teams having to be cut as they went along, the forests and canebrakes being impenetrable. Reaching Smith Fork they settled in and around what is now Liberty, and being of a hardy, industrious nature, were in an incredibly short time comfortably housed and domiciled. Among those who composed the colony were William and John Dale, Thomas West, William and George Givens, Thomas Whaley, Josiah Duncan, James and William Bratton, Henry Burton, the Walks, Fruits and others. Between 1800 and 1820 many new comers settled in various parts of the county, among whom were Jesse Allen, Allan Johnson, Martin Phillips, Britton Johnson, James Lockhart, John Martin, James Davis, Giles Driver, I. H. Hayes, Tobe Martin, Levi Bozarth, Alex. Martin, John Robinson, George, Samuel H. and John Allen, John C. Kennedy, Milton Ward, John Wooldridge, John Frazier, David Taylor, Nicholas Smith, D. League, John Maynor, Henry Cameron, P. G. Magness, Zachariah Lafever, Jacob and Abraham Overall, Robin Forester,

Reuben Evans, Matthew Sellers, James Powell, James Tubb, Jack Reynolds, Reddick Driver, Thomas Given, William Boyd, Thomas Duncan, Spencer Kelley, Bernard Richardson, William Kirby, Edward Hooper, Thomas Durham, David and William Adcock, William Floyd, Hezekiah Bowers, James Powell, John Vantrees, Jonathan and Stewart Dorse, E. Turner, James Goodner, Wm. Grandstaff, Thomas Simpson, William Wright, Benjamin Garrison, Anderson Pickett, Isaac Jones, James Jones and Edmund Turner, Sr.

Adam Dale erected the first mill, which was a log, water-power cornmill, on Smith Fork, near Liberty, built in 1800. The patronage of the mill came from the immediate Dale settlement, for the benefit of which it was established. Other early mills of the county were those of Leonard Fite, at Big Springs, on Smith Fork; Jesse Allen, on Eagle Creek; Thomas Durham and — Farrington, on Pine Creek; James Lick, on Cane Creek, and Nicholas Smith, on Smith Fork. In connection with Allen's mill was a cotton-gin and distillery, probably the first established in the county. The same gentleman also established and operated for a number of years an iron forge on Pine Creek, the ore being secured in the neighboring mountains. Between 1805 and 1815 the settlers would make frequent trips to New Orleans in keelboats, taking to market furs, produce, etc., and returning with salt, which would be sold in the settlements at as high a price as $10 per bushel. The voyagers were embarked on Caney Fork, floating into the Cumberland River, then the Ohio and into the Mississippi. From four to five months were required to make the trip to New Orleans and return. The principal mills of the county at present are as follows: Brown Bros. & Donnell's steam flour-mill, at Alexandria; J. H. Overall's steam flour, meal and saw-mill, and Hale Bros.' water-power grist-mill, at Liberty; Allen T. Wright's steam woolen-mill, and W. T. Robinson's steam grist-mill, at Dowelltown, and T. H. W. Richardson's, Wash. Reynolds', James Oakley's, W. G. Crowley's, John Bone's and James Kelton's grist-mills in various parts of the county.

De Kalb County is bounded on the north by the counties of Smith and Putnam, east by Putnam and White, south by Warren and Cannon, and west by Cannon and Wilson. The county was established by act of the Legislature passed in 1837, the territory for the new county being cut off from the counties of White, Warren, Cannon, Wilson and Jackson. The act creating and naming the county is as follows: "Be it enacted by the General Assembly that a new county be and is hereby established of parts of White, Warren, Wilson, Cannon and Jackson, to be called De Kalb, in honor of Baron De Kalb, the friend of American liberty, who fell at the battle of Camden in the Revolutionary war." The act also provided for the holding of the first sessions of the different courts at the house of Bernard Richardson, on the bank of Fall Creek, one quarter of a mile east from the present county seat, and for the appointment of a committee to locate a permanent seat of justice, lay out a town and sell the lots of the same, and with the money derived from the sale, erect the necessary public buildings. The county was formally organized at Richardson's house in March, 1838. A committee composed of Joseph Clark, Thomas Allen, Joseph Banks, Watson Cantrell and Thomas Durham, was appointed to select a site for a permanent seat of justice and erect a courthouse and jail. Of the commissioners, Joseph Clark is still living. A site was selected on the land of Bernard Richardson, who donated fifty acres of the same to the county, which was at once surveyed and laid off into lots and the same sold at public sale, and the town named Smithville in honor of John S. Bryan, who was known as and called Smith. A log courthouse and jail were at once erected, which stood and were used until about 1840, when the buildings of the present were erected. The courthouse is a square, brick building, two-story in height, and cost about $6,000. It is out of repair, and a new house will soon be a necessity. The jail is also a brick building, and cost about $2,500.

The population of the county in 1840 was 5,868; in 1850 it was 8,016; in 1860 it was 10,573; in 1870 it was 11,425; in 1880 it was 14,000 and in 1886 about 15,000. In 1886 the voting population was about 3,000, of which about 1,800 were Democrats and 1,200 Republicans.

In 1870 there were 182,726 acres assessed for taxation in the county, valued at $1,510,563, and the total valuation of assessed taxable property amounted to $1,960,031. In 1886 the number of acres assessed was 192,704, valued at $1,192,315, while the total valuation of assessed property amounted to $1,408,775; the tax agregate for 1886 shows taxes assessed in the county as follows: State, $4,226.32½; county, $4,226.32½; school, $3,521.93¾; poor, $704.38¾; highway, $1,127.02; poll, $1,450.

The live stock of the county in 1870 amounted to 3,390 head of horses and mules, 3,885 head of cattle, 11,473 head of sheep, and 20,999 head of hogs. In 1886 the estimated live stock amounted to 5,000 head of horses and mules, 11,000 head of cattle, 7,100 head of sheep, and 2,800 head of hogs. In 1870 the cereal products of the county amounted to 81,412 bushel of wheat, 486,823 bushels of corn, 32,250 bushels of oats, and 1,492 bushels of rye. In 1886 the estimated products were 76,000 bushels of wheat, 863,200 bushels of corn, 21,200 bushels of oats, and 4,000 bushels of rye.

De Kalb County is without railroads, the nearest one being the Lebanon branch of the Nashville, Chattanooga & St. Louis Railway, but has the next best thing, *i. e.*, a splendid turnpike, leading from Lebanon, Wilson County, to Smithville, the county seat, upon which the towns and villages of the county are situated, and over which a daily mail and passenger stage is run, affording good transportation, express and mail facilities; at intervals of five miles toll-gates are situated, the income of which is ample to keep the pike and bridges in excellent repair. While the other highways of the county are poor in comparison with the pike, they afford good travel during the spring, summer and fall months. There are no bridges in the county of importance off the pike, there being no necessity for them, as the streams are fordable at almost any season of the year.

On Monday, March 5, 1838, James Goodner, Jonathan C. Doss, Lemuel Moore, Reuben Evans, Joseph Turney, Thomas Simpson, John Martin, Watson Cantrell, David Fisher, William Scott, Samuel Strong, Henry Burton, Martin Phillips, John Frazier, Joel Cheatham, Jonathan Fuston, Peter Reynolds and James Batey, all holding commissions as justices for De Kalb County, met at the house of Bernard Richardson, on Fall Creek, and organized the county court by electing Lemuel Moore, chairman. The several county officers produced their certificates of election, qualified and entered upon the discharge of their respective duties, and the wheels of the Government were set in motion. The court continued to meet at Richardson's house until the completion of the log courthouse. The circuit court of De Kalb County was also organized at Richardson's, the first session being held on the second Monday in August, 1838, over which Judge A. J. Marchbanks presided. The chancery court was organized at the courthouse in Smithville in March, 1844, by Chancellor B. L. Ridley.

Among the first lawyers of De Kalb County were Jonathan L. Farrar, M. M. Brien, W. W. Wade, Sr., J. J. Ford, John H. Savage and Monroe Savage. The lawyers who have practiced since the war, and are at present members of the bar of the county are as follows, in about the order given, some of whom are not at present residents of the county: John H. Savage, M. M. Brien, Robert Cantrell, James A. Nesmith, Robt. C. Nesmith, W. W. Wade, Jr., T. M. Wade, J. S. Gibble, W. B. Stokes, B. M. Webb, B. G. Adcock, J. T. Hollis, B. M. Cantrell, John B. Robinson, A. Arant, R. M. Magness, P. T. Showers, Joseph Clark, Will T. Hale, D. O. Williams, J. J. Ford and J. W. Batts.

The following is a list of the county officers who have served from the organization of the county:

County court clerks: Pleasant M. Wade, William Lawrence, Washington Isbell, M. T. Martin, G. W. Eastham, P. G. Magness, E. J. Evans, Z. P. Lee and H. K. Allen, present incumbent.

Circuit court clerks: David Fite, William J. Given, J. B. Gibbs, J. T. Hollis, W. T. Haskins, T. M. Christian and T. W. Shields, present incumbent.

Clerk and masters: Thomas Whaley, Washington Isbell, J. T. Hallin John P. Robertson, W. W. Wade and M. A. Crowley, present incumbent.

Sheriffs: Pleasant A. Thomason, James McGuire, E. W. Taylor, John W. Dearman, J. Y. Stewart, John Hallum, W. L. Hathaway, C. Hill, J. H. Blackburn, M. F. Doss, C. S. Frazier, B. M. Merritt, H. S. Gill and S. P. Maxwell, present incumbent.

Registers: Daniel Coggin, W. I. Isbell, David Fite, J. H. Haynes, John K. Bain, M. H. McHarner, Judson Dale, J. C. Kennedy, J. B. Attwell, John Harrison, B. M. Cantrell, E. W. Taylor and John G. Evans, present incumbent.

De Kalb County has furnished her full quota of soldiers for all wars since organization, sending a full company, under command of Capt. John F. Goodner, to the war between the United States and Mexico, under the second call for volunteers, the company being mustered into service in 1847 in the Third Tennessee Regiment of Tennessee Volunteer Infantry, and during the civil war between the North and South furnished a number of companies to both the Northern and Southern Armies.

The Confederate companies was as follows: Capt. John F. Goodner's company of the Twenty-fourth Tennessee Regiment of Infantry, raised at Alexandria in April, 1861; Capt. R. D. Allison's company of the Sixteenth Tennessee Regiment of Infantry (of which regiment Capt. Allison was elected colonel, and Boon Savage, of his company, elected major), organized at Alexandria in 1861; Capts. J. S. Reece's and R. V. Wright's companies of Allison's battalion of cavalry, raised at Alexandria by Col. Allison in 1862; Capt. Robert Cantrell's company of the Twenty-third Tennessee Regiment of Infantry, raised at Smithville in 1861; Capt. John Peck's company of the Forty-fourth Regiment of Tennessee Infantry, and Capt. Perry Adcock's company of the same regiment, both raised at Smithville in 1862. The Federal companies were as follows: Three companies of the Fifth Regiment of Tennessee Cavalry, organized at Nashville in 1862, of which W. B. Stokes, of Liberty, was elected colonel, they being Company A, captain, J. H. Blackburn; Company B, captain, S. Waters, and Company K, captain, E. W. Bass. Six companies of the Fourth Regiment of Tennessee Mounted Infantry were organized at Liberty in 1864, of which J. H. Blackburn was elected colonel, they being

Company D, captain, Martin E. Quinn; Company E, captain, McAdoo Vanatta; Company F, captain, William L. Hathaway; Company G, captain, James P. Paty; Company H, captain, John T. Thompson, and Company I, captain, John Simpson. Of the First Regiment of Tennessee Mounted fantry, organized at Carthage in 1864, one company, commanded by Andrew J. Garrison. It is estimated that from 150 to 200 soldiers went from De Kalb County into other regiments, they going in squads, of which there was no record kept.

For history of above regiments and companies see Confederate and Federal military chapters in state department of this volume.

Smithville, the county seat, is situated on the Lebanon and Smithville pike, eighteen miles from Alexandria, and has a population of about 800. The town was founded in 1838 by the commissioners appointed by the county court to locate a permanent seat of justice. W. W. Wade, Sr., Samuel Chandler and P. M. Wade were the first merchants. Following, in the order given, the merchants were Perry G. Magness, William P. Harvey, J. M. Allen, William H. Magness, John L. Dearman, George Beckwith, J. Y. Stewart, S. B. Whaley and Elijah Whaley. Dr. G. W. Eastham was the first hotel-keeper, and he was succeeded in turn by James Ervin and Bernard Richardson. In 1846 a stock company erected a frame hotel building, which is now conducted by Joseph Bozarth. The other hotel is conducted by Mrs. N. G. Tyra. The present business of Smithville is as follows: R. B. West, G. R. Smith & Son, Smith Bros., Black & Bond, T. B. Potter, S. D. Blankenship, all general merchandise; W. B. Foster, C. Parker, groceries; Hooper & Bro., hardware; D. S. Harrison, F. Z. Webb, drugs; A. L. Foster, saddles and harness; R. B. West and E. J. Evans, livery stables.

Among the early physicians of Smithville were Drs. G. W. Eastham; Charles Schurer, J. C. Buckley, ———— Barnes, J. C. Cox, and E. Tubb. Those of the present are Drs. J. Z. Webb, P. W. Eaton, M. L. Wilson and James Womack.

The early schools of Smithville were of little consequence, and of them there is no record. In 1842 a brick building was erected and Fulton Academy established. This school was a very good one, and was continued until 1883, when it was succeeded by Pure Fountain College, for which a large three-story brick building was erected, at a cost of $12,000. Prof. T. B. Kelley has charge of the college at present, and is meeting with success.

The first church erected was a brick, put up in 1848 by the Methodists. A frame building was erected in its place in 1856, and is in use at present. The next church was the Baptist, erected in 1858, the next the

Christian, erected in 1873, and the next the Cumberland Presbyterian, erected in 1886. Before the Methodist Church was built log houses were used for churches.

Alexandria, the largest town of the county, with a population of about 900, is on the Lebanon and Smithville pike, half way between the two places (eighteen miles from each), and was founded about 1815, by ———— Alexander, who named the town after his native town in Virginia. A charter of incorporation was secured in 1846, and the town was incorporated until 1879, when the charter was surrendered and the "four mile" temperance law given authority and force, in order to close out saloons.

Among the early merchants were Joshua Coffee, ———— Alexander, Samuel Young, Church Anderson, Jacob Fite, James Goodner, William Floyd, J. D. Wheeler, Bone & Bro., Thomas Crompton, Reece & Ford, Turner Bros., Wheeler & Jones, John F. Moore, S. W. Pearce, Lawrence & Ray, William Geltford, L. D. Fite, J. D. Beard, and Beard & Goodner, all of whom were in business prior to the war. During the latter part of the war the only firm in business was that of Dexter Buck. From 1865 and 1870 the business men were Dexter Buck, J. M. Beard, Stokes & Wood, Edward Turner & Bros., Dinges & Lincoln, Hurd & Co., Bridges & Smith, George Evans and M. F. Doss. Between 1870 and 1880: Dinges & Co., Rutland & Goodner, S. W. McClelland, Ray & Zergin, John Jost, John Garrison, Edwards & Rutland, and L. Tubb. The merchants of the present are as follows: Dinges & Co., Rutland & Goodner, S. W. McClelland, general merchandise; J. W. King, Edwards & Rutland, and Gould & Newman, drugs; Tubb & Schure, hardwood and groceries; John Jost, confectionery; John Garrison, fancy groceries; L. Tubb, dry goods; Batts & Garrison and H. C. Flippin, undertakers; D. W. Dingess, livery stable, and B. F. Bell, hotel.

The early physicians of Alexandria down to the war were as follows in the order given: Drs. John Overall, George Gray, ———— Dougherty, William Sales, Cornelius Sales, William and Richard Blythe, T. J. Sneed, T. F. Evart, and T. J. Sneed, Jr. Since the war: C. L. Barton, O. D. Williams, T. A. Gould and Thomas Davis. Present: O. D. Williams, T. A. Gould and Thomas Davis. The first school was taught in a log cabin by Wylie Reynolds, about 1820. Later a school was taught by John Collins in a frame house. The first building erected expressly for a school was a frame, about 1840. The Masonic Academy was next, in 1856, and in 1858 T. M. Lawrence College was erected, the latter two being in operation at present.

In about 1820 the Methodists erected a log church, and in 1835 the same denomination erected a frame church, and in 1885 put up their present handsome frame church. In 1835 the Christians erected a frame church, and the present frame church of that denomination was built in 1851. In 1881 the Cumberland Presbyterians erected a frame building, which they use at present. There is a Baptist organization but no building.

The Alexandria *Patriot*, a weekly paper, was established in 1860 by W. H. Mott, which was published until 1861, when it suspended. In 1882 the Alexandria *Enterprise* was established by J. W. Newman, and published for about two years.

Liberty, situated on the pike, seven miles from Alexandria, has a population of about 500, and was founded in about 1800 by Adam Dale, and named in honor of the founder's home in Maryland. The first house was built by William Givens. ——— Walk was the first merchant, and was followed by Fite & Duncan, ——— Young, Moore & Price, Benjamin Bloyds, Joshua Bratton, and Leonard Moore, all of whom were in business before the late war. Since the war, Eli Vick, Fate Hale, Overall & Hale, Columbus Vick and Elijah Bratton were the merchants, and at present the business is conducted by the following firms: Hale & Son, William Vick & Son, and James Pritchett, general merchandise; D. D. Overall, drugs, etc.; James Pritchett, hotel.

The Liberty *Herald*, the only newspaper published in De Kalb County, was established April 1, 1886, by Will A. Vick. The *Herald* is a neat and newsy weekly, well edited and extensively patronized. A power press for the *Herald* is among the probabilities of the near future.

One of the first, if not the first, school taught in Liberty was that taught by — Gay, at a very early date, in a log house. Other schools were taught afterward, but all were of an inferior class, and it was not until about 1870 that a good school was established. At that time a substantial two-story brick house was erected and the Masonic Normal School founded, which is in successful operation at the present.

Salem Baptist Church was erected in 1810, being the first church built at Liberty. This denomination erected a new frame house in 1849, and a third frame house in 1880. The other church of Liberty is the Methodist, the original house being erected in 1825 and the present one in 1869.

Dowelltown, two miles distant from Liberty, on the pike, has a population of about 300, with a good frame Methodist Church, built in 1880, and a frame schoolhouse erected in 1885.

CANNON COUNTY.

MORE than half of Cannon County lies in the Central Basin, and the remainder on the Highland Rim. Spurs shoot out from the highlands, forming numerous valleys, through which course mountain streams, giving the county probably as much varied and picturesque scenery as any in the State. The soils on the highlands are light colored, and are for the most part thin and unproductive, save of a rank, barren grass which affords good summer grazing. Fruits and tobacco will also grow, in the highland soils. The knobs of the Central Basin are usually fertile to the top, but limestone crops out in such abundance as to render much of the surface unfit for cultivation. In the basin, however, is found the valuable farm lands of the county. The soil is rich, loamy and pebbly, easily worked and highly productive. Bluegrass grows spontaneously and luxuriantly on the slopes and tops of the hills, and even in the glades, furnishing rich pasturage. The crops of the county are corn, wheat, hay, clover, tobacco and the grasses, while the timber embraces species of the oak, ash, poplar, walnut, hickory, chestnut, gum, maple, beech, buckeye, cherry and elm.

Stone River traverses the county from east to west, receiving the waters of numerous tributaries, and is the principal water course of the county. Other streams are Rockhouse, Carpenter, Rush, Lock, Hill, Hollis and Brawley Creeks, all emptying into Stone River, Carson Fork, emptying into Brawley Creek, and Barren Fork of Collins River, Clear Fork, Sycamore, Hurricane, Saunders and Marshall Creeks.

The country now embraced in Cannon County was settled as early as 1807 and 1809, though it then belonged to several other counties in part. The early settlers were chiefly North Carolinians, who, however, came here from East Tennessee, to which section they had previously immigrated in quest of homes, but pushed on over the mountains as Middle Tennessee opened up for settlement. Among the settlers living here in 1836, when Cannon County was organized, were Henry D. McBroom, John Wood, James and Edmund Taylor, Wm. Hollis, Noel Lilly, Isham Cherry, Alexander Hill, Philip Rough, Philip Hoas, Henry Ford, Benjamin Allen, Usibid Stone, George St. John, Wm. Mears, Melchesedec Self, Joseph Harrison, Samuel Lewis, Wm. Middleton, James and John Barklay, Richard Vincent, Alexander Orr, Wm. McFerrin, Calvin Carlee, Jackson Wherry, Daniel Travis, Arthur Warren, Philip Mouser, Joshua Barton, George Petty, Benjamin Arant, L. S. Gilliam, Reuben Evans,

Benjamin Blodes, Tilman Bethell, G. W. Duncan, Joseph Simpson, D. M. Stewart, James Ferrell, Archibald Stone, J. G. W. Rose, Joseph Clark, Asa Smith, Elijah Stephens, James M. Brown, John Wright, Pumphry Bynum, Charles Espy, Wm. Preston, Sr., Walter Wood, Benjamin Cummings, Sr., Warren Cummings, Wm. Cummings, Sr., John Stone, Andrew Melton, Caleb and Wm. Sevillirant, Joseph James, James Miles, Alexander McBroom, Kit and Wm. Pyburn, Cullin Corlee, Edmond Sutton, William, James and John Wood, Nathan Finley, Jesse and James Todd, Robert Carson, Jonathan Jones, Ambrose Petty, Thomas Williams, John McClain, Archibald Hicks, Thomas Fowler, Gideon Rucker, Jesse G. Moore, Louis Jetton, Gabriel Elkins, James Hawkins and Charles Evans, many of whom are still living. One of the first schools taught in what is now Cannon County was the one situated about seven miles west from Woodbury, of which James Barklay was the teacher. This school was taught as early as 1810 or 1812. Other early schools of the years between the above school and 1815 were taught by Jacob Mackleroy, on Hill Creek, one and a half miles east of Woodbury; by Bartlett Wade, in the same neighborhood, and later in that neighborhood by John Finley. In about 1814 James Rucker opened a school in Woodbury (then Danville), and a few years later Elliot Tunley taught a school in the Methodist meeting-house in town. The next school in Woodbury was taught by Thomas G. Wood. Laurens Academy was established in Woodbury in 1838 as a county academy, for which a frame building was erected. In 1859 the house was destroyed by a fire, when a substantial brick was erected, which is now occupied as a private residence. In about 1855 the Baptists established a school, which has since become the Woodbury College. The school building is a large two-story brick, and the school a most excellent one. The other schools of the county besides the common schools are those at Short Mountain, Auburn, Bradysville and Readerville, those at Woodbury and Short Mountain being chartered and working under the four-mile law. In 1838 the scholastic population of Cannon County was 1,961; in 1868, 3,559, and in 1885, as follows: White—male, 2,296; female, 2,251. Colored—male, 118; female, 179; total, white and colored, 4,844. Among the first churches of Cannon County were Brawley Fork Baptist Church, in what is now the Third District; Prospect Methodist Church, on Hill Creek, in the Sixth District; St. John Baptist Church, in the Sixth District; Ford Meeting-house, Christian, in the Sixth District, and Corlee's Meeting-house, on Brawley Fork, also in the Sixth District, all of which were log houses and built all along between 1815 and 1820. The first church erected in Woodbury was a log house, built about 1820 by the Methodists. This stood until about 1840, when the present brick was erected. The next was a frame church erected by the Baptists about 1841, which is still in use, and the next was the Christian Church, frame, which was erected about 1842 and is still in use. The Cumberland Presbyterians have an organization and meet in the courthouse, they having no building of their own. The churches of the county by districts are as follows: First District, New Hope, Christian; Second District, Berea, Christian; Third District, Marion, Baptist, and Corlee, Christian; Fourth District, Bethlehem, Christian, and Wesley Chapel, Methodist Episcopal South; Fifth District, Daniels' Chapel, Methodist Episcopal South; Seventh District, Cold Springs, Christian, and Walnut Grove, Methodist Episcopal South; Eighth District, Wood's Meeting-house, Christian, and Blue Wing, Methodist Episcopal South; Ninth District, Osment schoolhouse and Short Mountain, Methodist Episcopal South; Tenth District, Sycamore, Baptist, and Melton, Christian; Eleventh District, New Hope, Cumberland Presbyterian, Shiloh and Poplar Stand, Baptist, and Auburn, Christian; Twelfth District, Bradyville, Christian, and Thytira, Cumberland Presbyterian; Thirteenth District, Holly Springs, Baptist, and Parker's Chapel and Gilley Hill, Methodist Episcopal South; Fourteenth District, Pleasant Ridge Christian, and Pleasant Ridge Baptist; Fifteenth District, Jones' schoolhouse Methodist Episcopal South.

Among the early mills of the county were those of Nathaniel Moorhead, at Woodbury, on Stone River, about 1813; Chas. Ready's mill, on Stone River, at Readerville, about 1812; Thomas Rooker's mill, on the same stream, four miles west from Woodbury, about 1814; Bryant's mill, on same stream, eight miles west from Woodbury, about 1816; David Whittaker's mill, near town, at about the same time; Archibald Prater's mill, on a branch of Stone River, five miles east of town, about 1820, and Alexander Hill's mill, on Hill Creek, about 1821. The principal mills of the present are the Readerville flour-mills, owned by P. C. Talley; Isaac McBroom's mill on Stone River, in the Second District; W. F. Brerard's mill, on Stone River, at Woodbury, and J. L. Sheckley's mill, on Stone River, in the Second District, all of which are excellent flour and meal-mills, and like the above named old mills, are operated by water power. Upon almost every creek in the county are found small, water-power corn-mills, and there are from ten to fifteen portable, steam saw-mills at work in the county.

Cannon County was established by act of the General Assembly, passed January 21, 1836, and was organized the following May. It was named in honor of Gov. Cannon, and its county seat for Hon. Levi

Woodbury, of New Hampshire. The county is bounded on the north by the counties of Wilson and Smith, east by Warren and De Kalb, south by Coffee, west by Rutherford, and has an area of 420 square miles. The county court in 1836 ordered the erection of a courthouse and jail. The former was completed in 1838 after the style and plan of the Rutherford County Courthouse, and cost about $13,000. The building is in use at the present and bids fair to do service for the next fifty years. It is a large, square, two-story brick building and is very conveniently arranged. The jail was also completed in 1838, was a brick building, but being too near Stone River it was washed away in the freshet of 1850. A second brick jail was erected in 1852 which served until 1880, when the present substantial stone building was erected.

In 1840 Cannon County had a population of 7,163, of 8,982 in 1850, of 9,509 in 1860, of 10,502 in 1870, of 11,200 in 1880 and of about 12,500 in 1886. In 1870 there were assessed in the county for taxation 160,013 acres of land, valued at $1,452,220, and the total valuation of real and personal property was $1,669,240. In 1886 there were assessed for taxation 157,605 acres, valued at $997,460, and the total valuation of real and personal property was $1,079,260. The tax duplicate for 1886 shows taxes assessed as follows: State, $3,237.78; county, $3,117.90; school, $4,796.90; road, $539.63, and poll, $1,670, making a total of $11,692.21. In 1870 the live stock of the county amounted to 4,562 head of horses and mules, 3,533 head of cattle, 12,198 head of sheep and 23,550 head of hogs. In 1886 the live stock amounted to 4,839 head of horses and mules, 6,367 head of cattle, 6,327 head of sheep and 27,917 head of hogs. In 1870 the cereal products of the county amounted to 79,520 bushels of wheat, 564,330 bushels of corn, 26,870 bushels of oats and 3,167 bushels of rye. In 1886 the products were 94,150 bushels of wheat, 821,012 bushels of corn, 22,802 bushels of oats and 6,985 bushels of rye.

In May, 1836, Thomas Powell, Isaac Finley, Allen Haley, Joseph Simpson, Blake Sedgly, James L. Essary, John Pendleton, Isaac W. Eledge, Elijah Stephens, I. M. Brown, F. L. Turner, John Milton, Charles C. Evans, Samuel Lance, Wm. Bates, Wm. B. Foster, John Martin, John Frazier, Martin Phillips, Reuben Evans, Lemuel Moore, James Goodwin, Peter Reynolds, James Beatie, Joel Cheatham and Jonathan Fuson, all bearing commissions as justices, met at the house of Henry D. McBroom, which was the old hotel, in Woodbury, for the purpose of organizing the county court. The body was called to order by Leighton Ferrell, sheriff of Warren County, and the oath of office was administered by Eli Bailey, acting justice for Warren County. The court then organized by the election of Thomas Powell as chairman, and the wheels of government were put in motion.

The Cannon Circuit Court was organized at McBrown's tavern in Woodbury in 1836 by Judge Edmund Dillahunty, who presided in interchange with the regular judge, Wm. Anderson.

Judge B. L. Ridley organized the Cannon Chancery Court at the old tavern in Woodbury in 1836, and appointed Henry Tratt, first clerk and master.

Among the early lawyers of Woodbury were Jonathan Farr, Abraham Burger, Jr., M. W. McKnight, J. S. Barton and Thomas G. Wood. The present attorneys are J. H. Cummings, H. J. St. John, A. Finley, James A. Jones, John S. Wood, W. C. Huston, A. J. Smithson and W. H. Cummings. Of the above M. W. McKnight was attorney-general of this circuit for eight years, 1866–74; H. J. St. John represented the county in the Legislature, 1857–58; J. H. Cummings held the same position, 1875–76; W. C. Huston filled the same office, 1877–78, and James A. Jones represented this district in the State Senate, 1875–76.

County Court Clerks: Samuel Garrison, 1836–39; James M. Brown, 1839–40; Rezin Fowler, 1840–52; Brinkley Lassater, 1852–60; Thomas Smith. 1860–62; Josephus Finley, 1865–70; E. B. Vance, 1870–78; Wylie W. Gray, 1878–86; J. G. Moore, 1886, and present incumbent.

Circuit Court Clerks: Thomas G. Wood, 1836–44; John Q. Weatherford, 1844–52; James Wood, 1852–56; D. L. Elkins, 1856–68; E. T. Dillon, 1868–72; Thomas Finley, 1872–78; E. C. Preston, 1878–86; Josephus Finley, 1886, and present incumbent.

Clerk and Masters: Henry Tratt, 1836–42; Caleb B. Davis, 1842–47; Thomas G. Wood, 1847–62; J. S. Ridley, 1865–68; A. F. McFerrin, 1868–70; W. J. Wood, 1870–76; J. E. New, 1876–82; F. B. Martin, 1882, and present incumbent.

Sheriffs: George Grizzle, 1836–38; Higdon R. Jarrett, 1838–40; John A. George, 1840–42; Isaac W. Elledge, 1842–44; Samuel Vance, 1844–46; R. A. Smith, 1846–50; Clint Elledge, 1850–52; Baden Raines, 1852–54; Warren Cummings, 1854–62; A. F. Todd, 1865–70; George Finley, 1870–72; B. F. Vincent, 1872–76; James H. Mitchell, 1876–80; B. F. Vincent, 1880–82; James H. Mitchell, 1882–84; H. L. Preston, 1884, and present incumbent.

Registers: Alexander McFerrin, 1836–40; Isaac Finley, 1840–42; Thomas J. Williams, 1842–48; Barton S. Travis, 1848–52; Burrel Spicer, 1852–56; James Ward, 1856–58; Cicero Sowers, 1858–62; Jack Merritt, 1865–66; Jack McBroom, 1866–77; Zebediah Brevard, 1871–72; A. G. Brown, 1872–78; W. A. Moody, 1878–86; Adam Fuller, 1886, and present incumbent.

Cannon County, as a county, furnished soldiers to the wars of 1836 and 1846, but they went as individuals, there being no regularly organized bodies or companies raised in the county for either of those wars. Not so, however, with the late Rebellion, to which she furnished the following eight companies, all regularly organized within the county:

Three full companies to the Eighteenth Regiment of Tennessee Infantry, organized in May, 1861, and commanded by Capts. Richmond Rushing, A. J. St. John and Grand Wood; one company to Col. Barton's Mississippi Regiment of Cavalry, organized in the latter part of 1861, commanded by Capt. Timothy Ellison, who was killed in 1862, and succeeded by W. M. McKnight; two companies to Col. Hill's Fourth Regiment of Tennessee Infantry, organized in 1862, and commanded by Capts. M. M. Brin, Jr., and J. H. Wood, and two companies to the Fourth Regiment of Tennessee Cavalry, organized in 1863, and commanded by Capt. H. A. Wylie and J. W. Nichols.

The county was occupied first by the Northern and then the Southern Armies during the struggle, and numerous skirmishes were fought in the county, but none of sufficient importance or consequence to merit mention.

Woodbury, the county seat, was formerly Danville, and belonged to Warren County. Danville was founded in about 1819 by Henry D. McBroom and Henry Watt, who were the first merchants, and the former the first tavern-keeper. Other early merchants were Henry Watt, Jr., Wylie & Dunkerson, Nathan Neeley, and Wood & Wylie. In 1836, when Cannon County was established, the commissioners entrusted with the locating of a county seat, selected Danville, and the name of the town was changed to that of Woodbury. At that time there were not over 100 inhabitants in the place. Woodbury now has a population of about 600, and is situated on the south bank of Stone River, at the terminus of the Woodbury and Murfreesboro Turnpike, nineteen miles east from the latter town, and fifty miles southeast from Nashville, in the lovely valley of Stone River, surrounded by high, rounded hills, and having beautiful scenery and excellent health. Woodbury was incorporated in 1852, and with the exception of the years of the late war, worked continually under the charter of incorporation then secured until 1880, when the charter was surrendered in order to give the "four-mile" temperance law force and effect.

The first merchants of Woodbury were Henry Trott, Jr., James J. Trott, Joseph Ramsey, Ramsey & Garrison, Parker F. Stone, Thomas C. Wood, Bates & Hume, and Nathan Neeley. Henry D. Broom continued as tavern-keeper up to about 1857–58. The merchants of the present are Martin & Gribble, McFerrin & Wylie, Hoover & Mason, J. A. H. Thompson, C. P. Broom, J. G. Smith & Bros., and E. and J. T. Stephens, dry goods and groceries; R. H. Preston, groceries; William Brewer, C. C. Broom and J. H. Thrower, drugs; Z. Dillon & Bro., saddle and harness shop; T. J. Vance, livery stable; J. H. Thrower, undertaker and furniture, and W. A. Talley, hotel.

The *Cannon Courier*, W. T. Mingle, editor and proprietor, is the only paper published in the county. The *Courier* was established in 1882, is Democratic in politics and is prosperous.

The early physicians of Woodbury were Drs. Gowan, New, Barnes, Flowers and Tatum, and those of the present are Drs. Robert F. Tatum, B. F. Lester, L. B. McCreary, H. M. Hern and Dr. Barton.

The villages of the county, all of which are small and have only from fifty to one hundred and fifty inhabitants each, are Bradeyville, ten miles southwest from Woodbury, in the Twelfth District; Auburn, sixteen miles north from Woodbury, in the Eleventh District; Mechanicsville, at Short Mountain, ten miles northeast from Woodbury, in the Ninth District. Readerville, seven miles from Woodbury and twelve miles from Murfreesboro, on the pike, is part in Cannon and part in Rutherford County, the county line running through the town, yet it is placed in Rutherford County, and the postoffice is in that county.

WHITE COUNTY.

W. M. Anderson, an enterprising farmer of the Fifth District, was born in White County, November 4, 1824, the second son of Zachariah and Rebecca (England) Anderson. The father was born in 1790 in Kentucky. He was a Baptist minister and Whig, a farmer and stock raiser. He died January 15, 1867. The mother was born in 1792 in Knox County, Tenn., and died August 5, 1871. They were married in 1816. The subject of our sketch was raised on a farm, and received his education in the schools of the vicinity. From 1843 to 1847, he was keeper of a toll gate at Crab Orchard, Tenn. In 1848 he was elected tax collector of White County. He then began farming and stock raising. In 1852 he was elected magistrate to fill the unexpired term of David Beam, and in 1854 was re-elected and served six years. He has been very successful in life and accumulated some fine property. He is a useful and respected citizen, and a generous contributor to all worthy enterprises. He is a stanch Democrat. February 20, 1849, he married Nancy A., daughter of Harmon and Mary Little. This union resulted in the birth of Rebecca, born January 20, 1851; William and Alice, who are twins, born May 2, 1868. All are living, and have received excellent educational advantages.

Pleasant Austin, a prosperous agriculturist of the Second District, was born September 8, 1820, on the farm upon which he now resides. His parents were John and Catherine (Haston) Austin. The father was born January 6, 1779, in Virginia, of English origin. He immigrated to Tennessee at a very early day, where he died February 28, 1858. The mother is thought to have been of Dutch descent. She was a native of Tennessee and her entire life was passed in the State. Our subject was brought up on the farm, and educated in the school of the vicinity. After attaining his majority he purchased land in the county and farmed about six years. At his father's death he bought the homestead and moved to it, where he has since resided. He is a substantial, honorable and worthy citizen. He is interested in the advancement of education and all beneficial enterprises. He is a Democrat. September 14, 1852, he was united in marriage to Mary E., daughter of Bluford and Sarah (Yates) Warren. The father was raised in Halifax, N. C., and the mother in Halifax, Va. The grandfather Yates lived to the unusual age of one hundred and twelve years. Mrs. Austin was born October 15, 1825, in Tennessee, and is the mother of John W., William Bluford, Robert S., Sarah Alice (wife of Norman Gist, who resides near Sparta), Flora C. (wife of Lewis Akins), James Mc. and Frank P.

J. R. Bosson, a well known and enterprising farmer of Walling Station, was born in White County, April 17, 1846, of French-Swede and Scotch descent. He is a son of Charles T. and Sarah Bell (Reed) Bosson. The father was born April 17, 1796, in Rocksboro, Mass., and immigrated to Tennessee about 1842. After remaining at Rock Island a short time he moved to the falls of Caney Fork, where he lived until the late war. He there located at Murfreesboro, where he died about 1865. The mother was a native of Lexington, Ky., and died April 17, 1846. Our subject was raised on a farm, and owing to delicate health, received but a limited education. At the age of seventeen he engaged as a salesman in the merchandise business at Murfreesboro, so continuing until the close of the war. He then began farming in this county to which occupation he has since given his attention, and in which he has been very prosperous. He is a valuable and respected citizen, interested in the advancement of educational, and all enterprises of a beneficial nature. He is a Republican. In October 8, 1868, he married Miss Amanda, daughter of Carter and Caroline (Sparkman) Dillon. The fruits of this union are Charles T.,

Edward E., Sarah B., Carter D., Caroline B., Sue M., James R. and Francis M.

Chas. V. Bronson, of Anderson & Bronson, livery stable, was born in Sparta October 13, 1858, the son of Robt. L. and Mary A. (Rodgers) Bronson (the widow Mrs. Lane), both of whom are of English origin. The father was born in Ohio, February 24, 1836, and the mother January 11, in White County, both now residents of Sparta. The father, a carriage-maker most of his life, has at times been a successful farmer. The parents of three children, and are members of the Christian Church. After completing a good education at Sparta he for eighteen months read law under C. Marchbanks. He then abandoned the law and after a year in photography and one as deputy county clerk of Henry County under Jos. Doyle, he returned to Sparta in 1882, and at the beginning of the next year entered his present partnership. He is unmarried. He is a liberal man and a decided Democrat.

J. F. Bruster, a well known farmer of the Fifth District, was born November 26, 1845, in White County. He is the youngest child of William and Kittie (Finley) Bruster. The father was born in 1796 in Virginia, and married in 1820. He immigrated to Tennessee in 1825, arriving here without funds. He made shoes at night while learning the tanners' trade. For twenty-five years he was a tanner at Sparta, where, in 1841, he purchased a farm and engaged in farming and stock raising, making a specialty of blooded stock, amassing considerable wealth. He was a Whig. His death occurred in 1852. The mother was born in 1803 in Kentucky, and died in 1884, a consistent member of the Methodist Episcopal Church South. Our subject was educated in Alabama and Tennessee. In 1866 he began farming and stock raising. In 1876 he entered into the mercantile business, and sold out five years later to W. J. Winstead. He married, in 1866, Amanda, daughter of Daniel and Rachel Sinvil of this county. Eight children were born to this union, seven of whom are living. Mr. Bruster is a stanch Democrat. He and his wife are earnest and esteemed members of the Methodist Episcopal Church South.

William S. Burgess, a prominent citizen and a well known, enterprising planter of White County and resident of the Twelfth Civil District, was born in Putnam County August 24, 1830. He is the son of Charles and Margaret (McBride) Burgess. His father was of Irish descent, a native of North Carolina, born in that State in 1806, and died in Putman County December 6, 1886. He was engaged in agricultural pursuits, and made life a fair success. He was a member of the Christian Church and died in that faith. Mr. Burgess' mother's ancestors came from Scotland. She was a native of White County, born in 1808. She is still living, a resident of Putnam County. Mr. Burgess is the second of thirteen children. He secured a common-school education, which has been supplemented by extensive reading. At the age of twenty-one he went West with the intention of going to California, but when he reached Missouri unfavorable news of the Pacific Coast caused him to stop in that State. He was one of the first settlers of Kansas. For three years he gave his attention to farming in Kansas and Missouri. In 1854 he returned to his father's home and purchased a farm in White County, where he lived five or six years. In the fall of 1862 he entered the Confederate States Army, and joined the Eighth Regiment of Cavalry, commanded by Gen. Dibrell. He served with credit the remainder of the war with this general, and took part in many of the battles and skirmishes fought. December, 1864 he was captured while on a scouting expedition, and kept prisoner of war until the battle of Nashville. In the spring of 1865, after an absence of three years, he returned home and resumed farming. Mr. Burgess has been an active business man. He began with nothing but an honest heart and a strong will, and now owns 1,200 acres of land in White County, also a half interest in a large water mill on Falling Water Creek, near the Putnam County line. The falls on the streams are remarkable beyond description. There are four falls, Mr. Burgess and his younger brother, Winfield, owning the first three. On March 13, 1855, he was united in marriage to Miss Ricy O. Barnes, a most excellent lady, who was born June 14, 1834, and reared in White County. To this union have been born three children—one son and two daughters. Although not a member of the church, Mr. Burgess and wife are in sympathy with the Baptist Church.

Wm. Cooper, a resident and manufacturer of Holden Station, was born March 2, 1843, a son of Wm. and Margret (Moat) Cooper, both of whom were natives of Luzgin, Ireland. The father was born about 1810, and died in Belfast, about 1852. The mother was born at Carrick Fugus, about 1819, and is still living. Our subject received his education at Belfast, and immigrated to America in 1853. He worked at the carpenter's trade until the late war, when he entered the Confederate service, Company C, Twenty-fifth Tennessee Infantry. He was captured at Cumberland Gap, but paroled at Williamsburg, Ky., and rejoined his regiment at Mobile, Ala. In 1863 he was captured at Rock Island, Tenn., but made his escape. Being unable to reach his old company he joined Carter's cavalry, and remained with them until the close of the war. He returned home and resumed his trade; he spent 1870 in Delaware, and the following year was engaged in the saw-mill business in Texas. A year later he came back to Tennessee and again worked at his trade. In 1874 he built a saw mill in this county, and in the last few years has extended his business into Alabama, North Carolina and Arkansas. In 1884 in partnership with his brother, John S. Cooper, he erected the Tennessee Planing Mills. He is also engaged in the general merchandise business at Holden Station December, 1884. December, 1885, the firm changed to Holden & Cooper. February 4, 1865, he married Mary Jane Witt, who died in 1876, a consistent member of the Missionary Baptist Church, and mother of one child, Lyla. Mr. Cooper's second marriage was with Amanda Webb, who has borne him one child, James W. Our subject is an enterprising, substantial and worthy citizen, a member of the Missionary Baptist Church, also of the I. O. O. F. He is a Chapter Mason and a Democrat.

J. S. Cooper, a junior partner in the Tennessee Saw & Planing Mill Company, was born in Malone County, Ireland, June 28, 1848. His parents, Wm. and Margaret (Moat) Cooper, were also natives of Ireland. The father died at Belfast about 1852. The mother was born about 1821 and immigrated to the United States in 1855, first locating in the State of New York, and remaining about two years. After spending some time in Maryland she moved in 1858 to Jamestown, Tenn., and one year later to White County, where the entire family now reside. The subject of this sketch received his education principally at Bird College. He took a law course at the Cumberland University, and began the practice of law in the early part of 1872. Two years later he engaged in school-teaching, which he carried on quite successfully for eight and a half years, seven of which he taught at Snow Creek Academy. In 1881 he entered into his present business with his brother William, in which he has been very prosperous. He is a worthy, substantial citizen and self-made man, whose education was acquired, and property accumulated by his own efforts. He is a stanch Democrat. In June, 1880, he was married to Miss Belle, daughter of James and Elizabeth High, of Carthage, Tenn. Three children have been born to their union: D'elma, Vernon and Willie Landis.

Malachi A. Cummings was born July 12, 1854. He is of Irish and Scotch origin. His grandfather, Joseph Cummings, of Irish descent, emigrated from near Richmond, Va., to this State over 100 years ago. He served in the Revolutionary war and was with Washington at the surrender of Cornwallis, and his maternal grandfather, William Dunny of Scotch descent, came from Kentucky to this State, both settling at a place now known as Cummingsville in Van Buren County, then White County. His grandparents lived to an extreme old age. His father, W.

B. Cummings, was born May 11, 1810, and filled the different offices of sheriff, circuit court clerk and county judge in his county with credit and honor. After the war he read law and in 1868 was admitted to the bar, and died October 22, 1884. Malachi was raised on the farm and after working through crop times, would go to school in the neighborhood in the fall. He received his principal education at Burritt College, paying for his tuition part of the time by sweeping the college building. In 1875 he attended the law school of Cumberland University at Lebanon, Tenn., and graduated in 1875, and was duly licensed to practice in all the courts of Tennessee. While attending the law school he received the honor of representing the Philomatian society as orator at the commencement exercises. After staying at Spencer and Sparta awhile he permanently located at Sparta, where he is now engaged in the practice of his profession.

L. D. Cunningham, a well known farmer and stock raiser of the Tenth District, was born in White County, July 2, 1837, the youngest child of Edmond and Nancy (Anderson) Cunningham. The father was born in Virginia June 5, 1792, and married November 11, 1814. He came to White County about 1810, and engaged in farming, stock raising and making brandy and whisky. He was a Whig and an industrious, thrifty man. He accumulated considerable property. His death occurred June 2, 1858. The mother was born May 4, 1795. They were of Scotch-Irish descent, both faithful members of the Baptist Church. Our subject spent his early days on the farm, receiving his education in the schools of the neighborhood. In 1857 or 1858 he began agricultural pursuits on his own responsibility. In 1863 he enlisted in Company G, Twenty-eighth Tennessee Infantry, under Gen. Cheatham. He took part in several battles, one of which was at Murfreesboro. He was a brave and gallant soldier. In 1860 he married Martha, daughter of John and Hannah (Moore) Mitchell, of White County. Mrs. Cunningham died November 3, 1872. February 14, 1874, our subject wedded America, daughter of Jesse and J. (Shockley) Dodson, of White County. To this union four sons and two daughters have been born, two sons deceased. Mrs. Cunningham is a member of the Methodist Episcopal Church South. Mr. Cunningham is a believer in religion but is not connected with any church. He is a stanch Democrat.

G. G. Dibrell. Of the prominent men who have lived in White County was Hon. John Catron, afterward judge of the United States Circuit Court, under appointment from President Jackson. Thomas K. Harris, the first representative White County ever had in Congress was a citizen of Sparta. He was killed in a canvass he was making for a re-election near Shellsford, in Warren County, by his competitor, Gen. John W. Simpson of White County. Gen. Simpson lived in White County until he died in 1862. He was a lieutenant-colonel in the war of 1812, and distinguished himself for his gallantry in the battle of New Orleans on the 8th of January, 1815. Gen. George W. Gibbs, the first president of the Union Bank of Tennessee, at Nashville, and afterward the founder of Union City, Tennessee; was for many years a citizen of Sparta. He was a senator in the State Legislature at Knoxville, Tenn., when he resigned, came home, and raised a company during the war of 1812, and made a fine record. His wife was a sister of Anthony Dibrell who located in White County, in 1811. Mr. Dibrell was born in Buckingham County, Va.; moved to Wayne County, Ky., when a youth; married Mildred Carter, who was raised in Wythe County, Va., and located in White County, where he died in 1875 aged eighty-seven years. Anthony Dibrell was a descendant of Christopher Dubray, who was a Huguenot refugee from France in the year 1700, and settled on the James River thirty miles above Richmond, Va. He was said to be an eminent physician, and died about the time of the birth of his first born, a son, Anthony. His widow married again, when Anthony was apprenticed to a farmer, who afterward moved to Buckingham County, Va. After Anthony obtained his majority, he changed the name from Dubray to that of Dibrell, and from him all of the Dibrell family have sprung. He married a Miss Lee, from a noted Virginia family, and raised a large family, and he was the grandfather of Anthony Dibrell of White County, Tenn, who was for many years receiver of the land office at Sparta; was twenty-two years clerk of the circuit court; was a director in the Bank of Tennessee; member of the Legislature, and ten years treasurer of the State of Tennessee. He raised a large family in White County. His only son, now in White County, is Gen. George G. Dibrell, who was born April 12, 1822, was raised upon a farm, and educated in the common schools of the county, except one session at the university at Knoxville. Before he was eighteen years of age, he was elected clerk of the branch of the Bank of Tennessee at Sparta, which office he held for six years, when, having married Mary E. Leftwick, the daughter of a merchant in Sparta, he retired from the bank and engaged in merchandising and farming until 1848. He was elected clerk of the county court, and was three times re-elected, until he voluntarily retired in 1860. He continued his mercantile business and farming interest. In February, 1861, he was the Union candidate for the State convention, and was elected by a very large majority. He opposed secession, but always declared his adhesion to the South, but said that secession was not the way to settle the impending difficulty, and declared if war was forced upon the country, he would fight for the South. In 1861 he was elected to the Legislature without opposition, receiving every vote polled in the county except one. He assisted in raising and organizing the Twenty-fifth Regiment of Tennessee Infantry, and at the organization, August 10, 1861, he was elected lieutenant-colonel; S. S. Stanton, colonel, and Tim H. Williams, major. This regiment was afterward assigned to Gen. Zollicoffer brigade. At Mill Springs, Ky., he was given control of all the outposts and picket lines, and cavalry officers of equal and superior rank ordered to report to him. His first hard-fought battle was at Fishing Creek, when, Col. Stanton being wounded early in the engagement, he assumed command of the regiment, which made a gallant resistance to the overwhelming forces of the enemy, and was the last to retire from the battlefield, and in the retreat across the Cumberland River the night following at Mill Springs, he and his regiment were the last to leave the fortifications, and the last to cross the Cumberland River just before daylight next morning. In front of Corinth, Miss., May 7, 1862, he commanded the outposts that had an engagement with Gen. Pope's advance, who telegraphed that he had routed the rebels and captured 4,000 prisoners, when Dibrell had only 200 men engaged, out of which his loss in killed, wounded and captured was forty-one. At the reorganization of the regiment he was defeated for re-election as lieutenant-colonel for local caucus, and returned to his home, intending to enter the cavalry service. He had only a letter from Gen. John S. Marmaduke and Gen. W. I. Hardee, who had witnessed his fight with Pope's advance, when he went to Richmond for authority to raise his cavalry regiment. That letter was so complimentary, that he was informed by the Secretary of War (Randolph) that he could have all the troops he wanted. He returned and raised his cavalry regiment (Eighth Tennessee) within the lines of the enemy; was assigned to the brigade of that great cavalry leader, Gen. N. B. Forrest; was engaged in several battles around Nashville, Franklin and in West Tennessee; at Parker's Cross Roads, at Spring Hill, Triune. On the retreat from Tallahoma, he assisted in the command of Gen. Forrest's old brigade, after the wounding of Col. Starnes, and commanded that brigade until the close of the war; was in two battles on Wild Cat Creek, in White County; began the fight at Chickamauga on Friday morning, September 18, 1863; was at Cleveland, Sweet Water, Philadelphia, etc., and then in many engagements under Gen. Wheeler on the retreat from Dalton to Atlanta; was under Gen. Longstreet in his East Tennessee campaign; won a battle at Philadelphia, and various other places, including Dibrell's Hill, and moved back to Georgia; was with Gens.

Wheeler and Hampton, in the campaigns through Georgia, South Carolina and North Carolina, and had many hard fights, such as Waynesboro, Buck Head Church, Averysboro, Barkerville, Stony Point and others; was ordered from Raleigh, N. C., to report to President Davis at Greensboro after the fall of Richmond; made the march, eighty-five miles, in two nights and a day, and escorted President Davis with all the archives, to Washington, Ga., where they surrendered, and were paroled May 19, 1865. After furnishing the President with an escort, he marched his men in a body back to Tennessee; found his home devastated, and his family almost suffering for the necessaries of life. He at once, with his son who had stood all the hardships of war with him, went to work on the farm, to try to build up his lost fortunes. When the war came on, he was in easy circumstances, clear of debt, or nearly so, and had good prospects. Now his property was all gone, debts unpaid, involved largely as security for friends, and $70,000 damage suits brought against him by unprincipled Loyalists, but he never faltered, and was never sued upon a debt of his own in his life. Kind friends furnished him supplies upon which to raise his crops, and to engage in a small mercantile business again. His friends stood by him, and he prospered; was elected to the Constitutional Convention, in 1869, which framed our present Constitution; was the author of several clauses in it; was elected president of the Southwestern Railroad Company in November, 1869, and through his efforts and good management secured the completion of that road to Sparta, and has now succeeded in having it again extended to the Bon Air coal mines, one of the finest coal properties in Tennessee. While president of the Southwestern Railroad Company he held $78,000 of State bonds issued to said road, which he refused to use or expend, and turned them back to the State, being the only railroad official in the State that ever returned a bond issued to a company. In 1874 he was elected to Congress by a majority of over 4,600 and four times re-elected, voluntarily retiring in 1884, and giving his whole attention to his farm and developing the Bon Air coal mine. He has seven sons living; his only daughter married and died, leaving two children he is now raising. He has been a member of the Methodist Church for forty-four years; twice sent as a delegate to the conference of that church.

G. W. Douglas, a well known druggist of Doyle Station, was born in Coffee County, Tenn., in 1855. His father was of Scotch-Irish descent, and his mother of English-Dutch. Our subject received a good education at Beach Grove. He taught and attended school alternately for a period of seven years, also devoting some time to the study of medicine. He entered the old medical college at Nashville in 1881 and 1882, after which he practiced about two years near Bellbuckle, Bedford County. August, 1885, he located at Doyle Station and engaged in the drug business, in which he has met with great success. The firm is Dainess & Douglas, the latter being the prescriptionist. They have a first-class stock, and are receiving a fair share of patronage. Mr. Douglas is an elder in the Cumberland Presbyterian Church, and a member of the Masonic order, Manchester. He is a Democrat, an energetic, worthy and respected citizen.

Dr. P. H. Earls, a well known physician of Perilla, was born in White County May 1, 1851. His parents, Martin and Titia (Robertson) Earls, were of English descent and natives of North Carolina. The father immigrated to White County, where he died in 1852. The mother's death occurred in 1851. Our subject became an orphan at an early age. He worked on a farm until he was eighteen. Having had but limited educational advantages, he secured the place of janitor in the Manchester College which he held four years, thus paying for his board and tuition. In 1872 and 1873 he attended Bird College, where he completed his schooling. He immediately began the study of medicine, and attended the Nashville Medical College, after which he entered upon his practice in the neighborhood of Perilla, where he has met with considerable success and received an extensive patronage. In 1883 he was interested in the mercantile business at this place. He is a self-made and highly respected man, who by his own efforts has accumulated a comfortable amount of this world's goods. He is a member of the Methodist Episcopal Church South and a Democrat. December 24, 1873, he wedded Miss Nancy N., daughter of William and Mattie Cole. Their union has resulted in the birth of three children: May L., Carrie E. and Ella E.

J. A. P. Fancher, a prosperous farmer and grist-mill proprietor of the Sixth District, was born February 26, 1841, in Overton County, Tenn. He is a son of Thomas H. and Susan A. (Officer) Fancher, of White (now Putnam) County. The father was born January 24, 1799, of English-Irish descent. He was an extensive stock raiser, and a man of considerable prominence and a Democrat; was a major of militia, a justice of the peace and magistrate of Overton County, and was instrumental in relieving the county of debt. He was several times urged to represent his county in the Legislature and Senate. From 1843 to 1846 he resided in Arkansas, after which he came to White County. He died April 5, 1884. His wife was born August 17, 1817; was married February 16, 1840, and died May 31, 1850. She was a consistent member of the Methodist Church South. Our subject was raised on a farm and received a fair education. Since his twenty-fifth year he has been engaged in agricultural pursuits, and with decided success. In 1861 he enlisted in the Confederate Army, Sixteenth Tennessee, under command of Col. John H. Savage. After two years' service his health failed, when he hired a substitute and returned home. Later he was arrested by the Federals and taken to Rock Island, Ill., prison. He was offered his liberty if he would take the oath of allegiance, but he refused. In 1865 he returned to White County, where he has since resided. October 9, 1867, he married Jane, daughter of Rev. James K. and Jane S. (Simpson) Lausden. Mr. Lausden is of Scotch-Irish descent, and his wife of Irish. To Mr. and Mrs. Fancher four sons and three daughters were born, one now deceased. Mrs. Fancher, who was a consistent member of the Cumberland Presbyterian Church, died May 18, 1884. July 6, 1884, our subject married Levina T. Lausden, his sister-in-law, who has borne him one child. Both are members of the Cumberland Presbyterian Church. Mr. Fancher is a stanch Democrat, and a liberal contributor to, and supporter of, all laudable enterprises.

W. W. Gooch, a well known merchant and farmer of Goochville, was born in 1844 in White County. He is of Irish-Dutch descent, a son of Joseph and Lavinia W. (O'Connor) Gooch. The father was born in 1793 in North Carolina and immigrated to White County at an early date, where he died about 1847. The mother was born in White County in 1815, and died in Texas in 1868. The subject of this sketch spent his early days on a farm and received a good education in the country schools. He was in the Confederate Army, Company I, Eighth Tennessee Cavalry. He served during the entire war, and although he took part in many of the famous battles, was neither wounded nor captured. After receiving an honorable discharge he returned home and began farming. In 1878, in connection with his agricultural interests, he engaged in merchandising. He is a man of untiring energy and ability. He now owns 240 acres of valuable and productive land, on the Calf Killer River. He is a Democrat, a member of the I. O. O. F. and one of White County's best men. In 1868 he married Melcena, daughter of Joseph and Margaret Gist. To this union have been born Joseph J., James W., Henry L., Wyman D., Addella M., Dora A., Wade H., Everett B. and Haden E.

W. H. Gracey, a prosperous farmer and stock raiser of the Sixth District, was born in White County August 8, 1846, the eighth child of Hugh and Ann (Hitchcock) Gracey. The father was a native of Ireland, and immigrated to this county when quite a young man. He was a successful agriculturist and stock raiser, a Whig and sheriff of the county. He died in November, 1854. The mother was of Irish descent, born in

White County in 1816, and now lives on the old homestead. The subject of our sketch was educated in the schools of the neighborhood, and worked on his mother's farm until his thirtieth year. January 2, 1876, he wedded Malvine, daughter of Frank and Louisa (Lydie) Boyd, of White County. Their family consists of Lillie, born March 12, 1877; Franklin, born May 15, 1880; Quillie, born March 12, 1882. Mr. Gracey has for two terms been overseer of the road. He has by careful management and industry accumulated considerable good property. He is at all times a generous contributor to all charitable and educational enterprises. He is member of the Cumberland Presbyterian Church and a stanch Democrat. Mrs. Gracey is a consistent member of the Methodist Episcopal Church South.

E. S. Haston, a well known farmer of the Second District, was born September 11, 1850, in Van Buren County, a son of Isaac T. and Elizabeth (Sparkman) Haston. His father was born March, 1828, also in Van Buren County, and died in 1875. His father (grandfather of our subject), David Haston, was a pioneer settler of Tennessee. Subject's mother was born about 1826, and died in 1882. E. S. Haston is of Irish descent; he was raised on a farm and educated at Spencer, Bird College. In 1871 he began business for himself. He was interested in merchandising at Spencer from 1877 to 1880, at which time he closed out and has since been exclusively engaged in farming. In 1884 he moved to present place of residence. He is a self-made, industrious and substantial man. By judicious management and economy has accumulated his possessions. He is a Democrat, a member of the I. O. O. F. and belongs to the Masonic Lodge at Spencer. In November, 1880, he wedded Miss Maggie Cummings, a native of Van Buren County. To their union four children have been born: Fred Dexter, Walter Eugene, Willie Burt and an infant.

Richard Hill, a well known and influential citizen of Sparta, and president of the First National Bank of the town, is a native of White County, born in the Ninth Civil District February 24, 1839. He is the son of William and Isabella (Brown) Hill. His father was of Irish descent, and was born in Virginia about 1795, and died in White County August, 1840. Mr. Hill's mother's descent is not known. She was a native of Tennessee and born in 1812, and is still living, a resident of White County. Mr. Hill is the youngest of three children. In his youth he secured a limited education, and has been engaged in farming all his life. He frequently traded in live stock, and has made the raising of fine stock a specialty. In the fall of 1861 he entered the Confederate States service, joined Dibrell's cavalry, and followed this gallant soldier through the remainder of the war. He returned home and resumed the peaceful occupation of farming. He lost almost everything he had by the war, and was yet more embarrassed by reason of heavy security debts against him, but being a man of remarkable energy, in a few years he was again in prosperous circumstances. In March, 1865, a State bank was established at Sparta, and Mr. Hill was made vice-president. In January, 1877, the bank was changed to a national bank and the stock increased from $40,000 to $50,000, and Mr. Hill was elected president, in which he has a bank stock of $8,500. On June 3, 1869, he married Miss Martha J. Officer, an excellent lady, born in Overton County, Tenn., July 2, 1840. Her father, James C.. Officer, was born in Overton County, October 21, 1808, and died in White County, October 22, 1868. Her mother, Leeann (Glenn) Officer was born in White County, January 14, 1813, and died in White County, November 1, 1868. Mr. Hill has two children—one son and one daughter: Robert L., born July 10, 1871; Mertie, born March 11, 1873. Mr. Hill owns a farm of nearly 2,000 acres. He is not a member of any church, but is a man of good morals, and is in sympathy with the Christian Church, while his wife is a member of the Methodist Church South.

Dr. R. V. Hobson, an eminent practicing physician of River Hill, was born March 15, 1837, in Richmond, Va., of which State his parents were also natives. His father, Richard Hobson, died in 1847; he was a son of Samuel Hobson, a Virginian of English descent. Subject's mother was Mary Ann, daughter of Frank Pearce, who was also a native of Virginia, and thought to be of French origin. Mrs. Hobson departed this life about 1848. Our subject was raised and educated in his native State, principally at Charlottesville, Oaklong Academy. He graduated in 1852, and immediately began the study of medicine, under guidance of Drs. Hughes & Leech. In 1859 he entered upon his practice at Alexandria, Va. In 1861 he moved to Baltimore, Md., remaining there about two years. During the following ten years he traveled extensively, also practiced four years at Perrysburg, Ohio. In 1876 he came to River Hill, where he has succeeded in building up a large and lucrative practice. He is recognized as one of the leading and most able practitioners of the county, and is universally respected. He has been an earnest member of the Christian Church for the past twenty-eight years, and is a Republican.

J. D. Holder, a well known merchant and farmer of Holder Station, was born December 3, 1838, in Tennessee, a son of Spencer and Elizabeth (Hopkins) Holder. The father was born in 1788 in Tennessee, and died May 8, 1876. The mother was born in 1795 in North Carolina, and is still living at the advanced age of ninety-one. The grandfather, John Holder, was of Irish descent, born in Virginia in 1760. He immigrated to Tennessee just prior to the birth of Spencer, and died in May, 1863. Our subject was raised on a farm, and educated at Antioch College, Van Buren County. In 1861 he entered the Confederate service, Company D, Eighth Tennessee Cavalry. In November, 1863, at Rock Island, he was shot in the left hip and disabled for life. After the war he went to Texas, where he was engaged in the saw-mill and merchandise business for nearly two years. He returned to Tennessee and entered into the merchandise business with his father at Holder Station, continuing until 1876. He then managed the concern six years on his own resources. In 1882 he closed out and began farming and stock raising. In 1885 he resumed his former business, in which he has been very successful. He is partner in the firm of Holder & Cooper. After the war he commenced without capital, but by judicious management and economy has amassed a fair share of the world's goods. He is an enterprising and esteemed citizen, a member of the Christian Church, a demitted member of the I. O. O. F. and a Democrat. In 1860 he married Miss Susan, daughter of Cary and Sarah Gillentine. Seven children have been born to their union: Sallie E. (wife of J. J. Gissom), Charley, Josie, Martha M. Spencer S. T., Allie May and Johnnie E., who died in March, 1885.

Hon. Eliphalet Jarvis, lawyer, and senator of the Ninth Senatorial District, was born five miles north of Sparta January 14, 1850, the son of Reziah and Margaret (Sapp) Jarvis. The father, born in North Carolina about 1794, died in White County, Tenn., in 1868, and the mother, a native of Tennessee, is still living in White County. The father, coming to White County in early life, was a successful farmer and a Democrat, and the misfortune of blindness befell him in 1857. Our subject, educated chiefly at Cumberland Institute in White County, worked on the home farm and taught school until he began the study of law in 1875 under Col. W. J. Farris, of Sparta. Since obtaining a license to practice in the early part of 1876, he has been exclusively devoted to the law. In August, 1886, unexpected to himself, he was nominated candidate for State senator of the Ninth Senatorial District (eight counties) by the Democratic party. Mr. Jarvis' majority over the Republican nominee, J. W. Dorton, of Cumberland County, was 1,001. At the first meeting of the Senate our subject was placed on six different standing committees, the judiciary, and that of finance and ways and means being the most important. He is a promising young lawyer, and fast winning his way to honorable distinction. December 28, 1876, he married Mollie Gilliland, a lady born in Polk County,

Tenn., in 1857. They have had five sons. Mr. Jarvis and wife are members of the Methodist Episcopal Church South. He is distantly connected with ex-Gov. Jarvis, of North Carolina.

S. J. Johnson, a well known farmer and stock raiser of the Eleventh District, was born in White County June 9, 1839, the third child of Joseph and Mary (Hargess) Johnson. Both were natives of Putnam County, of Irish-Dutch descent. The father was born November 25, 1809, and married about 1832. He was a prosperous agriculturist and stock raiser. Although a religious and good man, he never united with any denomination. He died in 1873. The mother was born March 20, 1811. She is a consistent and respected member of the Baptist Church. Our subject was reared on the farm, receiving but limited educational advantages. At the age of sixteen he engaged as clerk with Robertson & Johnson, of White County, remaining with them about ten years. January, 1861, he accepted a position with Hill & Bradley. July 25, 1861, he entered the Confederate Army. He was first lieutenant of Company K, Twenty-fifth Tennessee, under command of Col. S. S. Stanton. He was in the battle of Fishing Creek, Murfreesboro and Chickamauga. January, 1864, he was promoted to rank of captain, which he retained until he was captured at Drury Bluff, Va. He was taken to Fortress Monroe, Virginia, Point Lookout, Fort Delaware, Morris' Island (S. C.), Pulaski, Ga., and then back to Fort Delaware. After his return home he clerked for W. C. Johnson. In 1867, in partnership with J. H. Officer, he embarked in the mercantile business. Two years later he bought his partner out and carried the business on alone until 1883, and in the meantime was interested in farming. In 1880 he went into the mill and lumber trade. He has always been an energetic and able business man. He is self-made, and has accumulated a fair share of this world's goods. August 30, 1867, he married Fannie, daughter of William and Cynthia (Holeford) Officer, of Overton County. Three sons and five daughters have been born to this union, all of whom are living. Mr. Johnson is a true Democrat. He and his wife are active and sincere members of the Cumberland Presbyterian Church.

David C. Lowrey, a well known and enterprising planter of White County, and resident of the first civil district is a native of this county, and was born January 24, 1850. He is the son of Charles and Kittie (Hudgens) Lowrey, both natives of White County. Mr. Lowrey's father was of Irish descent and was born in 1820, and died in 1883, in the county that gave him birth. He was married in 1844, and was engaged in agricultural pursuits, to which he associated the raising and trading in live stock. He made life a good success, was an old line Whig before the war, and a Democrat after the war. Mr. Lowrey's mother's ancestors came from France. She was born in 1826, and is still living a resident of White County. The Lowreys originally came from Pennsylvania, and Mr. Lowrey's ancestors on his mother's side came from Kentucky. His great-grandmother on his mother's side was a niece of Daniel Boone. Our subject is the third of five children. He was educated at the Sparta Seminary and Burrett College, Van Buren County. He has been a merchant, a trader and a planter, and has been successful in them all. In 1867 he settled with his father on the farm where he now lives. Being a live enterprising man all of his life, he has secured a fair competency of this world's goods, and owns a farm of 625 acres in White County. On January 18, 1877, he was married to Miss Maggie Meredith, born in Texas in 1858, though raised in White County. Unto this union are born three children—two sons and one daughter. Mr. Lowrey is a stanch Democrat, and always supports that party. He is not a church member, but a firm believer in the Bible, and is in sympathy with the Christian Church. His wife is a deserving member of the Christian Church.

W. H. Magness, Jr., merchant, was born in De Kalb County May 15, 1856, the son of Rev. Perry G. and Martha J. (Webb) Magness, both of Irish origin, and natives of what is now De Kalb County. The father was born in 1826 and died in De Kalb County September 29, 1877. The mother, born in 1831, is still living in Warren County. The father's ancestors came from North Carolina. He was a prominent Primitive Baptist minister, and was county clerk of De Kalb eight years after the war. Receiving a liberal education at Water's & Walling's College, McMinnville, in 1876 he established a general store at Magness' Mills in De Kalb County. In 1880 he came to Sparta and has since been in the merchandise business. January 31, 1878, he married Florence Crowder, who was born in White County March 20, 1859. Three children were born to them—one son and two daughters. He is a Democrat politically, and is a member of the church to which his wife belongs, the Primitive Baptist.

J. F. Mitchell, a prominent farmer of the Tenth District, was born in White County September 12, 1852, the fourth child of John W. and Hannah (Moore) Mitchell. They were English-Irish. The father was born in White Connty June 16, 1823. He was justice of the peace for fifteen or twenty years, a prosperous agriculturist and self-made man and a stanch Democrat. He died September 23, 1863. The mother was born in Van Buren County July 15, 1827, and died October 5, 1871. Both were respected members of the Methodist Episcopal Church South. The subject of this sketch was raised on a farm and received a fair education in the country schools. He began farming for himself at the age of nineteen, and has since been quite successful. He is a worthy citizen and true Democrat. September 5, 1872, he married Nancy A., daughter of Joseph and Ann (Denny) Cummins. To them were born Willie, born June 17, 1873; Tobitha, born July 1, 1875; Joseph A., born September 28, 1877; Denny, born March 11, 1880, and Sallie J., born December 11, 1882. Mrs. Mitchell died January 14, 1883. Mr. Mitchell's second marriage took place February 11, 1883, to Nettie, daughter of James and Loirja (Brown) Davis, of White County. By this union are two children: Bertha E., born November 28, 1883, and James W., born June 12, 1886. Mr. and Mrs. Mitchell are members of the Methodist Episcopal Church.

Andrew L. Potts, a well known and enterprising planter of White County, is a native of this county, born in the Eleventh Civil District, September 13, 1819. He is the son of Patrick and Catharine (Price) Potts. His father was of Scotch-Irish descent, and was born in South Carolina about the year 1797, and died in White County in 1881. He was a farmer, and made life a success. Before the war he was an old line Whig, and after the war a Democrat. He was a member of the Methodist Church. Mr. Potts' mother was of English descent, and was born in North Carolina in 1804, and died in Arkansas in 1878, and was a member of the Christian Church. Our subject secured a good education in his native county, and early began the cultivation of the soil. At different times he has traded in live stock. In 1860 he was elected high sheriff of White County, and nominally held this office until the close of the war, at which time he was forced to relinquish it to W. F. Carter, who was appointed to this office by Gov. Brownlow; but in 1867 or 1868 Mr. Potts was re-elected high sheriff of White County, and served one term. In March, 1840, he married Miss E. M. England, native of White County, and born February 15, 1821. To this union were born nine children—four sons and five daughters. They have lost by death one son and two daughters. He has been a live, enterprising successful man all of his life. Though he began life rather poor he now owns a handsome farm of 680 acres in White County. He is a Democrat, is not a member of any church, but is a firm believer in the Christian religion, and is in sympathy with the Missionary Baptist Church. His wife is a member of this church, and is a woman of great piety.

J. S. Roberts, a prominent farmer and stock raiser of White County, was born February 25, 1832, in Overton County, the eldest child of William and Sarah (Matthews) Roberts. The father was born February

28, 1806, in Charlotte County, Va., and married in 1830. He was a saddler at Livingston, Tenn., and a Democrat. His death occurred in 1872. The mother was born February 20, 1805, in Overton County, and died in 1883; both were of English descent and members of the Baptist Church. The subject of this sketch worked at the saddler's trade in his youth, but began farming when he attained his majority. In 1856, he was elected trustee of Overton County; at same time was postmaster at Livingston. In the fall of 1862, he entered the Confederate Army, under Forrest's command, and served until 1864. In 1870 he was elected circuit court clerk of Overton County, and held that office three terms in succession, in connection with which he was engaged in the lumber business and farming. In 1882 he abandoned the lumber trade, and has since devoted his time exclusively to farming and stock raising. July 3, 1858, he married Mary, daughter of Carter and Margaret (Shelly) Allison, of Overton County. Five sons and five daughters are the fruits of this union. Mr. Roberts is a Democrat. He and wife are both members of the Cumberland Presbyterian Church.

Sam Scott, a well known farmer and stock raiser of the Eighth District, was born in White County, January 24, 1822. He is the seventh child of Jonathan and Elizabeth (Milican) Scott, both of whom were natives of Tennessee. The father was born in 1784; he was an extensive and prosperous farmer and stock raiser, and cultivated the second crop grown in White County. Although uneducated, he took great interest in the advancement of all educational enterprises. By industry and judicious management he accumulated considerable property; was worth at least $20,000. He died in 1852. The mother was born about 1786, and died in 1840. Our subject remained on the home farm until 1850, when he began farming for himself. In the spring of 1861 he entered the Confederate service, enlisting in the Sixteenth Tennessee Infantry, under command of Col. John H. Savage. He participated in the battle of Chickamauga; August, 1862, was discharged at Chattanooga, on account of his age. In 1863 he went out with Gen. John H. Morgan's cavalry. He fought at Charleston, Tenn.; was in a battle at Saulville, Va., while in G. G. Dibrell's command, in which he continued to the close of the war. He returned home and resumed his farming, and has met with unusual success. He is a liberal contributor to all charitable and educational enterprises, a valuable and esteemed citizen, and stanch Democrat. November 18, 1862, he married Francis, daughter of John and Mary (Scott) England. Twelve sons and one daughter were born to their union, all living but one.

Col. W. G. Smith, lawyer, of the firm of Snodgrass & Smiths, was born in Granville County, N. C., September 25, 1828, a son of George C. and Martha (Gooch) Smith, the former of German-French ancestry and the latter of Welsh descent. The father was born in Virginia in 1806, died at his son's, Dr. Henry P. Smith, whom he desired to have treat him for dropsy of the heart. He died of pneumonia April, 1, 1875. The mother was born in North Carolina, August, 10, 1809, and died in White County, December 24, 1881. The father, a tailor, was an apprentice in the same shop with Andrew Johnson in Raleigh and Oxford, N. C. The parents were married near Oxford, May 10, 1826. In 1848 they began a five-years' residence in Rutherford County, and then came to McMinnville where they were living at the time the father died. The mother then made her home with her son, Rev. J. D. Smith, who is a popular minister in the Cumberland Presbyterian Church. Our subject, one of nine children, was educated in the Oxford Academy of his native State; has been an extensive reader also. Preceding his parents a few months to Tennessee, he came to Nashville where he worked at the gilder's trade, painting mirror frames for three years. In 1853 he established a general store at McMinnville, but the following June lost the whole of his small earnings. Beginning again he continued as salesman for four years, working for a firm at Increase. In 1857 he came to White County and bought a stock of goods from James A. Hill, but in 1861 he left his business with a brother, and became captain of Company C, Twenty-fifth Tennessee Infantry (Confederate), and afterward lieutenant-colonel of the Eighty-fourth Tennessee Regiment Infantry, and took part in the battles of Shiloh, Corinth, Murfreesboro, Chickamauga, and from Dalton to Atlanta. After the war he returned home and resumed his business at Cave, White County, and added the tanning business also. In 1866 he began the study of law and was licensed a few years after, and since that time has been before the Sparta bar. After 1869 he was on his farm in the Third District until 1886, when he came to Sparta. May 10, 1857, he married Amanda R. Templeton, born in White County, Tenn., September 24, 1836. They have seven children, of whom W. T. is a member of the law firm. Our subject is a Democrat, and he, his wife and four children are members of the Christian Church.

T. W. Stewart, a well known farmer of the Third District of White County, was born March 3, 1843, in Person County, N. C. When about seven years of age he immigrated to Tennessee with his mother and located in Hawkins County, E. Tenn., and came to White County in 1859. His mother, Frances (Epps) Stewart, was of Dutch descent, born in 1806, in Lunenburgh County, Va., and died in White County in 1867. The father, David S., was born about 1800, in North Carolina, where he died in 1844. His mother was an English lady, whose maiden name was Drummond. Our subject was raised on a farm and educated in the country schools. At the age of eighteen he entered the Confederate Army, Company I, Eighth Tennessee Cavalry. He served during the entire war, and was in several of the most famous battles, but received no serious injury. After the restoration of peace and his return home, he spent one session at school and then engaged in farming, to which occupation his attention has since been given. He is one of the most substantial and enterprising agriculturists in the county and an esteemed citizen. He is a Democrat. October 31, 1866, he married Martha M., daughter of William and Betsy Anderson. This union resulted in the birth of William A., Elizabeth F., Lizzie Gertrude, Mary Lucinda, Lillian May, Martha Maranda, Leonie and Joseph Wyatt.

W. F. Story, of Story Bros., lawyers, was born in Fentress County, December 20, 1846, the son of Noah W. and Catherine (Woolsey) Story, both of English ancestry. The paternal ancestors came over with William Penn, one of whom, Thomas Story, assisted in the colonization of Pennsylvania. The father, born in North Carolina, died in White County, Tenn., March 30, 1879. The mother, a native of Fentress County, died in White County, August 15, 1885. The father came from Fentress County to White County in 1865. He was a farmer and a member of the same church as his wife, the United Baptist Church. After completing a liberal education, our subject taught school for two years, and in 1872 he began the study of law under Col. Calms, of Sparta, with whom he became partner, after he had the same year secured a license to practice. In 1873 he established a firm of his own, since which time he has been practicing. In 1885 Gov. Bates appointed him to the newly created office of White County judge, to which he was elected in 1886. For the last twenty-seven years he has been associated with his younger brother, Ephraim, in their present very successful firm. April 3, 1878, our subject married Hattie E. Cole, a cultivated lady born at Elkhart, Ind., in 1847. Of their four children a son and daughter are living. He is a sound Democrat and he and his wife are members of the Cumberland Presbyterian Church.

J. W. Taylor, a prominent manufacturer of jeans and woolen goods, and proprietor of a grist-mill, was born in September, 1833, in White County, Tenn., of Irish descent. His father, Creed A. Taylor, was born about 1809, in Virginia, and immigrated to White County about 1818. His death occurred in 1857. The mother, Sarah (Walling) Taylor, was born about 1811 or 1812, a daughter of Joseph and Katie Walling. She died in 1866, while on a visit to relatives in Arkansas. Our subject was reared on a farm and educated in the county schools. After farming a short time he engaged in the grist-mill business in 1863, and has met with unusual success. He added wool-carding machines to his business. In 1876 he put in five looms, and several more since that time, until he now has ten, with a capacity of 250 yards per day. The mill has a fine central location; is on Calf Killer River, six miles south of Sparta; is known as the Tebo Woolen Mill. Mr. Taylor has between $17,000 and $18,000 invested and is doing an extensive and lucrative business. He is a self-made man, his possessions being the fruits of his own efforts and industry. His eldest son, Creed A., is a partner in the mill. In 1862 our subject married Miss Margret Smallman, a cousin of the distinguished Judge Smallman, of Warren County. To their union four sons and six daughters have been born. Previous to the war Mr. Taylor was a Whig, and is now a Democrat. He and his wife are consistent and esteemed members of the Christian Church.

J. H. Towles, a leading merchant of Onward, was born May 1, 1854, in Warren County, a son of John W. and Lucinda (Wilson) Towles. The father was born March 31, 1819, in Warren County, Tenn., where his father, Joseph Towles, a Virginian, emigrated in 1818. The mother was born November 4, 1824, and died in July, 1865. They are thought to have been of English descent. The subject of this sketch was raised on a farm and received a liberal education. About the time of his majority, he engaged in the merchandise business in Smithville. October 20, 1875, he moved his stock to Towles' Mills, now known as Jesse. In 1879 he went to Cross Roads, Warren County, and remained until October 20, 1884, when he came to Onward, where he has been most successful. He was the first to build at this place, and has done much toward its improvement and advancement. Through his efforts the high school was established in 1886. He is a valuable and highly respected citizen, a member of the Christian Church, and a stanch Democrat. March 14, 1877, he married Miss Emma J., daughter of Christopher C. and Lavenia (Hudson) Zwingle, of Irish descent. To this union four children have been born: Mary E., Oliver J., Lavenia L. and Baxter Benton. Mrs. Towles is an earnest member of the Cumberland Presbyterian Church.

Wm. Turner, a prominent farmer and stock raiser of the Eighth District, was born in White County March 13, 1839, the third child of James and Ann (Lyda) Turner. The father was born about 1814, in Tennessee. He was a successful farmer of White County; he died in 1840. The mother is of Dutch descent, born about 1816. She is an earnest and respected member of the Methodist Episcopal Church South. At the age of nineteen our subject began farming on his own resources.

In July, 1861, he entered the Confederate Army, Company E, Twenty-fifth Tennessee Infantry, under command of Col. S. S. Stanton. He took active part in the battles of Murfreesboro, Chickamauga, Drury Bluff and Knoxville. April 2, 1865, he was captured and imprisoned at Johnson Island, Ohio, and was retained till June 19. He returned home and resumed farming. In March, 1870, he was elected trustee of White County, and served two terms. In 1874 he again gave his attention to agriculture, stock and cattle raising, so continuing up to present date. He is a prosperous, energetic and universally respected man, and a stanch Democrat. March 26, 1872, he married Ann, daughter of W. B. and Jane (Simms) Cope, of White County. To this union three children have been born: James, born August 19, 1873, died August 4, 1880; Frank, born November 22, 1875; Mary, born December 31, 1877. Mr. Turner belongs to the Methodist Episcopal Church South, and his wife to the Cumberland Presbyterian.

H. B. Ward, a prosperous farmer and lumberman of Wards Station, was born April 26, 1844, in Milan, Ohio; a son of Elam and Christianna (Byard) Ward. The father was born in Connecticut, in December, 1806, and moved to Ohio in 1809 with his parents. His father was Col. Jared Ward, a native of England and a gallant officer of the war of 1812. Mrs. Christianna B. Ward was a native of New York State, of Scotch descent. Our subject was raised on a farm near the place of his birth, and received a good academic education. At the age of eighteen he enlisted in the Federal Army, Company C, One Hundred and Thirty-seventh Ohio Infantry, Ohio National Guards. He was honorably discharged December 15, 1864, and has now the discharge paper, issued at Washington, D. C., bearing Abraham Lincoln's signature. Our subject then joined the One Hundred and Seventy-seventh Ohio Infantry Company, and served until the close of the war. He returned home, where for two years he engaged in farming, On account of feeble health he immigrated to White County, where he introduced and operated, for a short while, the first saw-mill in the county. Since that time he has been almost exclusively in the farming and lumber business. He is an energetic, able business man and good citizen; by industry and careful management he is now in very comfortable circumstances. He is a member of the K. of H., I. O. O. F. and is a Republican. April 7, 1870, he married Sallie, daughter of Wm. and Betsy Anderson. She was the mother of two children: Norman A. and Bessie. Her death occurred February 24, 1879. She was a member of the Missionary Baptist Church. November 9, 1880, our subject wedded Ella M., daughter of James and Margaret Davis, native of Connecticut, where Mrs. Ward was born February 19, 1855. This union has resulted in the birth of three children : Sallie M., Annie Pearl and Maggie C. Mr. and Mrs. Ward are earnest members of the Missionary Baptist Church.

E. Winstead, a prominent farmer of the Fifth District, was born November 17, 1822, in Hawkins County, Tenn., the fifth child of Ephraim and Margaret (Martin) Winstead. They were of Irish-Welsh descent. The father was a farmer and stock raiser. He was a Whig, and his death occurred in Hawkins County October 27, 1832. The mother was an excellent Christian woman, a member of the Baptist Church. She died October 24, 1872. The subject of our sketch was raised on the farm. His educational advantages were very limited. At the age of fourteen he took charge of his mother's affairs, and managed them with success. After attaining his majority he went to farming on his own resources. In 1859 he located in White County. In 1865 he was appointed magistrate, but did not serve. He has been a school director for nearly thirty years. He is a stanch Democrat, and a highly respected, valuable citizen. May 28, 1848, he married Emeline, daughter of David S. and Mary (Mitchael) Rogers, of Hawkins County. This union resulted in the birth of five children: J. W., born January 27, 1850; Nancy J., born September 28, 1851; W. W., born March 17, 1854; Serener E., born July 27, 1856, and Mary M., born November 10, 1858. Each received a good education. Mr. and Mrs. Winstead are earnest and respected members of the Baptist Church.

Oliver F. Young, a prominent merchant and farmer of Simpson's mills, was born January 4, 1825, in Jackson County, Tenn., a son of James and Elizabeth (Draper) Young. The father was born in North Carolina about 1787, and immigrated to Tennessee in 1797 with his parents, John and Sarah Young. John Young, when six years of age, was captured by the Indians, and retained by them until he reached his majority, at which time a treaty was made between the whites and Indians, and prisoners exchanged. He was thus restored to his friend, his parents having been massacred at the time of his capture. James (subject's father) located in Sumner County, and lived for a number of years in the only settlement of the western portion of the State. He afterward moved to Jackson County, where he died in 1860. He was sheriff of the county for fourteen years, and a member of the Legislature two terms— the first at Murfreesboro and the last at Nashville. His wife was born in 1787, and died in 1872. She was a daughter of Thomas Draper, one of the early pioneers of Tennessee. Our subject was reared on a farm, receiving the education of the average country boy of that day; he engaged in the merchandise business at Bagdad, Smith County, until 1852, when he moved to Hickman, Ky., continuing in the same business. In 1859 he went to New Orleans, where he was a commission merchant until 1862, when he suspended business until after the restoration of peace in 1865, when he again resumed and continued till 1869. He then moved to Paducah, Ky., and in 1870 to White County, where he has been, and ll is, interested in the merchandise, farming and milling business, in which he has been very successful. He is a self-made, industrious and able man. His possessions have been amassed by his own exertions and careful management. He is a member of the Christian Church, and a Democrat. In 1848 he married Nancy E., daughter of James and Rebecca Wilson, of Monroe County, Ky. She died in January, 1855. She was the mother of four children: Hayden M., Samuel A. (who died December 11, 1858), James E. (who died June 29, 1855) and an infant. In July, 1857, our subject wedded Virgie R. Watson, who bore him six children, four of whom are still living: Bettie C. (wife of the Hon. L. D. Hill), Prof. Frank S., Sallie R. and Dr. W. B. Mrs. Young died in August, 1868. July 31, 1870, our subject was united in marriage to Mrs. Eva Metcalf, nee Simpson. Her father, Gen. John W. Simpson, took a prominent part in the war of 1812.

Charles C. Young, a well known and enterprising merchant of Sparta, was born in this town February 25, 1845. He is the son of William M. and Matilda (Wallace) Young, His parents were married December 1, 1842. Mr. Young's father was of Scotch descent and was born in Jackson County October 23, 1807, and died in White County November 13, 1862. His mother was born in White County, November 5, 1822. She is still living and a resident of Fayetteville, Tenn. The grandfather of Mr. Young came from North Carolina at an early date and settled in Jackson County, and filled the office of high sheriff of that county for fourteen years, and was then in the Legislature for two sessions. At the age of eighteen Mr. Young's father, after spending his boyhood days on the farm, went to Nashville and served apprenticeship at the tanning business three years, after which he came to White County and with his small earnings established a tannery near Sparta and continued in the business about ten years. In the meantime he married a daughter of Woodson P. White. At different times before the war he was cashier of the Sparta branch of the Bank of Tennessee, of which he was a stockholder. Mr. Young received a liberal education in his native county, and at the age of fifteen entered the mercantile business as a salesman for the firm of D. P. & J. C. Shackleford at Fayetteville, Tenn., and remained one year. In the spring of 1861 he made an effort to join the Confederate States Army but was rejected on account of his age. In the fall of the same year he made the second attempt to join the army and was successful. He enlisted in the Forty-first Tennessee Regiment Infantry, and remained until the close of the war. He was twice captured, first at Fort Donelson, and kept a prisoner eight months at Camp Morton, Ind.; was exchanged at Vicksburg, and captured the second time at Franklin, Tenn., being wounded twice during the engagement, and unable to retreat with the army was sent to Camp Chase, Ohio, and remained a prisoner eight months again. He returned home in the spring of 1865, after an absence of nearly four years, and engaged in farming. Beginning in 1870 he followed tanning in Putnam County three years and then farmed three years. In 1876 he came to White County with about $1,000 cash, and established a store of general merchandise at Sparta. In 1882 he formed the partnership of Young & Dryer, doing a good business for two years. At the close of 1884 he bought out his partner and has since conducted the business alone. The firm does a business of about $20,000 a year. Besides owning and controlling the above business, Mr. Young owns three dwellings and one-half interest in the business house he now occupies. On June 19, 1872, he married Miss Nettie C. Burton, a cultured lady who was educated at the McMinnville Female College; she was born in Putnam County, May 12, 1846. To this union were born four children: Stephen H., born September 13, 1874; Mary E., born December 25, 1876; Minnie L., born December 22, 1879, and one other. Mr. Young is a Democrat, while he and his wife are members of the Christian Church.

WARREN COUNTY.

J. C. Biles, clerk and master of the chancery court of Warren County, Tenn., and resident of McMinnville, was born in this county June 27, 1843, the third of nine children born to Robert B. and Nancy (Ramsey) Biles, both natives of Warren County, where they were married in 1838. The father was born in April, 1810, was a farmer and stock raiser. He was a heavy loser by the war, was an old line Whig in politics and a member of the Methodist Episcopal Church South. He died in his native county in April, 1873. The mother was born in September, 1816, is a member of the Methodist Episcopal Church South, and is now living at McMinnville, Tenn. The paternal grandfather of J. C. emigrated from North Carolina and settled in Warren County in 1806. J. C. received a practical education and in the spring of 1861, when but seventeen years old, he enlisted in Company C, Sixteenth Tennessee Regiment Infantry, with D. M. Donnell as captain of the company and John H. Savage, colonel of the regiment. The regiment at first united with the forces of Gen. Zollicoffer, but in July, 1861, was transferred to Lee's army and remained with him until the following December, when it was sent to the coast of South Carolina. After the battle of Shiloh the regiment joined the Army of the Tennessee, where it remained throughout the war. Mr. Biles participated in the battles of Perryville, Ky., Chickamauga, Missionary Ridge and all the battles of Johnson's retreat from Dalton to Atlanta. He was captured after being wounded at Perryville, Ky., and sent as prisoner of war to Chicago, Ill., where he was kept until April, 1863, when he was exchanged and rejoined the army at Tullahoma, Tenn. July 22, 1864, at Atlanta he received a severe wound, and after his recovery, when on Hood's raid into Tennessee, he was again captured and sent to Camp Chase, Ohio, where he was held a prisoner until the close of the war. In the spring of 1865 he returned home and in August of the same year was appointed deputy clerk and master of the chancery court of Warren County, which position he held until 1871. In 1867 he in partnership with Charles R. Morford established a grocery and hardware store, in which he still owns an interest. January, 1877, he was appointed clerk and master of the chancery courts of his county and in 1883 was reappointed and still holds that office. In 1884 Mr. Biles was made a member of the State Democratic executive committee and was reappointed in 1886 and is now an honored member of that body. June 27, 1867, he married Miss Jane Morford, born in Warren County in July, 1848. Mr. and Mrs. Biles are members of the Cumberland Presbyterian Church.

Thomas Black, M. D., was born in McMinnville, June 13, 1837, the son of Alexander and Mary A. (Smith) Black. The father was of Scotch origin, was born in Kentucky in 1804, and died in 1859 in Orange County, Tenn., while on a tour to Virginia. The mother, probably of English ancestry and born in Kingston, Tenn., about 1810, died in Nashville in 1873. Soon after their marriage in Kingston they moved to McMinnville, where the father was in mercantile business during his life. One of nine children, our subject received a good education in his youth; in 1858 he entered the medical department of the University of Nashville, Tenn., attending one course of lectures. In 1861 he enlisted in Company F, Sixteenth Tennessee Regiment Infantry, colonel, John H. Savage, and served in the medical department during the war, having charge of various hospitals. He returned home in 1865, located near McMinnville, practiced his profession, and after attending lectures as before in 1867-68 he graduated. He then practiced in Nashville up to the fall of 1874, when he came to McMinnville where he has since controlled probably the largest practice in the county, with the experience gained also in the cholera epidemic of 1873 in Nashville. February 13, 1867, he married Emma J., daughter of Dr. J. S. Young, secretary of State of Tennessee, and born in the old Campbell house on the site of the capitol building at Nashville. Of their three sons and seven daughters, two sons are dead. Mr. Black is a Democrat and is a prominent member of the Cumberland Presbyterian Church, of which his wife is a member also.

Thomas F. Burroughs, a prominent citizen of McMinnville, is a native of Tennessee; was born in what was then Franklin County, but is now Coffee County, November 25, 1831, the eighth of ten children born to Dr. Peter and Elizabeth P. (Atkinson) Burroughs, both natives of Amherst County, Va., where they were married November 26, 1816, and in 1825 they immigrated to Tennessee and settled in what was then Franklin County, where they spent the remainder of their days. The father was born April 11, 1796; he served in the war of 1812, a volunteer at the age of sixteen years; was a practicing physician and made life a fair success. He was a Whig in politics and died in 1840 in Coffee County. The mother died in the same county in 1837. Thomas F. secured a good education and after its completion was for seven years engaged in the mercantile business at Livingston, Overton County. In 1859 he moved to Increase, Warren County, and here he established a store of general merchandise in connection with farming. In 1870 Mr. Burroughs came to McMinnville and opened a grocery and hardware store and continued in this until 1881. In the meantime in 1875, in partnership with Charles Ohlenmacher, he established a spoke and handle factory at McMinnville and later another partner, J. H. Hughes, was added to the firm, but in August, 1881, Mr. Burroughs became sole owner of the factory, which is valued at $45,000, and is now running it with good success. He also owns a fine house and lot in McMinnville. November 5, 1857, he married Miss Nancy A. Smallman, a native of Warren County, born June 27, 1838. To this union have been born three children: John S., born September 16, 1858; James M., born August 14, 1862, and Mattie E., born January 12, 1865. Mr. Burroughs is a Democrat and a member of the Methodist Episcopal Church South for about twenty-two years and a steward in the church for the last twelve years. Mrs. Burroughs is a member of the same church.

H. J. Cardwell, a well known planter of Warren County, was born near Cumberland Gap, Claiborne Co., Tenn., in 1825. He is the son of Francis and Judy (Leboe) Cardwell. The father was of English descent, born in Virginia, and in about 1806 immigrated to Tennessee and settled in Warren County. He was a farmer by occupation, a member of the Methodist Episcopal Church South, and died in 1844. The mother was of German-French origin, born in Claiborne County, Tenn. She was a member of the same church as her husband and died in 1867. H. J. received only limited educational advantages in youth, but has greatly improved his education by select and extensive reading. Early in life he began farming and now gives his time and attention principally to fruit raising. October 15, 1847, Mr. Cardwell married Louisa, daughter of Jeremiah and Annie (Boyacin) Jaco. This union resulted in ten children—six sons and four daughters—two sons and one daughter deceased. He was commissioned militia officer by Aaron V. Brown and held this office at the beginning of the late war. He has several times been solicited to represent his people in the State Legislature, but has always declined. He is a liberal supporter and contributor to all educational and religious institutions. He has given each of his children a good academical education and has one son who is a successful teacher, and one in the mercantile business at Shell's Ford, Warren County. Mr. Caldwell is a stanch Democrat in politics, and he and wife are firm believers in the Christian religion.

B. M. Coulson, a well known and enterprising farmer and native of Warren County, was born April 11, 1809, the fifth of eleven children born to David and Sarah (Cox) Coulson, who were of Irish ancestry and natives of Virginia. The father immigrated to Kentucky about 1800, where he remained a few years and then moved to White County (now Warren County), Tenn. He was a farmer by occupation and made life a success. May 26, 1836, our subject married Mary Hammons, a daughter of Leroy and Mary (Hampton) Hammons, who were of Dutch descent. Mr. Coulson received a good education, and when twenty years of age he, with his brother James, took charge of his father's farm, which they conducted twelve years with good success. In 1845 he moved to the home of his wife's parents, and remained there about thirteen years, when he came to his present home in Warren County. Mr. Coulson is a stanch Democrat and was elected constable in 1860, which office he held ten years. He is a member of the Methodist Episcopal Church South, of which his wife, who died in June, 1881, was a member.

George W. Cunningham, farmer and merchant of the Fifteenth Civil District of Warren County; was born in that county June 16, 1821, and is the son of John and Sarah Cunningham. The father was born in Virginia about 1792, and died in Warren County, Tenn., about 1857. He was of Scotch-Irish descent. His father, our subject's grandfather came to Tennessee in 1810, and located near the celebrated falls of Caney Fork, being among the first settlers of Warren County. He was in the war of 1812, and his father was in the Revolutionary war. John Cunningham was a farmer and tanner by occupation, and a Democrat in politics. The mother of our subject was born in Hyde County, N. C., October 25, 1799, and is now living with her son, George W. She has a limited education, but has a very strong mind for one of her age. She is a member of the Baptist Church. Our subject is the fourth of six children born to his parents, and now lives on the farm where he was born. His occupation in life has been that of a farmer until 1885, when in connection with his farm he engaged in the mercantile business at Rock Island, Tenn. He formed a copartnership with his grandson, Willie A. Moore, under the firm title of Cunningham & Moore. They carry a stock of goods valued at $2,500 and Mrs. Cunningham also owns 215 acres of land in Warren County, with the principal part under cultivation. This is the result of economy and judicious management. In August, 1842, he married Miss Sarah A. Hennessee, a native of Warren County, born about 1823, and the daughter of A. W. and Jennie (Neal) Hennessee. To them was born one child, a daughter, named Amanda.

G. H. Etter, farmer, of Warren County, Tenn., and now a resident of the Seventh Civil District, was born near Irving College, Warren County, February 3, 1831, and is the son of George and Harriet (Rowan) Etter. The father was born in Greenbrier County, Va., January 8, 1794, and was of German lineage. He followed the occupation of a tanner up to the late war, since which event he has tilled the soil. The mother was born in Hawkins County, Tenn., about 1809, and was of Irish descent. She died August 10, 1884. Our subject was the fifth of fifteen children. He remained under the parental roof until 1856, when he and his brother formed a partnership and engaged in the tanning business. His brother died in 1860, and he continued the business by himself until 1861, when he enlisted in Company H, Sixteenth Tennessee Infantry (Confederate Army). He remained in the infantry three years and then enlisted in the Eighth Tennessee Cavalry, and was in service until the close of the war. He was captured four times but was never in a prison. He received a wound at Buck Run, and while on his way from Dublin Station to Lynchburg, Va., with his regiment, the train ran off the track and he was severely injured. At the close of the war he came to his present location and began the life of a farmer. January 3, 1867, he married Mrs. Woodlee (wife of the late Elijah Woodlee). To them were born six daughters: Mary M., Lillie L., Georgia, Myrtle, Cleopatra and Harriett B. Mrs. Etter is a worthy member of the Christian Church.

Capt. W. G. Etter, merchant and farmer, was born near Irving College, Tenn., August 21, 1841, and is the son of H. R. and Jane Etter. The father, born in Hawkins County, Tenn., January 6, 1818, died January 6, 1880. He came to Warren County in 1837 and engaged in merchandising in connection with farming. He was successful although broken up by the war. The mother was born near Trenton, Ga., and died in Warren County, September 20, 1859. She was a member of the Cumberland Presbyterian Church. Our subject, the third of ten children, lived at home until May 18, 1861, when he enlisted in the Sixteenth Tennessee Infantry, Col. J. H. Savage, Company H, Capt. Meadows. He was first lieutenant, but after Chickamauga, was made captain. He was slightly wounded at Perryville and Chickamauga, and was at Chilton Hill, Cheat Mountain, Port Royal, Murfreesboro, Mission Ridge, Resaca, Pilot Knob, New Hope, Kenesaw Mountain, Marietta, Beech Tree Creek, Stone Mountain, Jonesboro, Lovejoy, Bentonville and the surrender at Greensboro, N. C. He then returned to Irving College, where he has since been engaged in farming. In 1871 he and his father engaged in the mercantile trade with a $4,000 stock, which, after his father's death, he conducted alone. From May until September, 1883, the business was owned by C. R. Martin, but afterward J. J. Meadows bought an interest with our subject. He has a good education and would have had better but for the war. He is a member of the Christian Church, and is a decided Democrat. December 19, 1867, he married Charlotte, daughter of J. W. and Mary Hill, and who was born October 1, 1843. She was a member of the Christian Church and died September 19, 1876. Three of their four children are living: E. Bruce, Lemma, Charlotte B. and Mary J., who was born May 1, 1871, and died November 12, 1883. February 17, 1880, he married Electra, daughter of W. and Sarah J. Meadows, and born in Warren County September 27, 1854. She was educated at Burritt College and is a member of the Christian Church. Their two children are Cecil and Alda.

David Fairbank, farmer, was born in Knox County, Tenn., September 1, 1829, and is the son of John and Sarah Fairbank. The father, of English ancestry and born in North Carolina about 1807, died about 1857. He came to Tennessee about 1829, and settled in Ray County. He was a farmer and a Democrat. The mother, born about 1808, was of English origin, and died about 1840. Our subject, the youngest of three children, lived with his parents until fourteen years of age, and then with an uncle, W. Lowry. In January, 1851, Julia A., daughter of W. J. and Malinda Cartwright, and born in Warren County, Tenn., January 25, 1830, became his wife. She is a member of the Christian Church. Seven of their eight children are now living: William W., Arminta M., Sarah L., John P., Levy L., Nancy A., Emery L. and Andrew J. (deceased August 2, 1886, in his twenty-second year). Our subject has had a life of hardship, but has succeeded, although limited in education. He is a Democrat, and is a member of the Christian Church. In the fall of 1861 he enlisted in the Fifth Tennessee Infantry, Confederate, and served under Col. Ben Hill in the battles of Shiloh, Shelton Hill, Richmond and numerous skirmishes, but was soon after discharged on account of ill health.

Thomas H. Faulkner, manufacturer, was born near McMinnville, Tenn., April 19, 1842, the son of Asa and Anis Faulkner. The father, born July 16, 1802, in Edgefield District, South Carolina, of German descent, came to Hickory Creek, Tenn., in 1808, and was apprenticed to Mr. Biddleman, a machinist. With little education he learned the manufacture of wool cards. His first venture was a mill on Hickory Creek in 1830. In 1846 two others joined him in building the cotton factory, two and one-half miles from McMinnville, called the Central Factory. In 1861, with S. B. Shurlock, he erected on Barren Fork, near McMinnville, a cotton factory named in honor of his wife, and which had a capacity of 2,500 yards of cotton goods daily. In 1863 this factory was used by the Confederates, who took possession of the products, and gave Gen. Rosecrans excuse for destroying it April 21, 1863. They were rebuilt in 1866 with a capacity of 24,000 yards daily, and is still in operation. February 19, 1827, he married Anne Wolfe, born in Scott County, Va., about 1804, and who died March 25, 1851. She was a member of the Baptist Church. Our subject, the tenth of fourteen children, left home in 1861, and enlisted in Company A, Sixteenth Tennessee Confederate Army, under Col. Savage, and after seventeen months on account of ill health received a furlough and returned home, remaining there until his marriage, October 10, 1866, to Mary, the daughter of Judge Robert and Martha C. Cantrell, and born in Smithville, Tenn., November 26, 1847. She is a member of the Methodist Episcopal Church South, and was educated at the Baptist Female College, and Minerva College, Nashville, and finally graduated from Corina Institute, Lebanon, then under Dr. Kelley's control. Their eight children are Robert A., born May 23, 1871, and deceased September 7, 1878; Carrie L., born February 5, 1875, and deceased March 30, 1877; Mattie L.; Charles H.; Kate C.; Thomas H.; William P. and Maryetta. Our subject began life for himself by manufacturing wool cards, his present business, but in connection with this he and his brother Clay became partners in manufacturing woolen goods two and a half miles from McMinnville, and in 1877 they also formed a partnership in a wool factory two miles from McMinnville with Robert Cantrell. In 1879 he dissolved partnership with his brother, and the firm is now Cantrell & Faulkner. Seventy-five thousand dollars is the capital invested in this factory, with a capacity of 1,000 yards of woolen goods daily, and a force of sixty-two men. Our subject never finished his education on account of the war. He is a member of the Methodist Episcopal Church and also of the K. & L. of H.

Clay Faulkner, owner of the Mountain City Woolen Mills, was born near where he now lives April 11, 1845. He is the son of Asa and Annie (Wolf) Faulkner, of German and Scotch descent respectively, the former born in South Carolina July 16, 1802, died in Warren County July 22, 1886, and the latter born in Scott County, Va., February 24, 1806, died in Warren County March 25, 1851. The father lived in Warren County after the eighth year, and was a great builder of cotton and woolen-mills on the various rivers in Warren County. Our subject, one of fifteen children, eleven of whom are living, and all but one of whom reached their majority received an academical education, and in 1866 with his brother J. J., took charge of the Butler Flouring Mills on Charles Creek in addition to his farming. In 1873 his present mills came into his and his brother, Thomas H.'s, possession, and new machinery was put in, and in the spring of 1879 Mr. Faulkner became sole owner, since which time his entire attention has been given to their interest. They are mentioned elsewhere in the history of Warren County. October 22, 1873, Mr. Faulkner married Mary K., a cultured lady and daughter of David Saunders, of Carthage, Tenn. She was born September 23, 1848. Their three children are Margie, born August 8, 1876; Herschel C., born March 2, 1878, and Daisy, born June 10, 1880. Mr. Faulkner and his wife are members and supporters of the Methodist Episcopal Church.

W. J. Fuston, farmer and miller, was born at Gath, Tenn., June 26, 1838, and is the son of Samuel and Nancy (Mullican) Fuston. The father was born near Knoxville, Tenn., November 8, 1807, and by occupation a farmer, is still living at Gath, Tenn., where he came in 1833. He is a member of the Methodist Episcopal Church South, and is very quiet and reserved in his habits. The mother was born in Warren County, Tenn., in 1802 and died in 1863. She was a member of the Methodist Episcopal Church South. Our subject, the fourth of five children, left home at the age of eighteen, and settled where Gath now is, and largely made Gath what it now is. Besides his occupation as farmer, in 1879 he engaged in mercantile pursuits at Gath, and was appointed postmaster there. In September, 1886, he moved to his present location, and built his mill, and now besides this business, he contemplates going into mercantile business at his home. He is a self-made man, beginning with nothing, but now owning 250 acres in Warren County, his mill costing $4,100, and $1,000 worth of stock in the Tullahoma National Bank. He is a member of the Christian Church. March 5, 1855, he married Catherine, daughter of Hamilton and Sallie Neal, and born in Warren County August 20, 1839. She is a member of the Christian Church. Their six children are Mary E., Samuel, Hamilton T., William N., Bell D. and Authur. Mr. Fuston is a member of the I. O. O. F. lodge.

John P. Gartner, a well known citizen of McMinnville, Tenn., was born in Hesse Darmstadt, Germany, October 15, 1838, and is the son of Leonhardt and Anna Gartner, both natives of Hesse Darmstadt. The father was born about 1780, and was a farmer by occupation. He died about 1854. The mother was born about 1800, and died about 1880. John P. is the youngest of ten children. In 1856 he immigrated to the United States with very little means at his command, and settled in Ohio, where he remained three years. He then traveled over the South and West. While in Ohio he learned the blacksmith trade, which he followed after locating at McMinnville, Tenn., in 1867. He is also engaged in the manufacture of wagons and buggies. He has a German education and is a good citizen. He has been elected alderman several times, and is now school trustee. He is a Democrat in politics, a member of the Cumberland Presbyterian Church, I. O. O. F. and the K. & L. of H. December 25, 1867, he married Misouri Polk Hoodenpyl, a native of McMinnville, Tenn., born in November, 1844, and a daughter of Philip and Hyxsy Hoodenpyl. Five children blessed this union, all living: Leonhardt P., Alline, John W., Henry and Florence. Mrs. Gartner is a member of the Cumberland Presbyterian Church.

A. J. Gribble, an enterprising and well known farmer of Warren County, and a resident of the Third Civil District, was born March 12, 1815, in Warren County, Tenn., and is the son of Thomas and Hannah (Shanks) Gribble. Thomas Gribble was born about 1777 in North Carolina, and died in Warren County, Tenn., August 12, 1849. He was of Scotch-Irish descent, and came to Warren County about 1814. He was an elder in the Cumberland Presbyterian Church for over forty years, and was a member of the Democratic party. The mother of the subject of this sketch was also of Scotch-Irish descent, and was born about 1778 in North Carolina, and died in Warren County, Tenn., August 3, 1868. She was also a member of the Cumberland Presbyterian Church. The subject of this sketch was married October 18, 1834, to Miss Mary P.

Randolph, who was born October 18, 1814, in Warren County, Tenn. She was the daughter of Rev. John and Polly Randolph, and died January 26, 1844. This union resulted in six children, four of whom are now living. The two who have died were John T. (who was born October 10, 1835, and was killed December 31, 1862, while fighting for the South, at Murfreesboro, Tenn.), and an infant, who died eight days before its mother's death. Mr. Gribble was married August 6, 1844, to Miss Catharine H. Bristow, who was born in Warren County, Tenn., April 26, 1825, and who is a daughter of James and Nancy Bristow. This union resulted in twelve children, five of whom are dead: Hannah P. (born September 4, 1852, died October 16, 1852), Lovia T. (born January 19, 1866, died January 22, 1875), James B. (born February 22, 1849, died an infant), Henderson C. (born December 25, 1850, died November 25, 1851), and Robert L. (born August 10, 1868, and died an infant). When our subject began life for himself he moved to the Fourth District, Warren County, living there two years, when he changed to his present location, where he has a farm of 300 acres. He had nothing when he commenced; and his experience in youth was one of hardship and toil, but by a life of industry and economy he has accumulated a comfortable competence. He is a stanch Democrat and a member of the Cumberland Presbyterian Church.

Joseph R. Grove, a farmer and fruit distiller of the Fifth Civil District of Warren County, Tenn., was born May 23, 1843, at Robertson Springs, Van Buren Co., Tenn., and is the son of Wm. M. and Peggy (Robertson) Grove. The father was born in Warren County, Tenn., December 10, 1809, and passed his life there. He was sheriff of the county for eight years, a Democrat in politics and a member of the Christian Church. The mother was born in Warren County March 10, 1809, and is still living. She is also a member of the Christian Church. W. M. and Peggy Grove were married February 3, 1831. Our subject was the seventh of ten children. After remaining with his parents until August, 1862, he enlisted in the Confederate Army in Company L, commanded by Capt. Brewster, but afterward by Capt. Rust, of the Eleventh Tennessee Cavalry, commanded by Col. D. W. Holdman. He was in active service for three years, and received a very severe wound. He was elected orderly sergeant when he enlisted, which position he held up to the surrender. He was in all the battles in which Forrest's command was engaged, and was a brave and gallant soldier. After returning home he remained with his parents until June 3, 1866, when he married Mary E. Forrest, a native of Warren County, Tenn., born September 12, 1848. This excellent lady has been well educated and is a member of the Missionary Baptist Church. She is the daughter of Capt. C. M. and Annie Forrest. Her father, Capt. C. M. Forrest, was born in Warren County, Tenn., January 21, 1817, received an excellent education, and is a minister in the Missionary Baptist Church. In 1877 he moved to Bell County, Tex. He was captain in the Fifth Tennessee Regiment Confederate Army, and is a Democrat in politics. The mother of Mrs. Grove was born in Warren County, Tenn., in 1817, and is a member and an active worker in the Missionary Baptist Church. The result of our subject's marriage was the birth of six children, four of whom are living: William, Charles F., Flora J. and Minnie. The two deceased are George D. and Albert. George D. was born in April, 1874, and died in July, 1874. Albert was born in November, 1875, and died in December, 1875. Our subject began business for himself as a farmer and was also engaged in trading in stock, which he continues up to the present. In 1872, in connection with farming he engaged in the fruit distillery business, which he also continues. He is a Democrat in politics and an active and enterprising man.

J. S. Harrison, M. D., a well known physician of McMinnville, was born in Wilson County, Tenn., May 8, 1831, the second of five children born to Edmond R. and Rebecca M. (Hawkins) Harrison. The father was born March 1, 1807, was a successful farmer, and died in 1881. The grandparents were natives of Virginia, and were of English ancestry. The mother was born May 1, 1805, in Virginia, but immigrated to Tennessee at an early day, and is still living. J. S. was reared on a farm, and his early education was obtained in the common schools, and he finished his literary course at Alpine College, Overton County, after which he began the study of medicine under Dr. J. L. Thompson, of Smith County. In the fall of 1854 he entered the old medical college of Nashville, from which he graduated in the spring of 1856. He then began the practice of his profession at Liberty, DeKalb County, and continued there until the breaking out of the war, when he entered the Confederate service, enlisting in Company C, Second Tennessee Cavalry. He was appointed sergeant in 1862, and later elected lieutenant. He was wounded in the right arm at the battle of Harrisburg, and was disabled for service for five weeks. At the close of the war Dr. Harrison returned home, and engaged in the practice of his profession at Smithville, De Kalb Co., Tenn., and continued there until November 1, 1883, when he moved to McMinnville, where he has built up a good practice. December 23, 1856, Dr. Harrison married Julia E., daughter of John and Mary West. She was born February 1, 1834. Dr. Harrison is a self-made man, and by economy and judicious management has accumulated a fair competency.

J. W. Hash, a wide-awake farmer of Warren County, Tenn., was born November 24, 1818, near Rock Island, Warren County, and is the son of William and Elizabeth (Baldwin) Hash, both natives of North Carolina. The father was born in Ash County in 1783, was married about 1808, and immigrated to Tennessee about 1810. He was an old line Whig in politics, and he and wife were firm believers in the Christian religion. He died October 1, 1851, and the mother died about 1872. Our subject was the fifth of eight children born to his parents, and remained at home until twenty-four years of age, when he began for himself. October 13, 1842, he married Nancy Franks, a native of Tennessee, born in 1822 in White County, and the fruits of this union were eleven children—eight of whom are living: Elizabeth, born May 6, 1843, and died May 25, 1862; Mary, born January 18, 1845, and died June 24, 1867; James H., born August 3, 1851, and died November 5, 1866. Those living are William H., Margaret L., Lean, Tabitha, John W., Jefferson D. and George W. Henry. They have also one grandson named Monroe G., son of Mary. Our subject and wife are members of the Separate Baptist Church. Mr. Hash now owns 200 acres of good land, the principal part of which is under cultivation. Before the war he was an old line Whig, but since that event has been a decided Democrat.

Hon. George H. Hash, a prominent and enterprising farmer of Warren County, is a resident of the Third District. He was born December 16, 1839, and is the son of Thomas and Drucilla (Howell) Hash. Thomas Hash is a native of Virginia, having been born there April 2, 1792. He came to Warren County, Tenn., about the year 1810, settling where the subject of this sketch now lives. He married Miss Drucilla Howell, who was born in Grayson County, Va., about 1794. About the year 1815 Thomas Hash was an enterprising and successful man. The subject of this sketch lived with his parents until the spring of 1861, when he enlisted in Company C, Twenty-fifth Tennessee (Confederate) Infantry, under Col. S. S. Stanton, and remained in the service until the surrender of Gen. Lee, having been engaged in numerous heavy battles and having received several severe wounds. Previous to his discharge from the army he was promoted to the captaincy of his company, in which capacity he was serving when he surrendered with the rest of the army at Appomattox C. H. He then returned to Warren County and engaged in teaching school about eight years, being at the same time engaged also in farming, the latter occupation having ever since occupied his time. In January, 1887, he became interested in a broom manufactory at Rock Island. In 1880 he was elected as a Democrat to represent his county in the Legislature. He has always been an ardent and devoted member of that party. In early life he acquired a good education, being a member of the senior class at Burritt College, at the breaking out of the war. He was married September 5, 1866, to Miss Sophia Mauzy, who was born in February, 1843, in Bledsoe County, Tenn. She is a daughter of Dr. Thomas and Jane (Floyd) Mauzy, is a graduate of Burritt College, a lady of refinement and a member of the Christian Church. Mr. and Mrs. Hash have four children: Victor H., Charles M., Jane L. and Ella D.

Hon. H. L. W. Hill, one of the most prominent and enterprising citizens of Warren County, now living in the Sixth District, was born March 1, 1810; son of Henry J. A. and Susannah (Swales) Hill. The father was of English-Irish descent, born in Edgecomb County, N. C., February 7, 1774, and died in Warren County, Tenn., August 1, 1825, from the result of an amputation of a limb that was injured in childhood. He moved to Georgia in 1800, and two years later came to what was then White County. A few years later he was a member of the Legislature and voted for the act separating Warren County from White County. While living in Georgia he was a member of the Baptist Church, but after moving to Tennessee he joined the Methodist Episcopal Church. The mother of our subject was born in St. Mary County, Md., December 31, 1767. She was also a member of the Baptist Church while in Georgia, but joined the Methodist Episcopal Church after coming to Tennessee. Her marriage resulted in the birth of seven children, of whom our subject is the youngest. He was born and has lived ever since where he now resides. After his father's death he continued to still live with his widowed mother till her death in 1846. He received his rudimentary education in the schools of the neighborhood, afterward taking a thorough course under Dr. F. H. Gordon and James B. Moores, at Porter's Hill, Tenn. After that he studied under Dr. Lawrence, at Carroll Academy, McMinnville, and then at Cumberland College, Nashville, of which Dr. Phillip Lindsley was president. After leaving Nashville he returned to McMinnville and taught school at Carroll Academy five months; then returned home and began farming and cultivating fine fruits, and distilling fine fruit brandies for medicinal purposes, which pursuits he continues to the present time. He began life with very little, but now owns considerable property. He has some very good farm lands in the valleys of Collins River and Hills Creek, some of which and some rich north mountain sides are in orchards, mainly apple. He also owns a considerable tract of mountain land, valuable for its deposits of iron ore, stone coal, timber and wild meadow and grazing grasses. He was elected to the House of Representatives in 1837, and re-elected in 1839 and 1841. He was elected to the Lower House of the XXX Congress in 1847, and represented the people in the State Constitutional Convention, in 1870. May 14, 1840, he married Miss Virginia A. Dearing, who was born July 3, 1823, and who is the daughter of Col. W. L. S. and Mary T. Dearing. This union resulted in the birth of ten children. Those living are Bertha born June 13, 1842; Virgil, born March 2, 1851; Susan, born April 19, 1853; Franklin, born July 20, 1855; Eliza, born January 23, 1858; Athelia, born December 29, 1859; Octa, born March 7, 1862; Mary D., born September 23, 1866. Two children, Dearing and Livingston, are dead. Col. Hill is a Democrat; has constantly maintained a first-rate character as a moral and most excellent citizen. He has never professed religion, been a member of any church or secret society. He firmly believes in the existence of and omnipotent, eternal living God, and he hopes for immortality.

Franklin Hill, farmer and stock raiser of Warren County, and now a resident of the Sixth Civil District, was born near his present home July 20, 1855, and is the son of Col. H. L. W. and Virginia (Dearing) Hill. The father was born in the Sixth Civil District of Warren County, Tenn., March 1, 1810, and is of English descent. His principal occupation has been that of a farmer, fruit raiser and distiller. In 1837 he was elected to represent Warren County in the Legislature, and was re-elected in 1839 and 1841. He was elected to the XXX Congress in 1847, and represented the people in the Constitutional Convention which met at Nashville in 1870. He has been a close student all his life, and is one of the influential citizens of the county. He is a Democrat and a Master Mason. The mother was born July 3, 1823. Our subject is the sixth of ten children. He lived with his parents up to the time of his marriage, which occurred June 24, 1875, and then moved to his present location. His wife, Leanora Myers, is a daughter of J. N. and N. Myers. She is well educated and a member of the Christian Church. To their union were born five children: Oscar, H. L. W., Virginia, Beatrice and Walter, who was born July 11, 1876, and died July 24, 1876. Our subject has a good education, which he secured at Water's & Walling's College, McMinnville, Tenn. He began life for himself by purchasing 400 acres of land of his father, which by hard work and good management has increased greatly in value.

I. P. Hill, farmer and stock raiser, was born near Irving College; Tennessee, January 19, 1825, the son of Isaac and Eliza Hill. The father was of English origin and born on Tar River, North Carolina, December 20, 1797, and came to Tennessee in 1806 with his parents and settled at Hill Creek, Warren County. He was a Democrat. His death occurred October 6, 1872. The mother, born February 4, 1800, in Jasper County, Ga., died in Warren County, Tenn., November 8, 1859. She was of English descent, and married August 20, 1818. Our subject lived at home until September 19, 1850, when he married Catherine, daughter of Thomas and Elizabeth Daniels, and born in Fairfax County, Va., October 10, 1830. She is of English descent and well educated. Five of their seven children are living: Isaac, Adia G., Ella M., E. Elizabeth and Andrew P. Melchisedec, born July 12, 1857, died December 16, 1857; Lillian L., born January 1, 1865, died April 2, 1882. Our subject was educated at Irving College, Tennessee, and is an active and enterprising man. When he began for himself his father gave him 300 acres of land, which he has increased to double its former value. He is a decided Democrat in politics.

Isaiah T. Hillis, an enterprising and well known farmer of the Fourth Civil District, Warren County, was born in the county October 23, 1839, and is the son of Isaac and Elizabeth (Drake) Hillis. Isaac Hillis is of Irish descent, and was born in Warren County, Tenn., in 1806. He had a good education and was a successful man, and died in 1877. His father was a native of North Carolina, and went from that State to Kentucky with Daniel Boone, but came to Tennessee and settled on Rocky River in 1804, thus being one of the first settlers of Warren County. The mother of Isaac T. Hillis was born in Carter County in 1808, and was of English descent. She was a well educated woman, and died in 1878. The subject of this sketch lived with his parents until the breaking out of the civil war, when he enlisted in Company I, Sixteenth Tennessee (Confederate) Infantry, and was in active service four years and seven days. He was at the battles of Chickamauga, Murfreesboro, Corinth, and numerous smaller battles and skirmishes. During the first two years he was in feeble health, and in different hospitals—Huntersville, Va., Rockbridge, Va., and Columbus, Miss. After his return from the war he lived with his parents until December 23, 1869, when he was married to Miss Marandie J. Moore, of White County, Tenn., a most worthy and well educated woman. She is the daughter of Alexander and Mary Moore, and is herself the mother of five children, all living: Charles M., Mary M., Ransom M., Isaac H. and Marandie J. When married, Mr. Hillis moved to his present location. In his youth he secured a collegiate education at Burritt College, situated at Spencer, Van Buren Co., Tenn. He is a very active and decided man, and a Democrat dyed in the wool. He has been elected by that party to the office of justice of the peace and other offices.

William Houchin, one of the proprietors of firm of Houchin & Biles' livery stable, is a native of McMinnville, born January 21, 1843, and by his own efforts secured a good education. He has nearly all his life been engaged in the livery business. Early in the year 1865 Mr. Houchin went to Nashville and for six months worked at the mechanic's trade but in July of the same year returned to McMinnville and in partnership with G. W. Hoodenpyl opened a livery stable, which they continued until 1869. In the meantime they had admitted another partner, J. D. Marshall. In January, 1869, N. W. Griswald entered the firm by purchasing the interest of Mr. Hoodenpyl. Mr. Houchin and Mr. Griswald then bought out J. D. Marshall and the firm was changed from G. W. Hoodenpyl & Co. to Griswald & Houchin. In September, 1878, Mr. Griswald died and Mr. Houchin closed out the property at public sale. The following November he opened another stable, having for a partner Mr. William Biles, and since then the firm has been very prosperous. They deal quite extensively in mules shipping from Warren and adjoining counties to the Southern States. January 18, 1886, they suffered a heavy loss by thirty-six mules being burned at Selma, Ala. Mr. Houchin is one of the rising business men of McMinnville and has a fair competency of this world's goods. He is an Independent in politics and although not a member of any church is a firm-believer in Christianity.

W. D. Hughes, farmer and distiller, was born near Irving College, Warren County, Tenn., November 7, 1858. He is the son of J. C. and Elizebeth Hughes. The father, of Irish descent, was born near the same place in 1831. He has been a farmer all his life, but for the past twenty years has been connected with a brandy distillery. He is a Democrat and a member of the Cumberland Presbyterian Church. The mother was also a member of this church, and was of English descent. She was born in North Carolina in 1827 and died August 1, 1877. Our subject, the fourth of nine children, began life for himself when twenty-one years of age, by becoming a partner of his father in the farming and distilling business. After four years he purchased his father's interest and continued the business in his own name. He is a member of the Cumberland Presbyterian Church and the I. O. O. F. order. Politically he is a Democrat and was educated at Burritt College, Spencer, Tenn.

Dr. E. H. Jones, a prominent physician and surgeon of Viola, was born near Murfreesboro, Rutherford Co., Tenn., and was the eldest of three children born to James and Cecilia (Overall) Jones. The father died in 1857. E. H. Jones, grandfather of our subject, an extensive planter and stock raiser in Rutherford County, reared and educated him, giving him a university education. At an early age he chose the medical profession, and in the spring of 1870 he entered the drug store of H. J. White of Navasota, Tex., as clerk, in which business he remained until 1875, when he returned to Tennessee and began the study of medicine under Dr. G. W. Overall of Murfreesboro, now of Memphis. In 1876–77 he attended the medical college of Vanderbilt University, Nashville, Tenn., and in 1877–78 he attended the medical college at Philadelphia, where he graduated with the highest honors. In 1878 he began the practice of his profession at Jacksboro, Tenn., where he remained one year, and in 1879 moved to Viola, at which place he has been very successful up to the present time. He was postmaster at Jacksboro, Tenn., for one year, and assistant postmaster at Viola three years. He was married March 11, 1886, to Fannie Potter, daughter of Thomas and Samantha (West) Potter of Smithville, Tenn. Both himself and wife are members of the Christian Church in good standing. Politically he is a stanch Democrat, and is highly respected in the vicinity both socially and as a physician.

James E. Jones is a native of Warren County, born near McMinnville, March 3, 1843, the third of eight children born to Zachariah B. and Eliza J. (Biles) Jones, both of English descent and natives of Tennessee. The father was born April 12, 1812. He was a farmer, a Republican and a worthy member of the Cumberland Presbyterian Church. His death occurred in Warren County in 1879. The mother, who is several years younger, is living a resident of Warren County. James E. secured a good education and early in life began farming. In 1870 he purchased a farm of 160 acres in the Tenth Civil District, where he soon after settled. The celebrated Nicholson Springs are situated on this farm. In 1872 he disposed of this farm and after making several changes in real estate, he purchased the farm he now owns in the Ninth Civil District. Mr. Jones has been successful in acquiring this world's goods, owning at present 250 acres of land, besides an improved lot in McMinnville. In February, 1877, he received the appointment of United States gauger and held this office ten years. He was assigned the section of country principally about McMinnville, and was a popular officer with both political parties. October 4, 1866, Mr. Jones wedded Miss Elizabeth T. Heneger, a native of Warren County, born April 9, 1849, a daughter of Geo. W. Heneger, deceased. Mr. and Mrs. Jones are the parents of six children—one son and five daughters—the son and one daughter deceased. Mr. Jones is a Republican, and he and wife and three children are members of the Methodist Episcopal Church South.

Robert Keaton, a resident of the Fifteenth Civil District of Warren County, was born near Liberty, Wilson Co., Tenn., December 25,

1830, and is the son of William and Susan (Hollandsworth) Keaton. The father was born near Richmond, Va., and the dates of his birth and death are unknown. He came to Wilson County, Tenn., after his marriage and remained in that county until his death. He was a farmer by occupation, a member of the Baptist Church, and a Whig in politics. The mother was a consistent member of the Baptist Church, and died in 1867. Our subject was the ninth of ten children; at the age of eighteen he left the parental roof and went to Mississippi, where he remained two years; he then came back to Wilson County, where his mother was living, and August 30, 1852, he married Miss Louisa Reider, who was born May 24, 1833, and who died April 1, 1862. To them were born five children, three of whom are living, viz.: Sarah A., Harriett A. and Mary M. Those deceased are William T., born June 1, 1853, and died March 1, 1856. Phoeba P. died in infancy. Mr. Keaton remained in Wilson County until 1855, when he came to Warren County, settled on his present location and engaged in farming. In 1864 he married Miss L. M. Wilson, a native of Wilson County, born May 24, 1843, a member of the Baptist Church, and the daughter of Allen and Elizabeth Wilson. In 1869 Mr. Keaton began preaching the gospel in the Missionary Baptist Church, which he continues to the present day. His last marriage resulted in the birth of four children. three of whom are living: Charles L., Parthenia C., Allen D., and one died in infancy. Mr. Keaton is well known and very much respected throughout the county.

Oliver Towles, farmer and merchant, is a son of John W. and Lucinda (Wilson) Towles. The father was born in Culpepper County, Va., March 30, 1819, and is now a resident of Warren County, Tenn. His parents came to Tennessee when John W. was quite young and settled in McMinnville, which was a very small place at that time. John W. has followed the occupation of a farmer, though at one time he was engaged in the mercantile and milling business. He has been a very successful man although he met with reverses during the late war. He is a member of the Christian Church, and a Democrat in politics. His wife was born in Warren County, Tenn., and although not a member of any church believes in the teachings of the Bible. Our subject was born near McMinnville, Warren Co., Tenn., March 14, 1856, and is the third of four children. In 1877 he and his brother formed a partnership and engaged in merchandising at Jessie, Warren Co., Tenn.; at the end of two years our subject sold his interest and moved to Daylight in the same county, where he formed a partnership with W. A. Robinson, and continued in business for one year. He then purchased the whole stock and continued by himself for two years, when his father purchased a half interest. At the end of one year he purchased his father's interest and came to his present location at Gath. In connection with his store he is also engaged in farming, and owns 153 acres in the Thirteenth District of Warren County, Tenn. March 11, 1880, he married Miss Isabel Wheeler, a native of Warren County, born about 1861 and died in 1881, leaving no issue. She was a member of the Cumberland Presbyterian Church. December 24, 1885, he married Miss S. L. Womack, a native of Warren County, born September 15, 1866, and to them was born one son, John W. Towles, Jr. Mr. Towles is a member of the order of I. O. O. F. and is a young, wide-awake business man.

William H. Magness was born in Warren County, Tenn., February 15, 1824. Being reared on a farm his education was limited to the meager advantages of the free schools. At twenty he was engaged as salesman in a dry goods store at Smithville, De Kalb Co., Tenn. In 1845 he commenced business at the same place on his own account, continuing at this with much success until 1881 when he moved to McMinnville. With the profits of his trade together with valuable tanning interests he was enabled to invest largely in the stock of several of the leading banks in the State. In 1874 he established the National Bank of McMinnville. At the organization he was elected president which position he has held with honor ever since. On the 25th of June, 1845, he was married to Miss E. J. West of De Kalb County, and it is to her habits of industry, prudence and economy that he attributes much of his success. There were born to them seven children, four of whom are now living: W. H., Edgar, Ella and Cordelia, wife of Judge Smallman. Strict habits of exercise and temperance have given him a robust constitution and his general health is good. His sons are connected with the national bank, W. H., Jr., being assistant cashier and Edgar bookkeeper. The father of our subject, P. G. Magness, was born in Spartanburg, S. C., in 1796. He moved to Warren County when twelve years of age and at eighteen was married to Mary Cantrell. The result of the union was twelve children. His father was a farmer, merchant and trader and secured a fair competency of this world's goods. He was remarkable for his unexampled energy and perseverance. He was a thorough Democrat and a strict member of the Baptist Church. His death occurred on March 1, 1884. It was quite a pleasure to this exemplary man to watch, in his old age, the multiplication and growth of the large family he had founded; and it was truly an object of gratification for there were born in direct line from him over 600 children, grandchildren, great-grand and great-great-grandchildren. Mr. Magness is a Democrat in politics and an influential member of the Missionary

Baptist Church; he is also a Past Master Mason. He wishes particularly to exhort the young men to be temperate. Then he thinks it will be revealed to them more clearly the wise words: "Do justice and love mercy."

Phillip H. Marbury, planter, was born in Buncombe County, N. C. April 24, 1810. He is the son of Benjamin and Mary (Hoodenpyl) Marbury, of English and Dutch descent respectively. The father was born in North Carolina in 1784 and died of small-pox in Arkansas in 1836; the mother was born in Warm Springs, N. C., in 1795, died in Arkansas about 1840. They were married in Grenville, Tenn., about 1808. The father, a successful farmer, and Democrat, was a personal friend of Andrew Jackson. Both parents were Baptists. Our subject, the oldest child, with exception of the time from 1820 to 1827 in Rhea County has since six years of age lived in Warren County. After completing his academic education he studied medicine one year under Dr. Hill, but abandoned it and in January, 1829, began a four years' clerkship for John Cain; then for twenty years after the spring of 1833 he was in partnership with Alexander Black as merchant at McMinnville. In 1852 Mr. Marbury was elected president of a railway stock company to build a road to McMinnville, and the road was built under his financial management, and as it was destroyed during the war, he, with the assistance of others, secured a grant of of $400,000 in bonds and rebuilt the road. In 1844 he became a planter near McMinnville and now owns 700 acres of good land and 400 under cultivation. Before the war he was connected with the bank of Sparta. He has been married three times: first in September, 1833, to Rebecca Mercer, a descendant of Gen. Fenton Mercer; second, to Mrs. Mary E. Scott, whose maiden name was Grundy, a granddaughter of Felix Grundy of State farm: third, to Mrs. Liley T. Garner, whose maiden name was Estell, a descendant of ex-Gov. Thomas of Maryland. Mr. Marbury was an old line Whig before the war, but has since been a Democrat, and always a liberal public worker. He is a member of the Cumberland Presbyterian Church.

E. G. Mead, of E. G. Mead & Co., barrel factory, McMinnville, was born in Warren County, Penn., February 3, 1824, the son of David and Climena (Owen) Mead, the former of English-German, and the latter of English-French descent, and both natives of Warren County, Penn., in which county the father was the first white male child born, the birth occurring June 16, 1800. He died in his native county in the fall of 1862. The mother, born about 1802, died in that county on July 3, 1825. They were married about 1822, after which he was a lumber dealer and in his later years also engaged in farming. The grandfather Mead built the first grist-mill in Warren County, Penn. The parents of our subject were members of the Methodist Episcopal Church, and the father a Jackson Democrat in politics. Having acquired a good education, our subject has been engaged in the lumber business most of his life. In 1868 he came to Warren County, and with his brother's assistance built the well known mills at Shelsford, in the spring of 1869. After running these mills successfully for fourteen years, he sold them in 1883, and in 1884 established his present prosperous manufactory. He is a liberal man, a Democrat, and a member of the Presbyterian Church. Mrs. Mead is his third wife.

William M. Meadows, a prominent farmer and stock raiser of Warren County, was born near Sparta, White Co., Tenn., August 28, 1822, and is the son of V. and E. (Lawrence) Meadows. The father was born in North Carolina the 14th of February, 1800, and died the 25th of December, 1886. He was of English descent, a farmer, and after the war a Democrat in politics. The mother was born in Warren County, Tenn., and was a member of the Methodist Episcopal Church. Our subject was the eldest of six children; at the age of eleven he was bound out to James Woodlee, of Warren County, Tenn., and lived with him eight years. He then went to Cannon County, and worked on a farm for one year after which he returned to Warren County, and lived with George Etter, Sr., for six years. May 29, 1846, he went to Mexico with Col. Campbell's regiment and Capt. Northcuts' company, and was gone four months. In January, 1849, he purchased his present farm, containing about 190 acres, but has since purchased 75 acres joining his land and 250 acres in the mountains. January 2, 1850, he married Miss Sarah J. Moffitt, a native of Warren County, Tenn., born January 15, 1831, and the daughter of Aaron and Harriet Moffitt. Mrs. Meadows is a member of the Methodist Episcopal Church and has a good common education. To them were born twelve children, nine of whom are living: J. J., E. Carlie, Ida E., Parizaide, Thulah B., Minnie L., William D., Aubrey D. and Francis M. The three children deceased are Virginia A., born in 1850 and died in 1856; Augustus F., born in 1859 and died in 1860; and Deborah, born in 1863 and died in 1863. During the war our subject was elected captain of the Home Guards, first by the Confederates and afterward by the Federals. He is a decided Democrat and is a self-made man in every respect.

L. D. Mercer, retired merchant, was born in Wayne County, Ky., November 23, 1810, the son of Richard and Mary (Mercer) Mercer, both of Scotch-Irish descent. The father, born in North Carolina about 1780, died in Wayne County, Ky., about 1855, and the mother, native of North Carolina, died about 1815 in Wayne County, Ky. They were married in Kentucky, and the father successfully passed his life as a farmer. He was a Democrat. Our subject was educated at Winchester Academy under a Mr. Witten and his son and daughter. In 1827 he entered the firm of Black & Mercer, at Cedar Bluff, Ala., as salesman, and after two years he spent one year in Kentucky. In 1831 he came to McMinnville, and with Alexander Blake established a store of general merchandise and for the next forty years in successful operation. Since 1879, when he closed out his business, as one of the most successful business men of the county, he has lived a retired life. June 2, 1840, he married Annie E. Hord, born in Hawkins County, Tenn., in 1821, and educated at McMinnville Female College. She died in 1851. Their only son, Foss H., born in 1847, is now a prominent member of the Pikeville (Tenn.) bar. Mr. Mercer is a decided Democrat, and a member of the Christian Church, to which his wife belongs.

W. H. Moore, M. D., a leading physician of Warren County, is a native of Cannon County, Tenn., a son of T. W. and Nancy (Ashly) Moore. The father was born in Indiana in 1823, of English-Irish descent. He is still living and resides at Beech Grove, Tenn. The mother was of English-French origin, born in Tennessee in 1828 and died in 1884. W. H. was reared on the farm and received a good academical education in youth and in 1875 began reading medicine with Dr. A. Norville, and in the fall of 1876 attended the medical department of the Vanderbilt University at Nashville, after which he began the practice of his profession at Hillsboro, Tenn., remaining there two years. He then moved to Viola where he has been very successful in his practice. March 10, 1881, Dr. Moore wedded V. J. Witherspoon, daughter of A. B. and Jane (Neely) Witherspoon, of Beech Grove. To this union three children have been born: Oges, born May 10, 1882; Lillie, born May 11, 1884, and W. H. born April 1, 1886. Dr. Moore is a Democrat and a member of the Christian Church. Mrs. Moore is a member of the Old Presbyterian Church.

J. F. Morford, merchant, is a native of McMinnville, born August 9, 1829, a son of J. F. and Jane B. (Taylor) Morford. The father was born in 1799, in Princeton, N. J., where he received a collegiate education. In 1820 he immigrated to Tennessee, and settled in McMinnville, where he began the practice of law, and was soon appointed clerk and master of the chancery court and served in this capacity thirty-five years. His death occurred in 1869. The mother was a native of Warren County. J. F., the subject of this biography, was reared and educated in his native county, securing an academical education, after which he entered the clerk's office and acted as deputy twelve years. In 1859 Mr. Morford established a mercantile store, but at the beginning of the war suspended business until 1865, when he reopened his store and has been very successful in acquiring a competency. He is director and vice-president of the Peoples Bank and a worthy and influential citizen. In 1854 he wedded A. E. Lusk, a daughter of J. D. and Pauline Lusk of this place. Mr. and Mrs. Morford are the parents of three children: Josiah J., Florence M. (Mrs. D. B. Carson) and C. M., of the firm of Morford & Co. He is a member of the Cumberland Presbyterian Church and a Democrat, but prior to the war was an old time Whig.

Ed W. Munford. The Munford family came from England, were early settlers in Virginia, and trace their lineage back to Simon De Montfort of Henry III time, of whom Green in his history of the English people thus speaks: "His life was pure and singularly temperate; he was noted for his scant indulgence in meat, drink or sleep. Socially he was cheerful and pleasant in talk, but his natural temper quick and ardent, his sense of honor keen, his speech rapid and trenchant." He also records an anecdote which displays this high sense of honor and promptness to repel any assault upon it. Green says that having for four years been seneschal of Gascony (one of the kingly provinces on the continent) and in that service advanced a large sum of money on the king's promises to repay it; upon reminding the king of this promise "Henry hotly retorted that he was bound by no promise to a false traitor. Simon at once gave Henry the lie" etc. (Vol. I, paragraphs 221, 223.) It is not known when or why the spelling of the name was changed into its present form of Munford, but the original "Montfort" is still adhered to by collateral branches whose blood relationship is known. Born near Danville, Ky., on the 16th of October, 1820, the subject of this sketch was the youngest child of William Munford, a "blue-grass farmer," and received at Centre College a classical education, but did not graduate. His father was the son of Thomas Bolling Munford, of Amelia County, Va., who on account of his high personal character was elected to a position of public trust by his fellow citizens without his ever having been a candidate for office. That, however, was in the good old time when "office sought the man," an amiable state of public sentiment which has long since been swept out of existence with other political excellences which had they been pursued might have prevented demagogues from supplanting the statesmanship of the country. A near relative of Thomas Bolling was the State reporter, William Munford, a ripe classical scholar who has enriched our literature by a translation of Homer's "Iliad," which critics, both American and European, have pronounced to be the most accurate and faithful in the English language. George Wythe Munford, the librarian, and secretary of the commonwealth for so many years, and the late excellent William T. Munford were his sons. Thos. Bolling Munford invested in lands in Kentucky for his sons, and four of them, James, Thomas, Richard and William, when quite young men settled upon their respective plantations in that State when it was still called the wilderness. William removed toward the latter end of the last century and the others not long after, Richard giving the name to Munfordville on Green River. William married Lettice, a daughter of Thomas Ball, a prominent citizen of the vicinity of Danville, and for his young wife's sake purchased a farm adjoining that of his father-in-law, and removed to it. Here his family of nine children were born and only after the mother's death was the farm sold. This was while Edward was a very little boy, so young that while he remembers his mother's habit of taking his brother Richard, his little sister and himself to secret prayer three times every day and other evidences of her deep piety, he has only a dim recollection of her features or appearance. Through her he is related to the Marshall and Breckinridge families of Kentucky. His father brought Edward with him in 1835 to Tennessee on a visit to his daughters, Mrs. Dr. McCorkle and Mrs. James C. Jones (afterward governor), and his two sons, Thomas and William, who lived at Lebanon and in the immediate vicinity. He died there in the following spring, leaving his young son to the guardianship of his brother William. At Lebanon he completed his interrupted studies under the late Rev. Thos. R. Anderson, who after its establishment became president of Cumberland College. Anderson was a famous educator, stern in appearance and bearing he was the terror of all bad boys, a number of whom were sent to him to be "broken in." To well inclined boys, however, no man could be more fatherly and kind. When the course of his studies ended and Edward was about leaving with his books Prof. Anderson called him back and said: "You are about to leave me; before you go I want to say something to you to be remembered. I am a judge of boys and you will make a man who will have a good deal to do with the world and the world with you. Now remember this in all your after life. 'If a man looks mean he is mean' and this he never forgot. At the age of sixteen years he began the study of his chosen profession, the law, under the late Judge Robert L. Caruthers, but after one year so spent removed with his guardian to Clarksville, Tenn., where for two years more he prosecuted it under the accomplished lawyer, George C. Boyd. The late senator, James E. Bailey, and himself were the only students Boyd would at that time accept saying that "most of the young men choosing the profession have no appreciation of its important and dignified duties and adopted it merely in the hope of leading lives of genteel vagabondage without labor." He had the spirit of the true lawyer, and inspired his two chosen proteges with his own aversion to pettifoggery, trickery and chicanery. Taking license at twenty at Mr. Boyd's earnest solicitation, he soon became involved in active practice. This so interfered with his regular studies that he adopted the plan of admitting no one to his office at night so that whilst the world slept he could dedicate the undisturbed hours to the acquisition of knowledge. For a long time 4 o'clock in the morning was his hour for going to sleep, and most dearly has he paid the penalty of this violation of the laws of health. Let all young men and women too be taught physiology and anatomy, and the great fact impressed upon them that not only is sound health the greatest of earthly blessings to its possessor and nothing can compensate for its loss, but that permanent success is more surely won by living in all respects according to enlightened rules of hygiene. In this particular there is great room for reformation and improvement in the method and matter of instruction in our schools. The Romans regarded the perfection of education to be attained only in "*Mens sana in corpore sano*," a sound mind in a sound body, and our boasted civilization has not yet attained this height of practical wisdom in the training and enlightenment of youth. The world would be made much happier by it, and it is now an accredited fact that much of the so-called vice of the land originates in bodily disease rather than original depravity of heart. In 1849 he married Amelia A., daughter of Paul J. Watkins, of Alabama, wound up his business at Clarksville in 1850, and opened a law office in Memphis early in 1851, where he at once found full employment. Although his health was delicate his professional employment was such that his labors were unremitting and in 1853 he was advised by his physicians that he had but two choices, viz.: "go off to the country where neither books nor courthouses are, take all the outdoor exercise you can, or stay here and die." He went upon a farm, did his own overseeing and in less than two years was restored to health. In the winter of 1854-55, being strongly urged to return to the city and this accompanied by the offer of a most advantageous partnership, his craving for mental occupation became irresistible and he resumed his practice there. In 1855 his young wife died leaving him a son and daughter, the latter following her mother in a few months. This was a blow almost too hard to be borne, for though books have always been a source of inestimable happiness to him yet his sweetest or his tenderest joys were found in the endearments of home. He now lived for his boy, and his profession, which he pursued till 1860, when having amassed a sufficient fortune, he retired from business that he might devote himself to the education of his son. It was his purpose to take him to Europe where he could learn the languages, more especially of France and Germany, from the lips and thus acquire their correct pronunciation whilst the vocal organs were yet flexible. The year 1860 was devoted to closing up his affairs and the spring of 1861 fixed as the time of his departure. By that time, however, the political troubles of the country he saw must result in a sectional war, and under an imperious sense of duty, he remained to share the fortunes of the South. Nothing but a sense of duty could have compelled this course, for in all the steps up to that time he had opposed secession. He honestly believed the questions at issue should be settled by statesmanship and not the sword, and until Mr. Lincoln issued his proclamation for 75,000 men to invade the Southern States, he clung to the hope that some masterly genius in state-craft might, even amidst the wild confusions of the hour, devise some plan by which war might be averted and the true interests of the country subserved. When that proclamation appeared he saw that "the time for debate was ended and the time for action had come," and at once devoted his energies and much of his means to assist the South in the coming struggle. When Gen. Albert Sidney Johnston assumed command of the Western Department he was announced in orders as a major on his staff and served by his side till his death on the field of Shiloh. Starting with the army of Bragg into Kentucky from Chattanooga in the fall of 1862 he was prostrated by disease, and did not recover sufficiently to appear again in the field till the Dalton-Atlanta campaign under Gen. Joseph E. Johnston. Lying sick in bed in southwestern Georgia, a paper brought into his room announced the evacuation of Dalton without a battle. Realizing that Gen. Johnston was short of men, he started next day to rejoin the army and was so feeble that at about six miles on his journey he was taken from his horse whilst in the act of falling off and laid in a roadside cabin for several days unable to rise. However, he finally met the army below Resaca and served as well as his enfeebled condition permitted till after the battles of the 22d and 28th of July in defense of Atlanta, when at the urgent solicitation of his superior officers, he went to the city of Macon, where all that kindest friends could do to alleviate his sufferings was done. His condition and positive refusal of an honorable discharge from service were represented to the president, who nominated him as one of the judges of Gen. Richard Taylor's Departmental Military Court, with the rank of colonel of cavalry. The senate confirmed the appointment, and he served in that capacity till the surrender. On being asked one day long since about his services during the war he laughingly replied: "Well, sir, since it now is all over I look back with pleasure upon the fact that I never killed more of the Yankees than they did of me, and as judge, never had a man either shot or hanged." His services, however, were more highly appreciated by others than they seem to have been by himself. Returning to Memphis after the war with a feeble frame, he eschewed all business and devoted himself to the restoration of his health and the care of the orphaned children of his brother, William, and their own and his sons' education. In the fall of 1867 his health was so far restored as to justify his marriage, and in November of that year he espoused Mrs. Mary E. Gardner, widow of Lieut. William Ross Gardner of Augusta, Ga., formerly of the United States Navy. She is a lady of rare grace and culture, the model, as he says, for a gentleman's wife. Once more blessed with love and home his health grew gradually stronger, and in 1872 he was offered and accepted the presidency of a company composed for the most part of Northern men who purposed investing large sums of money in mineral interests in Tennessee. This led him to remove to McMinnville, where he has since resided. In that bracing and invigorating climate he has builded up and now enjoys comparatively good health, but does not hesitate to say that to his gentle, affectionate and intelligent wife he is more indebted for this blessing than to all else besides. They are possessed of ample fortune for their wants, and in the midst of picturesque scenery, friends and books, the evening of their lives is being passed with more than the usual amount of human happiness. Col. Munford's conversation abounds in reminiscences of what he has read and whom he has known. He says that beyond doubt Albert Sidney Johnston, take him all in all, was the greatest man he ever knew, and he means true greatness, that rare and harmonious union of sound intellect, incorruptible integrity and large-hearted goodness, enlightened by culture and perfected by experience. He tells that since the war while he was a director in the Carolina Life Insurance Company, of which Hon. Jefferson Davis was president, one day in conversation he remarked that he believed Gen. Johnston was the ablest general the Confederacy had, when Mr. Davis with great animation, replied: "Ah, sir, he was the greatest man we had in or out of our army—the very greatest." Col. Munford retains as one of his most cherished memories that of the confidence and friendship with which Gen. Johnston honored him up to the hour of his lamentable death.

W. T. Murray, attorney at law, was born January 18, 1854, in Sparta, White Co., Tenn. He is the son of Thos. B. Murray, who was born in Jackson County, Tenn., and who was an able and successful attorney.

The father died at McMinnville January 15, 1878. The mother, Mary Murray, daughter of William P. and Jane (McKinney) Goodbar, is a native of Tennessee. Our subject is of Irish ancestry. He was reared in McMinnville, and on account of delicate health was unable to attend school closely, so he received but a limited education. He read law in the office of his father, however, and began practice at McMinnville, in May, 1872, and has acquired the leading practice of this bar. November 3, 1883, he married Fannie L. Snodgrass of Sparta, Tenn., the daughter of Jos. and Lue Snodgrass. Our subject is a self-made man, and is now worth about $15,000. He is a member of the Methodist Church, of the F. & A. M., K. of H., and K. & L. of H. orders. Politically he is a Democrat.

Hamilton Neal, farmer of Warren County, and now a resident of the Fourth Civil District, is the son of William and Hannah Neal. The father was a native Virginian, born November 10, 1777, and of English extraction. His parents immigrated to Tennessee when William was quite young, and here he married Hannah Jones, a native of Virginia born September 17, 1773. They came to White County, Tenn., in 1806, and were among the first settlers of the county. They were both members of the Baptist Church, and died in 1865 and 1860 respectively. Our subject was born in the Fourth Civil District of Warren County, Tenn., September 26, 1812, and was the eighth of ten children. He married Sallie Forrest, a native of Warren County, born April, 1806. She was a member of the Baptist Church, and died April, 1853. Their family consisted of the following children: Elizabeth, Hannah, Martha, Katherine, O. D. and John M. Those deceased are Mary Martha, and O. D.; the last named was born September 2, 1842, and in the spring of 1861 enlisted in the Confederate service, Sixteenth Tennessee Infantry, under Col. Savage. He died at Huntersville Hospital, September 3, 1861. December 11, 1854, our subject married Nancy Ann Burnett, a native of McMinn County, Tenn., born September, 1827, and a member of the Cumberland Presbyterian Church. This marriage resulted in the birth of these children: Jennie, Nancy Ann, Hamilton, Lula, Jesse E., P. L., Joseph B. and Robert L. Our subject is a member of the Cumberland Presbyterian Church, a good citizen and a Democrat in politics.

A. Northcut, planter of Warren County, was born in this county April 9, 1837, the fourth child of James and Susan (Hammons) Northcut, both natives of Tennessee. The father was born about 1810, was a successful farmer, owning before the war fourteen slaves. He began life poor, paying for his first horse by picking cotton in Mississippi. At the time of his death his property was valued at $16,000, although he had lost considerable by trusting his friends, and on this account at one time was in debt $4,000. Very little was known of his parents, but they are supposed to have come from England. He died in 1866. The mother's death occurred in 1868. Our subject was reared on a farm and at the age of twenty-one years began farming on his own resources and is now an extensive stock raiser. In January, 1867, Mr. Northcut wedded E. W. King, a daughter of Wilson and Elizabeth (Cellers) King, of Warren County, and to them have been born two children: Sanford, born March 16, 1868, and Susan A., whose birth occurred June 28, 1878. Father, mother and children are members of the Cumberland Presbyterian Church. Mr. Northcut served three years as school director and is much interested in educational institutions. His son is attending the Southern Normal at Bowling Green, Ky., and his daughter, the Viola Normal College. He is a stanch Democrat in politics.

Daniel Osborn, a prosperous planter of this county and a resident of McMinnville, was born October 6, 1822, in Wayne County, Ind. His father, Daniel Osborn, Sr., was born about the year 1792, at Long Island, N. Y., engaged during life at the different occupations of teaching, merchandising and farming, was a Universalist in religion and died in 1849, in Sioux County, Wis. Mary Washington, his wife and the mother of our subject, was a native of England, came to the United States with her parents when fourteen years old, and at an early day settled in Indiana, where she became Mrs. Osborn about the year 1820. She was a Baptist and died in Iowa, in 1876. Our subject is the eldest of twelve children. He obtained a fair education in youth, worked at the mechanic's trade for a time, but in 1852 began merchandising in Richland County, Wis., where he remained eight years. He then moved to Grant County, where he sold goods about four years, then went to Dexter, Iowa, and still later to Des Moines. He remained in the latter city five years as merchant, and in 1876 moved to McMinnville, Tenn., which has since been his home, and near which he owns a farm of 176 acres. He also owns two farms of 250 acres near McMinnville, and two fine residences in town. A large portion of his fund are in bonds. He wedded Miss Mary, daughter of Abraham Heed, March 31, 1858, and by her is the father of four children, only one, Daniel. now living. The mother was born in Belmont County, Ohio, December 25, 1836, and is a member of the Christian Church. Mr. Osborn is a Universalist in belief.

P. G. Potter, farmer and merchant of Warren County, and now a resident of the Thirteenth Civil District, is the son of Watson and Harriett (Magness) Potter, both natives of De Kalb County, Tenn.

The father was born in 1817, of English lineage, and is now a resident of De Kalb County. He has followed the occupation of a farmer and mechanic all his life. He is a member of the Primitive Baptist Church and a Democrat in politics. His wife was born in 1819 and died July 6, 1866. She was a member of the Primitive Baptist Church also. Our subject was born near Smithville, De Kalb County, September 27, 1842, and was the sixth of fourteen children. He lived with his parents until twenty-two years of age, when he moved to Warren County, where he remained two years engaged in farming. He then moved to the mouth of Mountain Creek, at Jessie, and was engaged in mercantile pursuits for six years, when he moved to his present location and followed the same business. He is a man of great energy and enterprise. Although he started with a very light capital, and was burned out once, he now carries a stock of $3,500 and owns 260 acres of land worth $7,000, with a good portion under cultivation. In the fall of 1863 he enlisted in the Twenty-Third Tennessee Regiment (Confederate Army), and was in service about one year when he came home on account of ill health. He was in the battle of Murfreesboro and numerous skirmishes. May 9, 1865, he married Miss Melvinia Webb, a native of Warren County, Tenn., born June 15, 1843, and the daughter of James and Mary Webb. To our subject and wife were born six children; only two are now living: Osee and Clyde. Those deceased are Ella, born in 1868 and died in 1883; Minnie, born in 1871 and died in 1884; James, born in 1873 and died in 1876, and Arthur, born in 1876 and died in 1878. Mr. Potter is a member of the Christian Church and a Democrat in politics. In 1878 he was appointed postmaster at Dibrell, which position he has held ever since; has done as much as any man of his means to build up schools and churches, and to advance the general interests of those he is intimately associated with; is a man of good moral habits and is an active worker in the church to which he belongs.

J. R. Ramsey, of Gwyn & Ramsey, merchants, was born in Warren County May 3, 1862, the son of William and Mary (Taylor) Ramsey, both of Irish origin. The father, born March 9, 1832, in Warren County, was a very extensive stock raiser. The mother was born February 22, 1841, and both were members of the Christian Church. Reared on the farm, our subject in February, 1885, engaged in merchandising at Viola, Tenn., a member of the firm Bonner & Ramsey, the former of whom sold his interest to C. R. Gwyn in March, 1886, when the present firm was formed. February 10, 1886, our subject married Mattie S., daughter of Col. Porter and C. S. Floyd, and of Irish extraction. Both he and his wife are members of the Christian Church, and among our best citizens.

R. M. Reams, editor of the *Southern Standard*, was born at Spring Hill, Maury County, June 20, 1857, a son of Joshua M. and Hattie (Haley) Reams. When eleven years old Mr. Reams went to Tuscumbia, Ala., and served three years' apprenticeship in the printing office of the *North Alabamian*. In the summer of 1876 he came to McMinnville, Tenn., and worked for six years in the *New Era* office, and was joint publisher of that paper with Mr. D. F. Wallace during the year 1880. In the fall of 1882 he, in partnership with Dr. J. B. Ritchey and H. P. Newton, purchased the *Southern Standard*, and under the style of the Standard Publishing Company they published this paper until the spring of 1884, when Mr. Reams purchased his partners' interests and has since been sole editor and proprietor of this journal. The *Southern Standard* is purely Democratic. It is one of the leading papers in this section of the country and has a large circulation. Mr. Reams is a member of the Presbyterian Church.

Cyrus Richmond, a prominent citizen of McMinnville, was born at Batavia, Genesee Co., N. Y., April 29, 1815. He is the third of five children born to Job and Ruth (Barrett) Richmond, both of English descent. Cyrus secured a good academical education in his youth, and early in life began the cultivation of the soil. He was engaged in farming until he immigrated to Tennessee, and for the past ten years has led a retired life. He spent the first thirty years of his life in his native county, and the next ten years in Niagara County. In 1860 Mr. Richmond went to Wisconsin, and settled in Sheboygan County, where he lived sixteen years. In 1876 he immigrated to Tennessee, and settled in McMinnville, where he now lives. He has been an enterprising and energetic man all his life, and has been very successful in accumulating this world's goods. In 1842 Mr. Richmond wedded Miss Caroline Willey, a lady of excellent worth, and a native of Berkshire County, Mass., born in 1822. Mr. Richmond is not a church member, but is a firm believer in the Bible and the Christian religion; Mrs. Richmond is a member of the Missionary Baptist Church.

George M. Smartt, an enterprising farmer of Warren County, is a native of the county where he now lives. He was born February 24, 1814, the fourth son of William C. and Peggie (Colville) Smartt. The father was a native of Virginia, born November 13, 1785, and of English descent. He immigrated to North Carolina in 1804, and September 13, of the same year, married his wife, who was a daughter of Joseph and Martha Coville. The father of our subject was a farmer and extensive stock raiser of Warren County, Tenn., to which State he moved in 1806. He was prominently connected with all enterprises that had a tendency to build up his county, and was a liberal supporter of religious institutions. He was the first sheriff of Warren County, and was several times solicited to represent his county at the State Legislature, but always declined, and was in the convention of 1834 that framed the first constitution of the State. He was a soldier in the war of 1812, and his death occurred June 18, 1863. The mother was of Irish ancestry, and died February 22, 1827; they were both members of the Cumberland Presbyterian Church. George M. was married December 22, 1840, to Ann Waterhouse, a daughter of R. G. and Elizabeth (Hackett) Waterhouse, of Rhea County. Mr. and Mrs. Smartt were the parents of nine children—three sons and six daughters—all living. The wife died December 2, 1870; she was a member of the Cumberland Presbyterian Church. September 3, 1872, Mr. Smartt married Cornelia, a daughter of G. W. and Ann (Zachery) Smartt, of Alabama, and to them have been born three children—two sons and one daughter.

W. H. Smartt, a well-to-do farmer of Warren County, was born in this county February 14, 1832, and was a son of William C. and Elizabeth (Hackett) Smartt. (For a brief sketch of the father, see biography of George M. Smartt of this county.) The mother was of Irish descent, a member of the Cumberland Presbyterian Church, and died in June, 1864. W. H. was reared on the farm, and in 1865 purchased the home place and engaged in farming, and has made this occupation a success. In connection with farming he turns his attention to stock raising. September 15, 1859, Mr. Smartt wedded Mary J., daughter of David M. and A. E. (Martin) Bell, of Hamilton County. Mr. and Mrs. Smartt are the parents of seven children—two sons and five daughters—one son deceased. Mr. Smartt is a stanch Democrat in politics, and he and wife and four children are members of the Cumberland Presbyterian Church.

Rev. George T. Stainback, pastor of the Cumberland Presbyterian Church of McMinnville, is a native of the Old Dominion, his birth occurring April 4, 1829, in Brunswick County, where he remained until about the age of six years. His parents, George W. and Lucretia T. (Eppes) Stainback, were both born in Virginia in 1795, the former in Brunswick County and the latter in Sussex County; they were of German and English descent respectively. Marrying in 1818, they immigrated to Limestone County, Ala., in 1835, thence to Memphis, Tenn., in 1842, where Mr. Stainback died two years later. He was a soldier of the war of 1812, was an honest, upright man, and with the exception of being in the livery business at Memphis, he followed farming through life. His widow died at Columbus, Miss., in 1874. The subject of this biography, George T., is the fifth of eleven children, and the only one now living.

After attending lesser educational institutions he entered the University of Mississippi, which, after four years' attendance, graduated him with the degree of A. B. in July, 1854; two years later the degree of A. M. was conferred upon him, and in 1867 he was further honored with the degree of D. D. In 1855 and 1856 he acted as assistant professor of Latin and Greek in his *alma mater*. He continued in charge of his pastorate at Columbus, Miss., thirteen consecutive years, and in 1872 removed to Huntsville, Ala., where he followed his calling two years. In 1874 he accepted a call from the First Cumberland Presbyterian Church of Memphis, remaining there four years, but in 1879 returned to his old charge at Columbus. Four years later he came to McMinnville, where he has since attracted much attention by his ability, eloquence and piety. Dr. Stainback not only preaches true Christianity but practices it as well, and is to-day recognized as one of the leading divines of the South. Miss Clara B. Grady, a native of Gibson County, Tenn., became his wife October 19, 1854, and died December 5, 1864. He wedded Miss Mary Mason of Columbus, Miss., January 4, 1871. To his first marriage four children were born, and to his present one three children.

Jacob Stipe, a prominent minister and farmer of Warren County, a resident of the Fourth Civil District, is a native of Tennessee. He was born March 25, 1834, and is the son of John and Glaphrey (Bowmen) Stipe. John Stipe was born in Tennessee April 19, 1811, was of German descent, and was by occupation a farmer. Politically he was a Democrat. He was married, in 1830, to Miss Glaphrey Bowmen, a native of Sparta, White County, who was born in 1811. They were both members of the Baptist Church. He was killed by guerrillas in Arkansas in 1863. She died in 1869. Our subject was the third of eleven children. He married Miss Angeline Hawkins, a native of Illinois, whose parents moved to Pikeville, Bledsoe County, when she was quite young. In youth she secured a good education. By her marriage with Mr. Stipe she has had eight children, all of whom are living and are members of the Baptist Church. Their names are Lucy E., Glaphrey O., Mary F., James P., Sarah M., George S., Dameris N. and John M. When the subject of this sketch left his father he began to farm in Bledsoe County, and remained there until the fall of 1870, when he removed to his present location. In 1860 he began life as a minister of the gospel. In 1875 he engaged in merchandising at his home, which he continues to the present time. His lot has been one of hardship and toil, but he has made life a success, as he now owns 600 acres of land on Rocky River, and 5,000 acres in the mountains. Politically he is a dyed-in-the-wool Democrat, and he is a Mason in good standing. In his youth he secured a limited education, but since then he has been a great student, and is on the whole a self-made man. Knowing the value of education he has always sustained the cause to the extent of his ability.

A. M. St. John, a leading merchant and senior member of the firm of St. John & Stubblefield, was born September 22, 1861, in Warren County, a son of John and Fatina (Sewell) St. John. The father was born in Tennessee September 21, 1829, and his ancestors are supposed to have come from England. A. M. was reared in Warren County, and received only a limited education in the country schools of his neighborhood. At the age of twenty-one years he began clerking in the mercantile business, which he continued until 1885, when he began business on his own resources. October 6, 1886, Mr. St. John wedded M. B., daughter of J. T. and Sarah Merritt. Mr. St. John is a man of high standing as a citizen of Viola, and is strongly in favor of all educational improvements, and is a liberal contributor to all such institutions. His views politically are Democratic, and he is an influential and worthy member of the Christian Church.

James Webb, farmer and stock raiser, is the son of James and Mary (Webb) Webb, and was born in the Fifteenth Civil District of Warren County, Tenn., December 25, 1818. The father was born in North Carolina about 1795, and was of English descent. He came to this county about 1813, and was one of the first settlers. He was a farmer, a Democrat and a member of the Baptist Church. He died in April, 1877. The mother was a native of North Carolina born about 1796, and also of English descent. She died about 1867. Our subject lived with his parents until the time of his marriage, which occurred August 25, 1842. Miss Mary Byars, a native of Warren County, Tenn., born in March, 1828, became his wife. She is the daughter of H. and J. Byars and by her marriage became the mother of sixteen children, eleven of whom are living: Malvina, Jane, Ascenith, A. J., H. B., Isham, G. H., James, Robert L., Mary E. Dovey and Joseph L. Those deceased are Thomas, Didama and three children that died in infancy. After marriage our subject began farming and now, by his good and judicious management, owns 1,200 acres of land. He has been elected constable of his district, also tax collector and justice of the peace at different times. At present he is tax assessor. He is a decided Democrat in politics and an excellent citizen.

B. C. Wilkinson, farmer, miller and merchant, was born in De Kalb County, Tenn., December 11, 1836, and is the son of George W. and Mary Wilkinson. The father was born in South Carolina about 1815, and was of Scotch-Irish descent. He was a farmer, a Democrat in politics, and died in Smith County, Tenn., about 1847. The mother was born in South Carolina about 1817, is still living and is a resident of southwestern Missouri, and a member of the Primitive Baptist Church. Our subject is the eldest of five children. He remained at home until after his father's death when he came to Warren County and lived with an uncle —C. A. Cantrell. He remained with his uncle until nineteen years of age when he returned to De Kalb County and attended school for one year. He married Miss Elizabeth Potter, March 24, 1859. She was born May 13, 1844, and is the daughter of Thomas and F. Potter, of French descent. Nine children were the result of this union, seven of whom are living: Thomas B., William D., John F., George L., A. L., Cleveland L., and Bell; those deceased are Mary, born in June, 1863, and died when an infant, and Fatima, born in January, 1881, and died when an infant. After marriage our subject began cultivating the soil and this he has continued up to the present time. In the spring of 1861 he enlisted in the Sixteenth Tennessee Regiment (Confederate Army) commanded by John H. Savage, and in Company A, commanded by L. M. Savage, and was in the battle of Perryville and many skirmishes. At the battle of Perryville he received a wound. At Ringgold, Ga., in 1863, he was taken prisoner and remained in prison at Rock Island, Ill., until the close of the war. After his return from the war he again engaged in farming. In 1873, in connection with his farming interest, Mr. Wilkinson engaged in merchandising at Bare Branch. In 1881 he closed out his business at the latter place and came to his present location where he followed his former occupation, but also engaged in the milling business. He has 250 acres of land well cultivated and is succeeding quite well in life. He is a Master Mason, a member of the Christian Church, and a decided Democrat in politics.

E. H. Williams, a prominent farmer of Warren County, was born in Onslow County, N. C., February 28, 1836, the third of a family of seven, born to N. W. and E. N. (Cox) Williams. The parents were married in 1830 in North Carolina, and in 1837 came to Tennessee, where the father engaged in farming until 1851, when he established a mercantile store at Tullahoma. Soon after his location in that town he was appointed postmaster and held that position until his death in 1853. He was of English descent, his wife of Irish. The subject of this sketch was reared on a farm and at an early age chose as his occupation, the carpenter trade. He worked at this trade until 1853 when he turned his attention to farming and has farmed very successfully until the present time. He has in connection with farming traded in stock very extensively and in 1883 and 1884 sold goods in Viola. April 29, 1861, Mr.

Williams' marriage with Fannie Cunningham was solemnized, and to this union one child was born, W. E., born July 14, 1865. Mrs. Williams died in 1867. January 15, 1874, Mr. Williams married Janie Albritton, of Snowhill, Ala. This union resulted in the birth of two children: Charley, born February 14, 1876, and Frank, born March 29, 1878. Mrs. Williams was a member of the Methodist Episcopal Church South, and died March 13, 1880. Mr. Williams married Nannie M. Finch, of Warren County, January 3, 1883, and to them one child has been born, Alice, born September 3, 1884. Mr. and Mrs. Williams are members of the Methodist Episcopal Church South, and he is a Democrat in politics. In 1876 Mr. Williams was elected justice of the peace and has held that office to the present time.

P. H. Winton, farmer, was born in Coffee County, Tenn., August 13, 1841, the sixth son of Stephen and Susan (Sayne) Winton, who were both natives of Tennessee. The father was of Scotch descent, born in 1791, was a life-long farmer, and a member of the Christian Church. He died March 1, 1878. The mother was born in 1801 or 1802, and was a member of the Methodist Episcopal Church South. Her death occurred January 11, 1864. P. H. was reared on the farm and received but a limited education. In 1858 he was engaged by G. Braly as salesman at a small salary and remained with him eighteen months, when he began as salesman for Dr. Davis and after one year with this employer he engaged in various occupations until April 27, 1861, when he enlisted in P. Turney's regiment, First Tennessee. In June, 1862, he was discharged on account of ill health, and in 1864 he began farming, which he continued until 1867, when he established a mercantile store in Viola, and one year later returned to the farm. For one year he farmed in connection with his father-in-law and then began farming on his own resources. In 1882 he raised 1,600 bushels of wheat on 100 acres of land, and has made farming a success. September 10, 1873, Mr. Winton wedded Lulillian Ramsey, a daughter of S. M. and O. (Smart) Ramsey, and to them have been born three children: McRamsey, born July 8, 1874; Harris S. (deceased), born January 12, 1876, and Emma O., born September 26, 1877. Mrs. Winton died September 17, 1881, a member of the Christian Church. Mr. Winton is a member of the same church, and a Democrat in politics.

Col. Edmund J. Wood, a well known and enterprising planter of Warren County, is a native of Tennessee, born May 15, 1828, in what is now Cannon County, but at that time was a part of Warren County. He is a son of John H. and Roxanna P. (Sutton) Wood. The father was of English descent, born in North Carolina in 1803, and while a child came with his parents to Tennessee. He was a farmer and merchant by occupation, a Democrat in politics, and died in Cannon County in 1879. The mother was of Scotch-English ancestry, born in Kentucky in the year 1806. Edmund J. secured a good education in youth and was principally educated at Irvin College, Warren County. After completing his education he was for three years engaged in the mercantile business at Woodbury, Cannon County. In 1853 he was sent to the State Legislature and represented Cannon County for two consecutive terms. In 1859 he was elected to the State Senate, representing the counties of Cannon, Warren, Grundy, Coffee and Van Buren one regular term and two extra sessions. In 1861 Mr. Wood moved to Warren County, and in September, the same year, enlisted in Company F, Fifth Confederate Regiment, with B. J. Hill as colonel. He was elected captain of the company, and at Corinth, Miss., was made lieutenant-colonel, but on account of ill health, caused by rheumatism contracted during the services, was not able long for active service. He spent his time as his health would permit with the army, but in 1864 returned home, and after the close of the war settled on his plantation, and has since been a successful planter. In the bloody and hotly contested battle of Shiloh he took an active and conspicuous part, and in the report of his commanding officer, was complimented for his gallant conduct upon the field, and referred to as the "bravest of the brave." In 1886 Col. Wood was defeated for the State Legislature by Col. John H. Savage, though he controlled a large vote of the citizens of Warren County. In March, 1887, he was appointed by President Grover Cleveland, postmaster at McMinnville, Tenn., which position he is now filling to the satisfaction of the public and the department. In 1854 he married Miss Lizzie Thompson, a most excellent lady, a native of Rutherford County. To this union have been born three children. Col Wood has done much in supporting the interest of the Democratic party in this part of the State, and he and wife are members of the Christian Church.

William T. York, a prominent and enterprising farmer of Warren County, residing in the Fifth Civil District, was born in the county July 9, 1849. He is the son of George W. and Martha (Lurk) York. George W. Lurk was born in North Carolina September 20, 1810, and died in July, 1876. He was of English descent and came to Tennessee when quite young with his parents, who settled on Rocky River. He was a successful farmer, was well educated, was a member of the Christian Church and of the Democratic party. Mrs. York was born in Warren County, Tenn., December 19, 1810, and died October 25, 1851. She was a well educated member of the Christian Church. William T. York was the ninth of ten children and lived with his parents until 1873, when he went to Texas and remained there two years. He then returned to Warren County on account of his father's illness. He then began the life of a farmer in the Fourth District, Warren County, living there until 1882, when he moved to his present location. When he began life on his own account his father gave him $1,000, which, by judicious management and energy he has increased to $4,000. He has an academic education, is a member of the Christian Church, a Mason and a Democrat. He was married December 27, 1881, to Miss Josie P. Myers, who was born in Warren County November 29, 1829. She has a collegiate education, secured at Burritt College, located at Spencer, Van Buren Co., Tenn. She, like her husband, is a member of the Christian Church. She is a daughter of Thomas S. and Martha J. Myers. The result of her marriage to Mr. York has been three children, all living: William L., born January 27, 1883; Byron M., born November 2, 1884, and Thomas W., born July 31, 1886.

COFFEE COUNTY.

William Alwood, a prominent citizen of Manchester, Tenn., was born September 22, 1850, in Fulton County, Ohio. He is the son of Levi S. and Delilah (McQuillin) Alwood—the former of Scotch descent, born in Ohio October 9, 1826, the latter of Irish descent and born June 22, 1830, in Ohio. The elder Alwood was married in 1848; engaged in farming and he came to Tennessee in 1873, his permanent home. He is a Republican and in sympathy with the Methodist Episcopal Church, of which his wife is a member. After completing his academical studies he was employed on his father's farm. In 1873 he married Ella Higgins, born September 27, 1853, in Ashtabula County, Ohio, the daughter of Harris Higgins. Our subject immediately moved to Coffee County near Manchester and continued farming several years exclusively, but in 1886 he came to Manchester and added lumbering, also for one year the livery business with J. H. Burger. A careful man, he now owns 550 acres in Coffee County, a Manchester improved lot and a half-interest in the livery valued at $3,600. He has four children and is a Republican.

Simeon Ashley, clerk of Coffee County Circuit Court, and a prominent citizen of Manchester, was born March 8, 1830, near Beech Grove, Tenn. He is the son of William and Mary (Weaver) Ashley, of English and

Scotch descent respectively—the former born in South Carolina, Lawrence District, February 14, 1789, and the latter, in North Carolina in 1790. Their parents came to Tennessee in early days, and the maternal father was a companion of James K. Polk's father in the then far West. After the marriage of the elder Ashley, in about 1812, they made Beech Grove their permanent home. He was a farmer, a stanch Democrat, and a Primitive Baptist in religion. The mother of our subject was a member of the Methodist Episcopal Church. The dates of the father's and mother's deaths were in 1870 and 1869 respectively. One of eight children, our subject received his early education at Beech Grove Academy, and taught and farmed about eight years. With W. T. Moore he established a general store at Bradyville in 1856. In 1861 he enlisted in the Confederate service Company E, Eighteenth Tennessee Infantry. His varied experiences may be seen from the following engagements: Fort Donelson, Murfreesboro, Chickamauga, Missionary Ridge, etc. After his long military life he returned and cared for his father until the latter's death. Since 1878 he has been in public service, as county clerk twice, and his present position of circuit clerk. He is a popular self-made man and property owner, having a farm in Coffee County, and Manchester lots. August 6, 1856, he married Ellender J. Roughton, born December 24, 1844, in Coffee County, and daughter of Elisha H. Roughton, Esq., of Coffee County, They have four children—three sons and a daughter. Mr. Ashley is a decided Democrat, and although not a church member he believes in the Christian religion. Mrs. Ashley belongs to the Christian Church.

John H. Ashley, high sheriff of Coffee County, and a prominent citizen of Manchester, was born in Rutherford County, June 13, 1848. He is the son of W. F. and Lidia A. (Mankin), both natives of Tennessee and of English descent; the former was born near Beech Grove in 1822 and died November 5, 1878; the latter, still living, was born in Rutherford County, in 1822. The elder Ashley was a farmer and a sound Democrat. Our subject was the oldest of seven children; received his academical education at Beech Grove Academy chiefly, and for sixteen years successfully pursued agriculture. In 1884 he was elected high sheriff of Coffee County and was honored by re-election two years later by a handsome majority. He has risen, a self-made man, to his present successful position. December 18, 1868, he was married to Mattie E. Hightower, born in Murfreesboro in 1859, and a graduate from the Female Institute in her native city. Two children were born to them: Freelin H., born February 11, 1881, and Mamie, born September 7, 1883. Mr. Ashley is a stanch Democrat and a member of the Separate Baptist Church, while his wife belongs to the Methodist Episcopal Church, and is an influential lady.

James G. Aydelott, lawyer, and one of the most prominent citizens of Tullahoma, Tenn., was born in Hickman, Ky., November 3, 1845, and is the son of John D. and Sarah (Grizzard) Aydelott. The father was born in Rutherford County, Tenn., in 1818, and died at Hickman, Ky., in 1852. The mother, born in Nashville, Tenn., in 1827, is the daughter of James Grizzard, the pioneer merchant of Tullahoma. When a small boy our subject removed with his mother to Tullahoma, where he has since resided. While a man of good education, his attendance at public school did not exceed three months altogether, having been taught entirely by his mother, who was a lady of fine education and more than ordinary attainments, educated as she was at the old Nashville Female Academy. In 1860 our subject entered the store of J. B. Witherby as clerk, remaining there until the occupation of Tullahoma by Gen. Bragg. He then entered the Confederate Army news depot, serving in that position until the Georgia campaign, when he went on duty at the headquarters of the Army of the Tennessee, where he remained until after the surrender in North Carolina, having been under Gens. Johnston, Bragg and Hood. At the close of the war he returned home and occupied a position as clerk in the store of Crane & Witherby, being at the same time a member of the firm of Aydelott & Stevens, manufacturers of harness, saddles, boots and shoes. In 1869 he entered into partnership with Joel Witherby in general merchandise, in which he was engaged until 1873, when the firm was dissolved by the retirement of the senior member to private life. He next became a member of the firm of Aydelott, Davidson & Co., in 1875, but retired from the same in a few months. In 1876 he formed a copartnership with John P. Bennett, and remained in the same until 1878. In 1880 he engaged in the lumber and produce business, continuing until 1883. For a year and a half he was actively engaged in developing coal mining in East Tennessee, in which he was largely interested, but in 1885 closed out the controlling interest, since when he has been devoted to his law practice and office work. Mr. Aydelott is, and has been for eighteen years a member of the county court, member of the board of aldermen, mayor of Tullahoma, twice, four and five years each time, and recorder the same number of times. He has been for the past twenty years an active member of the I. O. O. F., being elected in 1884 Grand Master of the Grand Lodge of Tennessee, and in 1885 was elected Grand Representative of the Grand Lodge of the Sovereign Grand Lodge, serving in that capacity at the session of the same at Boston, Mass., in 1886. His term of office will extend to and include the meeting of the Sovereign Grand Lodge in Denver, Col., in 1887. In 1886 he was elected Grand High Priest of the Grand Encampment, I. O. O. F., of Tennessee. He is also a member of the Tullahoma Lodge and Chapter, F. & A. M., and of Tullahoma Lodge, A. O. U. W., representing the latter in the Grand Lodge of Tennessee. In politics he is a Democrat and belongs to the progressive Democracy of the new South; while having never asked for office, he has always taken an active part in politics, and has been a delegate to every county, congressional and State Convention held by his party in fifteen years. He is a director of the Nashville, Chattanooga & St. Louis Railway, also a director of the Tullahoma National Bank and is prominently connected with various other corporations. Our subject was married March 20, 1872, to Sallie, daughter of George and Delilah (Troxler) Cortner, of Bradford County, Tenn. She was born in 1851. To them have been born three children, as follows: George Cortner, born August 5, 1873; John Doak, December 6, 1875, and Jessie Mai, January 9, 1881. Mr. Aydelott is a member of the Episcopal, while his wife is a member of the Cumberland Presbyterian Church.

A. W. Booth, M. D., a prominent citizen and leading physician of Tullahoma, Tenn., was born in Bedford County, Tenn., in 1858, and is the son of J. B. and Elizabeth (Vannoy) Booth. Our subject was reared on the farm, and educated in the public schools. In 1879 he began the study of medicine, and graduated from Vanderbilt University in 1881. The same year he began practicing in his native county, but soon removed to Tullahoma, where he has since lived and succeeded in building up one of the best practices in the town. October 29, 1884, he was married to Ella, daughter of Capt. C. H. Bean, of Moore County, Tenn. Mrs. Booth is a member of the Methodist Episcopal Church South, and our subject is a member of the A. O. U. W. Lodge.

E. A. Call, farmer and miller, of Coffee County, was born in Lincoln County March 6, 1825. His parents, Daniel H. and Nancy (Hinkle) Call, natives of Roan County, N. C., came to Tennessee about 1822, and began farming and distilling. He built the first steam distillery in Coffee County, continuing until about 1848 in the business. Our subject, one of nine children, entered the distillery at sixteen, and continued successfully for thirty-six years. November 9, 1850, he married Susan Timmins, of Lincoln County, by whom he had nine children. She died June 19, 1877. October 7, 1879, he married Francis E. Wildman, whose death occurred in July, 1884. He was married the third time to Lizzie, daughter of P. A. and Ellen (Rollin) Huffer. Politically he is a Republican.

COFFEE COUNTY. 925

James Carden, farmer and stock dealer in Coffee County, was born there September 28, 1831, and is the son of Lewis and Catherine (Simpson) Carden, of Scotch-Irish descent, the former born May 17, 1809, and now living, and the latter born about 1815, in North Carolina, and deceased July 16, 1869. Our subject lived with his father until twenty-four years of age, from whom he received 125 acres, living on this for nineteen years, when he came to his present place. He married Pharaba Simpson, born August 16, 1837, in Coffee County, in 1855, January 18. Twelve children were born to them, ten living: Peter R., Joseph S., Robert L., Emily P., Sarah E., Dora, John A., Mary L., Thomas F., Minnie O., William A. (died May 6, 1884), and Eva C., (died April 30, 1883). After five months in the Confederate service Mr. Carden was disabled and discharged. He owns altogether 562 acres of land and has always been in politics a Democrat.

George N. Carter, jeweler, dealer in watches and silverware, and a leading young citizen of Tullahoma, Tenn., was born in Tuscumbia, Ala., in 1859, and is the son of James Carter, a native of Virginia. His father immigrated when quite small with his parents to Bedford County, Tenn., where, in 1830, our subject's grandfather, grandmother, and five children were burned to death in their residence, the house having been set on fire from a stove. Reared in the town of his birth, he attended the public schools. In 1878 he succeeded his father in the jewelry business at Tuscumbia, continuing until 1881, when his health failed him, and he traveled for two years in the photograph business. In 1883 he entered the jewelry store of John W. Rooth, at Shelbyville, Tenn., remaining with him until January 2, 1883, when he came to Tullahoma, and opened his present establishment. Our subject is a member of the National Jewelers' League, and also of the Christian Church. In politics he is a Democrat.

John B. Carroll, proprietor of the St. James Hotel, member of the firm of Carroll Bros. & Co., and one of the energetic and prominent young citizens of Tullahoma, was born July 4, 1855, in Coffee County, Tenn. His father, H. W. Carroll, born in 1826, and his mother, Mary (Walker) Carroll, born in 1824, were both natives of Coffee County. His mother died in 1876. Both were members of the Methodist Episcopal Church South. His father is still living, and is one of the most prominent farmers of the county. Our subject was reared on his parents' farm, and received a good common-school education, and has developed into a thorough business man. He was married, December 20, 1876, to Eldora E., daughter of William and Narcissa (Taylor) Eoff, and born in Coffee County, Tenn., May 27, 1858. Her parents were natives of Tennessee also, and residents of Coffee County. To our subject and wife two children have been born: Goldie O. (October 4, 1880) and Norma E. (October 17, 1884). Mr. Carroll is a member of the R. A. M., A. O. U. W., and the K. of H. lodges, and carries life policies of $2,000 in the McMinnville (Tenn.) Mutual Life Insurance Company, $2,000 in the K. of H., and $2,000 in the A. O. U. W. lodges. He is a conservative Democrat, and is considered one of the substantial and prominent young citizens of Tullahoma.

J. A. Clark, farmer in Coffee County, was born in Rutherford County, August 22, 1822. His parents, Anthony and Sallie (Dunlap) Clark, natives of North Carolina, came to Tennessee in 1800 remained until 1850 and then went to Texas. Here the father died about 1871, and the mother a year later. They were of Irish and English descent. Our subject married Millie Wilkinson in 1844. Born to them are nine children: John, November 5, 1845; Rufus, November 10, 1846; R. S., January 19, 1849; I. M., November 5, 1851; Ellen, March 3, 1854; Sallie, April 4, 1856; James, April 7, 1859; Elizabeth, August 17, 1861, and Willie D., August 30, 1865. Mr. Clark, his wife and six children are members of the Christian Church. He has educated his children, one of whom is teacher in the Winchester Normal School, one principal of Hillsboro (Tex.), schools, and a third also teaching in Texas. Mr. Clark is a Democrat.

W. A. Clark, farmer of Coffee County, was born June 17, 1830, in Lebanon. His father, Joshua Clark, was born June 5, 1806, in Maryland, and came to Kentucky early, and finally to Lebanon in 1828, engaging at contracting and farming until 1847, since then he has been devoted to the latter. His mother, Sarah (Allen) Clark, daughter of "Billy" Allen, of Lebanon, was born February 14, 1807, in Tennessee. Our subject is of Scotch-Irish descent. Having learned the mechanic's trade, he left his father's farm when nineteen and worked at his trade until 1865, since when he has been a successful farmer. June 14, 1849, he married Elizabeth S. McGinn, a native of North Carolina. Their children are Joshua, William E., Robert H. and John D. Besides dealing in general merchandise at Bradyville, he was postmaster and collecting officer there several years; the planing mill business occupied his attention for a time also. Politically, he is a Democrat. His wife is a relative of Gen. Steele, of Saulsbury, N. C.

A. B. Conley, merchant, and a prominent citizen of Tullahoma, Tenn., was born in Rutherford County, Tenn., November 7, 1847; the son of A. W. Conley, a native of Tennessee. Our subject was reared on a farm in what is now a part of Crockett County. He acquired his education in the common schools and in 1867 began the study of medicine. He attended the Eclectic College at Cincinnati, Ohio, the medical department of the University of Louisiana at New Orleans, and graduated in 1884 from the American Eclectic Medical College of Cincinnati. From 1871 to 1880 he practiced in Louisiana and then went to Milan, Tenn. June 17, 1886, he came to Tullahoma and engaged in general merchandising, his present occupation. At the age of fourteen he ran away from home, joined the Confederate Twelfth Tennessee Cavalry. After a year's service he returned home on account of sickness. He was married in 1869 to Mattie J., daughter of Washington Mitchell of Rutherford County, Tenn. Three children were born to them—one girl and two boys. Our subject is a member of the Masonic, Odd Fellows, K. of P., K. of H., K. & L. of H. and A. O. U. W. orders.

G. R. Crane, druggist and a prominent young citizen of Tullahoma, Tenn., was born in Manchester, Tenn., November 26, 1858, the son of Dr. William and M. A. (Alexander) Crane. At the age of two years he with his parents came to Tullahoma, which has since been his home. He acquired his education in the public schools, and has added much thereto by his practical experience. He began life for himself when but fifteen years of age as a clerk. At the age of twenty-one he began in the produce business, and continued in this for one year, when he engaged in the drug trade, in which he has met with success. He was married November 3, 1881, to Mary E. Lambert, and to them one child, G. R., Jr., was born August 20, 1882. In 1884 our subject was elected recorder of Tullahoma, and in 1886 he was elected a member of the board of aldermen to serve two years. He is a member of the I. O. O. F. Lodge, is a Democrat, and himself and wife are members of the St. Barnabas Episcopal Church.

S. J. Crockett, farmer in Coffee County, was born June 9, 1809, in Georgia. His father, John, a native of South Carolina and pioneer of Tennessee in 1812, was born February 29, 1780, and died March 9, 1859. He was of Irish descent. His mother, Mary (Cowan) Crockett, was born November 17, 1779, in Georgia, and died in 1857. Leaving the farm when of age, after four years in general merchandising at Hillsboro, he began his career of farming. He was collecting officer for a time. March 15, 1835, he married Amelia Austell, born February 4, 1817, in South Carolina, daughter of Amos and Lucy Austell. Seven of their eight children are living: Eliza; Jno. G.; Bettie, wife of T. J. Brown; Sarah, wife of J. Gillam; Samuel A.; Cynthia E., wife of S. Willis of Texas, and Archia W. Of considerable wealth before the war our subject had to begin life anew after. A member of the Cumberland Presbyterian Church, he is politically a Democrat.

George W. Cross, a prominent lawyer of Manchester, Tenn., was born in Anderson County August 31, 1849. He is the son of William and Jane (Black) Cross, both of English descent and natives of Anderson County. The former, born in 1810, is still living; the latter, born about 1820, died February 26, 1885. Married in 1836 the elder Cross engaged in farming. He is a Democrat, and sympathizes with the Cumberland Presbyterian Church of which his wife was a member. Our subject, the fifth of eight children, was educated chiefly at Cumberland University, at Lebanon, Tenn., and the military school of Knoxville, Tenn., from which he graduated in 1874. After three years' teaching in Decherd and Salem, Tenn., in September, 1877, he took ten months at Vanderbilt University Law Department, and the professor granted him license to practice. Since 1878, when he came to Manchester, he has become one of the most successful lawyers of Coffee County and among the ablest in this section. January 17, 1882, he married Beulah Hickerson, born in 1861, the daughter of Judge W. P. Hickerson. She was a cultured lady. Her death occurred July 24, 1885. Mr. Cross is a decided Democrat.

F. E. Cunningham, proprietor of the Tullahoma Distillery, and a prominent citizen of Tullahoma, was born in Bedford County, Tenn., September 15, 1852, and is the son of M. T. Cunningham, a native of Pennsylvania. The father died in 1874. Our subject was reared in Bedford County, and educated in the town schools. At fourteen years of age he entered the store at Flat Creek as clerk, remaining there until four years later he was appointed United States revenue store-keeper, in which he was engaged about four years. In 1876 he purchased and conducted a distillery in Coffee County, but in 1882 came into his present establishment. Our subject is a member of the K. of H. Lodge, and a Republican in politics. He was married September 3, 1884, to Bell, daughter of Elijah Couch of Bedford County. They have two children: Mamie and Vester. His wife is a member of the Cumberland Presbyterian Church.

George W. Davidson, one of the oldest and most prominent citizens of Tullahoma, and a member of the Coffee County bar, was born in Lincoln County, Tenn., June 21, 1826, and is the son of Joel and Elizebeth (Henry) Davidson. The father was born at Beon's Station, Granger County, Tenn., in July, 1799, and died in August in 1848. The mother was born in Hillsboro, Orange Co., N. C., January 5, 1800, and died in November, 1883. Both were members of the Old School Presbyterian Church. Our subject was reared on a farm, and received a limited education. He learned the cabinet-maker's trade at the age of sixteen years, and followed the same for about four years. Until the breaking out of the war he was engaged at contracting and building. He then became drill master for first one and then the other army in the mountain counties of Tennessee, and in 1863 entered the Federal quartermaster's department, and served in the capacity of clerk until the close of the war. He was soon appointed postmaster at Tullahoma, and held the office until his resignation in November, 1885. During his postmastership he was also United States commissioner, and holds the office at present, together with that of recorder of Tullahoma. For several years he held the following offices at one and the same time: Postmaster, United States commissioner, recorder, justice of the peace, public school director, and notary public. Mr. Davidson was married February 24, 1864, to S. W. Cleveland, who was born in Lincoln County, Tenn., in 1844. To them have been born five children: Robert H. born May 17, 1865; Joan, September 10, 1869; Abraham L., May 27, 1873; William J. September 16, 1875, and Maud, January 25, 1879. Robert H. is at present deputy postmaster at Tullahoma. In 1870 our subject was licensed as an attorney by Judges Steele and Tillman. He is a Republican, but was a Whig previous to the war. He is conservative in his political views and has warm friends in both parties. He is a member of the Methodist Episcopal Church North, while his wife belongs to the Cumberland Presbyterian Church.

G. S. Deakins, farmer, of the Thirteenth District of Coffee County, Tenn., was born in Marion County (now Sequatchie) Tenn., in 1832, and is the son of William and Sarah (Richards) Deakins, natives of Tennessee. The father died in 1848 and the mother in 1836. Both were members of the Cumberland Presbyterian Church. Reared on the farm with a common-school education, he also attended Burritt College at Spencer, Tenn., and later, Emory and Henry College of Virginia. Having entered the law school of Lebanon (Tenn.) University in 1860, the civil war caused him to enter the Confederate service, in Company H, Thirty-fifth Regiment of Infantry. After the war and a resident in his native county for some time, he went to Jasper, Tenn., where he was appointed clerk and master of the Chancery Court, holding this until his resignation four years later. In 1884 he removed to Tullahoma, and after a year's residence there, began farming. In 1860 he was married to Mary, daughter of Judge Frazier of Nashville. She died in 1863. In 1874 he married Mary A., daughter of F. A. Lochmiller, a native of Tennessee. They have two children: Vernie S., born February 8, 1875, and Fredrick T., born March 26, 1886. Both our subject and wife are members of the Old School Presbyterian Church.

H. P. Dewey, lumber dealer, and a prominent citizen of Tullahoma, was born in Michigan in 1838, and is the son of Cyrus J. and Maria (Beulah) Dewey, natives of the Green Mountain State. The father was born in 1812 and died in 1864, and the mother was born in 1813 and died in 1853. Both were members of the Old School Presbyterian Church. Our subject was raised in Washington County, Mich., and educated in the public schools and at Monroe College, Mich. He farmed and attended school alternately until the fall of 1862; he became a member of Company H, Eighteenth Regiment Michigan Infantry, and served until honorably discharged in June, 1865. He then spent a year in Iowa at general merchandising. He returned to Michigan in 1867, and after a year's farming, engaged in steam saw-milling. In 1874 the firm removed their mill to Franklin County, Tenn., six miles below Winchester. In 1880 he was appointed United States guager in the revenue department, and in 1881 came to Tullahoma. He engaged in his present business in the spring of 1886. Mr. Dewey was married, January 16, 1866, to Minnie E., daughter of Nathaniel Gardner, of Coldwater, Mich., she being born in 1849. Their two children are Lillie E., born October, 1867, and Eddie L., born November, 1869. He was elected alderman in 1885, receiving 328 out of 368 votes cast. He is a Conservative Republican. Our subject, wife and daughter, are members of the Methodist Episcopal Church, he being a trustee and his wife class teacher of the same.

William M. Fariss, M. D., a leading citizen and physician of Tullahoma, Tenn., was born in Franklin County, Tenn., April 22, 1834, and is the son of William and Martha (Clardy) Fariss, natives of South Carolina. The father died in 1861 and the mother in 1874. Both were members of the Cumberland Presbyterian Church. Our subject was brought up on the farm and attended the public schools. In 1854 he began the study of medicine at Winchester, with Dr. Wallace Estill as preceptor. Later he attended several courses of lectures, and in March, 1858, graduated from the medical department of the University of Nashville. He at once began practicing in Franklin County, Tenn., and continued until he entered the Confederate Army, joining Company D, of Turney's First Regiment of Tennessee Infantry as private. He was appointed assistant surgeon and assigned duty with the Fifth Alabama Battalion. Subsequently he was elected first lieutenant of his old company with which he continued during the war. At the battle of Gettysburg he was seriously wounded in the thigh, captured and held as prisoner for twenty-one months. After the war he returned to his old home and took care of his aged mother, practicing his profession. In 1869 he removed to Tullahoma to practice where he has resided ever since, and built up a large and lucrative practice. October 17, 1867, our subject was married to Amanda M., daughter of C. J. Taylor of Franklin County, Tenn., and to them have been born nine children, two of whom are dead. Our subject and wife are members of the Methodist Episcopal Church South, and he is a member of I. O. O. F., F. & A. M., and A. O. U. W. lodges. Politically he is a Democrat.

J. K. Farris, M. D., a prominent physician of Coffee County, was born in Franklin County in 1836. His parents, William C. and Mahaley, (Kennerly) Farris, were natives of Franklin County, the latter, daughter of J. P. Kennerly, of Georgia. The father was a shoe-maker, and came to Tennessee in 1811. Our subject married Mary E. Austell in 1857, whose parents were natives of North Carolina. They have had eight children: Ellen K. (deceased), born in 1858; Samuel J., in 1860; John K., in 1865; Annas A. (deceased), in 1868; William R., in 1870; Sue J., in 1873; Mary E., in 1885, and Sophia C. (deceased), in 1878. His wife died in 1885. Reared on the farm and with an academic training, he began the study of medicine under Dr. J. E. Hough, of Pleasant Hill. After practicing in Arkansas, he came to Coffee County in 1861, where he has built up his present extensive practice. A self-made man, he has given his childern collegiate training.

Timothy S. Givan, editor and proprietor of the *Tullahoma Messenger*, one of the prominent weekly papers of Middle Tennessee, was born in Hardin County, Ky., October 8, 1845. He is the son of James M. and Mellona (Needham) Givan, both of whom were born in Kentucky, the former November 4, 1811, and the latter September 19, 1819. The parents, married October 9, 1834, had ten children born to them, six of whom were boys, and of these our subject is the youngest. The mother died April 5, 1854, and in 1856 the father married Rachael Clark. He died October 4, 1859. The childhood days of our subject were spent on the farm, and at the age of ten years he entered the office of the Cloverport (Ky.) *Journal*, where he served an apprenticeship of four years. Previous to the breaking out of the civil war, he taught a term of five months in his native State, and when the crisis came, enlisted in the Federal Army, joining at first, Company I, Thirty-seventh Regiment of Kentucky Mounted Infantry, and later, the Sixteenth and Second Regiments of United States Regulars. He was subsequently commissioned teacher and chaplain of the Second United States Regulars, and also post chaplain and librarian for the garrison at Mobile, Ala. At the close of the war he returned to Kentucky and re-entered the newspaper business in the position of local editor of the *Kentucky Intelligencer*, published by W. D. Givan, his brother, first at Munfordsville, and afterward at Caverna. In 1870 he purchased the material of the *Kentucky Templar* and *Kentucky Presbyterian*, and removed the same to Olney, Ill., where he established the *Western Guardian* and published it for eighteen months. His next literary work was as associate editor of the *Little Bouquet* and *Journal*, two religio-philosophical periodicals, and also superintendent of the Chicago publishing department from which they were issued. Four and a half years were spent in this capacity when he returned to Kentucky and in 1876 established the *Breckenridge News* at Cloverport. Two years later he came to Nashville, Tenn., and opened a printing house from which were published the *Weekly Protectionist*, the *Weekly Tennessee Farmer*, the *Weekly Progress*, the *Semi-Weekly Standard*, the *Weekly Tennessee Republican*, and the *Weekly Southern Broadax*. He was both editor and proprietor of the last two mentioned papers. The above publications were discontinued with the destruction of the office by fire in December, 1883. From Nashville he returned to Hardin County, Ky., purchased a farm, and for eighteen months engaged in farming and merchandising. December 8, 1885, our subject became business manager of the *Tullahoma Republican*, then owned by a stock company, and July 13, 1886, he formed a copartnership with J. A. Lewis and purchased the paper. During the same month he leased his partner's interest and became sole editor and proprietor of the publication. The following January the name of the paper was changed to that of *The Messenger*, while the policy became politically independent instead of Republican. Our subject is a man of recognized literary talent and attainments, and has contributed largely to the periodicals of the West and South. He is the author of the following works: "The Pearl of Great Price," "Happy at Last," "My Darling," "The Guardian Angel," and "Two Novel Marriages." In mentioning his connection with the *Breckenridge News*, the *Memphis Trade Journal* said: "We have received the initial number of the *Breckenridge News*, published at Cloverport, Ky. It is edited by T. S. Givan, whose contributions to the literature of the country have stamped him as an author of no ordinary merit. Maj. Givan is one of the brightest of the many brilliant writers of the West." Mr. Givan is one of the prominent citizens of Tullahoma, and his newspaper is enjoying merited success. He was married June 6, 1876, to Ellen Sloan, a native of Warren County, Tenn., who is the daughter of Rev. John L. and Mary J. Sloan, and was born May 12, 1860. Rev. Sloan was a minister of the Cumberland Presbyterian Church, and an author of considerable note. He died in 1863, and his widow is now a resident of Nashville. Four children have been born to our subject and wife as follows: Harry M., born July 24, 1877;

Minnie M., born March 31, 1879; Walter T., born February 26, 1881, and James Archer, born February 25, 1883. Mr. and Mrs. Givan are members of the Methodist Episcopal Church. W. D. and John F., brothers of our subject, were ministers of the Methodist Episcopal Church South. John F. died at Woodsonville, Ky., in the fall of 1866, and W. D. on New Year's night, 1883, at Nashville. The latter belonged to the Savannah District, Clifton Circuit, at the time of his death.

W. P. Hickerson, Jr., was born in Manchester, October 20, 1850, the son of Judge William P. and Mary S. (Martin) Hickerson, both of Scotch-Irish descent. The father, born in North Carolina, November 26, 1816, went when a child to Tennessee, and began life as a dry goods clerk at Manchester, and afterward read law under Col. Charles L. Ready of Murfreesboro, and for a number of years was the leading lawyer of that section. For sixteen years he was judge of the Fifth District, and was appointed by Gov. Marks as a judge of the State Arbitration Court. As a lawyer he was among the first in Tennessee. He died in Coffee County, of heart disease, April 18, 1882, and his wife just one year before. Both are buried in the old family graveyard near Manchester. He was a prominent Democrat in the State. The mother, born in Wilson County, Tenn., February 13, 1825, died April 17, 1881. Our subject, the second of five children (two living), was educated chiefly at Manchester College, and then for ten months was a contractor in building the Illinois Central Railway, through West Tennessee, then known as the M. C. Railway. Afterward with an uncle, L. D. Hickerson, he leased the McMinnville & Manchester, and the Winchester & Alabama Railways. Three years after he sold the lease to the Chattanooga Company, altogether a successful speculation. He then became conductor for the Chattanooga Company for a year, on the McMinnville & Manchester Railway. In 1879 he began the Stone Fort Paper Company's Mills, in which he has since owned a half interest, and which are the largest mills south of the Ohio River, and the only mills in the State that make the wood pulp. On October 17, 1877, he married Ella, daughter of James C. Ramsey, Esq., of McMinnville, and is a cultured lady. Their four children are William P., born July 2, 1878; Chisum R., February 23, 1880; Georgie M., January 26, 1882, and Nasion W., born March 31, 1884. His wife is a member of the Cumberland Presbyterian Church.

L. D. Hickerson, Jr., a prominent and progressive young citizen of Tullahoma, and cashier of the First National Bank of that place, was born five miles east of there January 13, 1861. He is the son of L. D. Hickerson, Sr., president of the above bank, whose father, John Hickerson, originally of North Carolina, founded one of the oldest and most respected families in this portion of the State. Our subject was reared in Tullahoma, and, after attending the public schools, took a course at Burritt College, Spencer, Tenn., and later took a complete course at Goodman's Business College at Nashville. Returning to Tullahoma he entered the saw-milling and contracting business in 1877, continuing at this until his election in 1885 as cashier of the bank. He is secretary and treasurer of the Caney Fork Coal & Iron Company, treasurer of Tullahoma, and is a member of Tullahoma Lodge, K. of H., of which he is Vice-Dictator. In local politics he is a "Mugwump," but in national affairs always supports the Republican nominees.

Wilburn Hiles, one of the substantial farmers of the Fifth District of Coffee County, Tenn., was born in Bedford County, Tenn., July 30, 1826. He is the son of Joseph Hiles, a native of North Carolina, who was born in 1796, and immigrated to Tennessee in early days. Our subject, brought up on the farm, attended the common schools. He was engaged in merchandising at Flat Creek, Bedford County, when he entered the service of the Confederacy, and was detailed to raise stock and grain for the Southern Army. Later he became a member of Norman's battalion, and at the battle of Chickamauga was wounded in the right leg, disabling him. He joined his parents, then refugees in Georgia, and after the war engaged in merchandising at Somerville, Tenn.; later he returned to Bedford County, then to Coffee County, and engaged in farming. He was married, in 1866, to Minerva Bobo, born in Bedford County in 1843. To them have been born the following nine children: Joseph E., born in 1868; W. Evan, in 1870; Mary E., in 1872; James W., in 1874 (died in 1885); Frank K., in 1876; Walter S., in 1878; Lena M., in 1880; Daisy D., in 1882, and Gracie T., in 1884. The mother is a member of the Primitive Baptist Church.

P. C. Isbell. His parents were both born in Warren County, Ky. His father was of English descent; his mother of German and a granddaughter of Frederick Stump, an early settler in Davidson County, Tenn. He was born in Warren County, Ky. His father moved to Jackson County, Mo., when he was a small boy, where he grew up in the dark backwoods and never attended school. He had a fine working education. His mother taught him to spell, read and write and a few rules in arithmetic, what she knew. He mastered Webster's "blue back," and then engaged as a school-teacher, which he followed for several years, working his way up to a high grade in the English language. After leaving the schoolhouse, he continued his studies in all the departments useful in practical life. He came to Tennessee in 1850, read law in the office of Hon. W. P. Hickerson, in Manchester, was admitted to the bar in 1852, and has continued in the practice at that place ever since. His father was a Whig and an uncompromising supporter of Henry Clay. He was schooled in the doctrines of the Whig party, and the old Baptist Church doctrine, which his parents held sacred. He is one of the few men who have gotten away from all of their early political and religious teaching. He works up all the great questions involved in human life. He is independent in thought and action, without the slightest tinge of superstition. He is anxious to have an intelligent people, grand in purpose, noble in sentiment and just in action. He thinks it can all be accomplished by a proper administration of government; that every man's home should be sweetened with prosperity and happy with affection, that people should be educated and developed in harmony with their organic constitutions, that the organic parts of man should be treated as sciences, that ignorant sentiment always has been a dangerous element; that ignorance is not the normal state of man, but that it is consequent upon an inefficient administration of government. He is not a member of any organization or society, is strictly conservative, and is deeply interested in the general welfare of humanity. He never hesitates a moment to advocate the right, and condemn the wrong. He has the utmost contempt for time servers and policy people. He never annoys any one with complaints about anything unpleasant. He has schooled himself on the bright side of humanity, and he keeps that side before the people. He delights in trying to make every one happy. His motto is

"The world is as we make it,
And life is as we make it."

D. C. Jackson, a prominent citizen of Summitville, Tenn., was born November 16, 1821, in Monticello, Ky., and is the son of J. B. and Dorcas (Cox) Jackson. The father was born in Lewisburg, N. C., in 1798, and when quite young came to Tennessee. For eight years, before he went into the mercantile business, he was clerk of McMinn County. The mother was born about 1797 in Tennessee. Both were members of the Methodist Episcopal Church, and he was a Democrat. In 1839 our subject began an extensive tour through Virginia, Missouri, Arkansas, Texas, Indian Territory and Mexico. He then returned to Coffee County and September 8, 1846, married Edna Taylor, of Granger County. She lived but a short time. After visiting California until 1851, he returned and married Mary F. Rhodes, of Coffee County, April 18, 1852. She died January 31, 1855. They had one child, John T., who died at four years of age. He visited California a second time, and April 23, 1860, married Elizabeth Chilton, of Jefferson County. They have six children.

In 1861 he enlisted as Confederate captain of the Thirty-seventh Tennessee Infantry; he organized a cavalry company a year later as captain also. Under Col. Adrian and others he continued until the war's close, receiving severe wounds at Chickamauga and Steubenville. Since the war he has been at Summitville, engaged in farming, as justice of the peace, and in his present position of postmaster.

Capt. A. Jacobs, a well known planter of Coffee County, Tenn., was born August 3, 1818, near his present home. His grandfather came from England as early as 1750, and was a soldier of the Revolution, living successively in Maryland, North Carolina and Bedford County, Tenn., where he died at the unusual age of one hundred and six years. Our subject is the son of Jeremiah and Rebecca (Rudd) Jacobs, natives of Tennessee and North Carolina, and born about 1793 and 1802 respectively. The father died about 1858, and the mother about 1871, in Coffee County. Both were members of the Cumberland Presbyterian Church, while politically the father was a Democrat. He was engaged in agriculture, the oldest of twelve children. Our subject has been a self-educated man and Bible student; engaged in mercantile business at Beech Grove about twenty years before and ten years after the war; in addition to his farming interests, he also dealt in live stock before the war. Losing much through the war and in securities, he has 300 acres of fine Coffee County land. He is a Democrat in political faith, while religiously the entire family are prominent workers in the Cumberland Presbyterian Church. December 1, 1842, he married Catherine, born October 27, 1822, in Coffee County, the daughter of James Dillard. Eight children were born to them.

Stokely Jacobs, a well known planter of Coffee County, Tenn., was born there February 26, 1840 (ancestors mentioned in biography of A. Jacobs). Our subject, after completing his education, was engaged in agriculture chiefly. In 1861 he enlisted in the Confederate Company G, Seventeenth Regiment Tennessee Infantry. He occupied various positions in Hardee's corps, and took part in the battles of Rock Castle, Perryville, Murfreesboro and Petersburg, where he was captured and sent as prisoner to Point Lookout and Elmira, N. Y. Paroled in 1865, he returned home, and after the close of the war began farming. Entering the store of his brother at Beech Grove, in 1868, he became a partner in 1880, but on the death of his brother in 1883, he again returned to his present occupation of farming. He is now the owner of 300 acres of land. February 1, 1866, he married Laura, daughter of William Blanton, born April 1, 1848, in Bedford County. They have nine children. He, his wife and three children are members and supporters of the Cumberland Presbyterian Church.

J. M. Jernigan, a prominent farmer of Coffee County, was born there March 27, 1843. He is the son of Alexander and Louisa (Shake) Jernigan, natives of Tennessee, the latter of whom died in 1863. His father then married Martha Ford, of Coffee County. Reared on the farm, our subject has clung to agriculture. In 1864 he married Mary Todd, but was divorced in 1867. He then married Elizabeth Fulton, and they have reared the following adopted children: W. E. Parker, E. R. Rosco, and Henrietta B. Daniel. He and his wife are members of the Methodist Episcopal Church, while his political faith is strictly Democratic.

W. T. Lawrence, deputy sheriff of Coffee County, and a prominent citizen living near Beech Grove, Tenn., was born October 22, 1847, in Coffee County. He is the son of John H. and Tabitha H. (Blankenship) the former born in 1812 (died in 1858) in Tennessee, and the latter born in 1810 in Virginia, and living in Coffee County. The father was a farmer, politically a Democrat, and belonging to the Methodist Episcopal Church. Our subject, one of nine children, received his education chiefly at Beech Hill Academy, when soon after his father's death the care of the estate was thrown on to him, soon after his eleventh year. After the settlement of the estate, through the good management of the mother and sons, he received his share about 1870, since which he has been devoted to the cultivation of his land. He at present owns over 210 acres of valuable land, he lives on a late purchase as mentioned above. August 26, 1869, he married Leona, born January 10, 1850, in Rutherford County, daughter of W. F. Astlay. They have had eight children— four sons and four daughters. Mr. Lawrence has been deputy sheriff three years, and justice of the peace for six years. Both he and his wife are members of the Methodist Episcopal Church, while politically he is a Democrat.

Mrs. C. J. Lyon, wife of the late T. B. Lyon of Coffee County, was born February 10, 1829, and daughter of James and Jane Mason, the former born August 3, 1789, in North Carolina, and the latter July 2, 1800, in South Carolina. The father's father came to Tennessee in 1780, living on Stone River, and in Bedford County. He died May 26, 1863. Jane Mason's parents came to Bedford County, in 1800; one was of Dutch and the other of Irish descent. Our subject, one of seven children, married Joseph Tillman, September 17, 1850. He was born February 4, 1826, in North Carolina, and receiving a wound at Shiloh, died in Holly Spring Hospital, April 25, 1862. He enlisted in the Forty-fourth Tennessee Infantry five months before his death. Six children were born to them: Mary A., Martha J., Eliza N., Flurina C., Joseph P. and Elizabeth. They were married in Bedford County, moved to Coffee

County, and located at her present home. April 23, 1879, she married T. B. Lyon, who was born December 31, 1812, and died February 3, 1885. Mrs. Lyon was educated, and is a member of the Cumberland Presbyterian Church.

W. A. Marshall, furniture dealer, and present mayor of Tullahoma, Tenn., was born in Lincoln County, Tenn., in 1842, and is the son of J. W. and Nancy T. (Neal) Marshall, natives of Prince Edwards County, Va. Reared on the farm of his parents, our subject received his education at the neighboring schools. At the age of thirteen he came with his parents to Tullahoma, and entered his father's store, remaining until the opening of the late war. He then enlisted in Company B (Confederate), of Turney's First Regiment of Tennessee Infantry. After the war he returned home, working at different occupations until 1876, when he opened a stove and furniture store. Selling his stock of stoves in 1885, he has since carried furniture only, the only establishment of the kind in the city. For several years Mr. Marshall served on the police force of Tullahoma, and for seven years was a member of the board of aldermen. February 4, 1886, he was elected mayor for a term of two years, the first man elected to that position by the people of that city. He is a member of the Odd Fellows' Lodge, and the Cumberland Presbyterian Church, and is a Democrat. In 1865 our subject was married to Lucinda C., daughter of Robert Darwin, deceased, of Tullahoma. They have had twelve children, four of whom are dead: Mary L., born January 3, 1867; Emma C., March 14, 1871; William R., April 15, 1874; Lottie L., November 29, 1875; Harry L., March 12, 1877; Daisy L., May 20, 1879; Josiah M., May 18, 1881, and Minnie V., born June 22, 1883. The mother died in April, 1885.

H. P. Maynard, a progressive young citizen of Tullahoma, and member of the firm of Maynard & Sons, wholesale and retail dealers in general merchandise, was born in Wisconsin in 1864, and is the son of I. F. Maynard, a native of Vermont, and born in 1815. With his parents at the close of the war, our subject came to Tullahoma, where he has since resided. He acquired a good education in the city schools, and has added much thorough practical experience. For a number of years he was employed by his father as clerk, but in 1884 was admitted as partner, his father and brother Charles being the other members. For the last three years our subject has also engaged in manufacturing rubber stamps. Politically he is a Republican.

P. H. McBride, M. D., a well known physician of Coffee County, was born in that county, December 27, 1825. He is the son of William S. and Milly (Conwell) McBride, the former born at Lynchburg, Va., and the latter born at Abbeyville, S. C. in 1801. They died in 1879 and 1877 respectively in Coffee County, where he was a farmer. Our subject, one of ten children, after his school life ended, was for two years a blacksmith. Serving in the Mexican war for over a year, he fought at Vera Cruz and Cerro Gordo. Returning to Coffee County he worked at blacksmithing and mechanics until 1861, when he enlisted in the Sixteenth Regiment Tennessee Infantry (Confederate), and was for one year its flag-bearer. In 1862 he organized a company of cavalry, and was their captain at Richmond (Ky.), Fort Donelson, Murfreesboro, Chickamauga, and with seventeen men, August 24, 1862, fought a regiment for fifty-five minutes. On account of ill health he was discharged in 1863. After blacksmithing at Beech Grove until 1869, he studied medicine and began his successful practice in 1871. August 27, 1848, he married Elizabeth A. Emerson, a cultured lady, born July 26, 1826, in Kentucky. Their children are William H., Thomas M., Pleasant H., Burr H., Mollie C., and Demillion E., who died in 1862. A decided Democrat, he was State senator in the XLIV Assembly. He has been several times justice of the peace and superintendent of weights and measures in Coffee County. In 1848 he was elected colonel of the Forty-eighth Tennessee Militia.

S. J. McLemore, a pioneer of Tullahoma, was born in Lincoln County, Tenn., December 29, 1822, and is the son of S. J. and Martha (Whitaker) McLemore, natives of North Carolina. The father died in 1825 and the mother in 1880. Our subject reared on the farm, remained there until his marriage to Margaret J. Ward in 1841, when he removed to Nashville and entered the produce business. In 1851 he came to Tullahoma. He sold goods until the civil war and after the close of the same entered the livery business. In 1876 he began merchandising, continuing at that until January, 1886. His wife died in 1881. In 1883 he married Ruthea J. Gross, a native of McMinnville. By his first wife our subject has six children: William H., John C., S. J., Lamyra, Henrietta and Laura. Our subject is a member of the Methodist Episcopal Church South, and his wife of the Christian Church. He is a member of Tullahoma Lodge, No. 101, I. O. O. F., of which he is the only surviving charter member. He has served several times as mayor and alderman of Tullahoma. He is a Democrat.

D. E. Mead, merchant of Hillsboro, was born September 7, 1839, at Greenville, N. Y. His father, W. R. Mead, was born about 1798 and died in 1879, in Vermont. His grandfather, Adolphus, was in the Revolution. Liddie (Colwell) Mead, his mother, was born about 1800 in Virginia, and died in 1882 in New York. Living on his father's farm until twenty-two years of age he began business at Logansport, Ind., but was soon commissioned sutler under Gen. Rosecrans. After the war he engaged in merchandising at Tullahoma until 1866, when he began his present occupation. He has served almost three terms as magistrate at Tullahoma and Hillsboro. Justice of the peace, secretary and president of the county fair, are offices with which he has been honored, and also served as postmaster from 1870 to 1886. October 27, 1864, he married Mary A. C., daughter of Rev. R. P. Gannaway, of Montgomery County. They have six children: Carlton E., Cora L., Ethea L., Lydia, David E. and James W. He is a Democrat politically.

F. N. Miller, editor of the *Manchester Times* and a prominent citizen of Manchester, was born at Port Hudson, La., December 5, 1853, the son of Albert and Delilah (Saunders) Miller, the former born October 18, 1822, in Indiana, and the latter May 1, 1832, in Kentucky, and still living in Port Hudson, La. The parents were married about 1846. In 1861 the elder Miller enlisted in the Confederate Company E, Twenty-first Mississippi Regiment Infantry, and was killed in the battle of Chickamauga in 1863. He was a successful brick-mason. Our subject is the third of five children, and after a good academical education he served an apprenticeship as printer at Woodville, Miss., for four years. In 1869 he made a nine years' tour of western cities, working in Texas, Missouri, Kansas, Colorado, Iowa, Kentucky and Nebraska. Returning to Tennessee in 1879 he spent a year in Union City, and then bought a half interest in a journal called *Our Country* in Dresden. A year later he went to Nashville and entered the *Banner* office, and in 1881 came to Manchester and established the *Times*, which, through his constant attention and ability, has become recognized as one of the leading Democratic journals of this section of the country. Published at $1 per year, it has a circulation of 600. December 14, 1880, our subject was married to Alice J. Castleman, born March 16, 1856, in Weakley County, Tenn. She is a lady of intelligence and culture. The two children who were born to them (both daughters) died in infancy. Mr. Miller is a stanch Democrat and the columns of the *Times* are made to mirror his political faith. He is a member of the Methodist Episcopal Church, while his wife is a Missionary Baptist. He is United States commissioner of the middle district of Tennessee.

J. S. Moore, chancery court clerk and master in Coffee County, was born August 24, 1837, in Wilson County. He is the oldest son of Alfred and Elizabeth P. Moore, the former born in 1802, in Tennessee, and died in Manchester in May, 1862. The father of Alfred M. was a native of North Carolina. Our subject, living on the farm until twenty years of age, engaged then in merchandising until the war. Soon after enlisting in Company K, Twenty-fourth Tennessee Infantry, he was attacked by fever, but on his recovery entered Douglass' battalion, with which he served until near the surrender. In 1870 he left merchandising to take the office of county trustee, serving six years. In February, 1877, he received his present appointment from Chancellor Marks. December 21, 1865, he married Nannie, daughter of Henry and Effie Powers. Nine children were born to them, seven of whom are living. He is a member of the Christian Church, and believes in prohibition and Democracy.

Lewis B. Morgan, lawyer and chairman of the county court, was born in Lincoln County, Tenn., in 1834. He is the son of Smith and Abigail (Alexander) Morgan, natives of Tennessee. The former was born in 1806, and the latter in 1809. They are now residents of Fayetteville, Tenn., and are members of the Baptist Church. Until his seventeenth year our subject lived with his parents on the farm, and then learned the blacksmithing trade, following that, together with farming for a number of years. In 1856 he went to Kansas with a company of 365 men, joining them at Montgomery, Ala., for the purpose of pre-empting lands, and while there joined the pro-slavery party, and took up arms against John Brown and his supporters. In the fall of 1856 he returned to Fayetteville, and worked at his trade until the breaking out of the war, when he enlisted in Company F, of the Fourth Tennessee Regulars, Infantry, commanded by Baxter Smith. He was afterward transferred to Company I, Fourth Tennessee Infantry. He served throughout the war, the latter part of which he was a member of Jefferson Davis' escort. At the close of the war he returned to Fayetteville, and for two years engaged in cotton raising. At the end of this time he came to Tullahoma and engaged in farming until 1880, when he opened a blacksmith shop and for four years worked at his old trade. He was licensed to practice law in 1879, by Judges Williams and Quarles, and in January, 1886, was elected chairman of the Coffee County Court, followed by re-election in January, 1887. In politics he is a Democrat. Mr. Morgan was married in 1861, to Hannah, daughter of Dr. Thomas and Hannah B. (Moore) Anderson, of Coffee County, Tenn., and born in 1838. They have had born to them the following children: Cassandria V., born April 28, 1862; Calladonia D. (deceased), born April 28, 1866; Percy A., born December 30, 1868; Lewis B., August 12, 1872; Barclay in 1874; Frank A., in 1879, and Grace M., born in 1882. Mrs. Morgan is a member of the Old School Presbyterian Church.

William L. Norton, postmaster and a prominent citizen of Tullahoma, Tenn., was born in Bedford County, Tenn., November 27, 1839, and is the son of Dr. William Norton, a native of North Carolina, who was born March 2, 1801, and is the oldest physician within a radius of a hundred miles of Tullahoma. He came to Tennessee, and at an early date, a pioneer of Bedford County. He makes his home with his son, our subject. Mr. Norton was reared in Bedford County and acquired his education in the common schools. He worked on the farm until his twenty-eighth year, and then began merchandising at Normandy, Bedford County. In 1876 he removed to Tullahoma and continued his business for six years, when he retired and entered a dry goods house as salesman. Hs entered the Confederate service, joining Company E, First Tennessee Infantry (Turney's), and served throughout the war, receiving several wounds, at the second battle of Manassas, and at Gettysburg, the first necessitating the use of crutches for six months. October 12, 1881, our subject was married to Allie, daughter of Leonard Marbry, of Shelbyville, Tenn. They have two children: Earl L., born September 3, 1882, and Glyndon Pearl, born January 14, 1885. The mother is a member of the Christian Church. Our subject is a member of the A. O. U. W. and K. of H. fraternities. He was appointed postmaster under President Cleveland and assumed the duties of his office November 16, 1885.

E. W. Pearson, an enterprising farmer of Coffee County, was born in Bedford County, November 23, 1856. He is the son of Charles and Mary J. (Wells) Pearson, natives of Tennessee. The elder Pearson was a manufacturer in Bedford County until 1871, when he was a farmer and millwright in Coffee County, and finally at Sparta, Tenn., where he is still milling. Our subject, the oldest of seven children, after an academic training attended Eastman Business College, Poughkeepsie, N. Y. Returning home he began the lumber business for I. W. Whitman, of Boston, and in August, 1878, was employed by the Stone Fort Paper Company. In 1879 he became contractor for Hicks & Pearson, Flat Creek, then began mercantile business at Gallatin. Returning to Coffee County. he erected a lumber dressing and bending factory near Manchester, soon moved it to Tullahoma. After a year in saw milling he built at Normandy a spoke and handle factory. After a time as drummer for Smith, Gifford & Co., of Nashville, he settled on his present farm. He married Fanny Price, of Manchester, October 28, 1880. Born to them were Charles L., December 29, 1882, and James P., February 20, 1885. Mr. Pearson is a decided Democrat, and is school director and road commissioner. He and his wife are members of the Christian Church.

W. Ramsey, a farmer of Coffee County, was born April 3, 1823, in Warren County. Samuel and Pollie (Strowd) Ramsey, his parents, lived in Warren County. The elder, Mrs. Ramsey's father, was one of the first settlers of that county. Our subject is of English and Irish descent. November 30, 1852, he married Rachel Parker, by whom he had four children. She was a member of the Christian Church and died March 15, 1862. August 5, 1865, he married Ellen Norton, daughter of J. M. and Mary (Wilkinson) Norton of Coffee County, They have one child. Our subject taught school, having been educated at the school which was the predecessor of Franklin College, also at Irwin College in Warren County. He, his wife and three children are members of the Christian Church.

R. H. Richardson, merchant and a prominent citizen of Tullahoma, was born in Bradford County, Tenn., in November, 1846, the son of Thomas E. Richardson, whose death occurred in Coffee County in 1850. When our subject was about six months old his parents moved to Coffee County, settling near Duck River in the Fourteenth District, where he was reared and attended the free schools. He finished his education at Manchester College. January 1, 1868, he came to Tullahoma and entered a store as clerk, and in 1878 began business for himself, and has since conducted a successful general store. He was married in November, 1868, to D. D. Zell, daughter of F. M. Zell of Bedford County. To them three children have been born as follows: Linda M., born November 8, 1880; Warren W. December 31, 1882; Thomas E., born October 30, 1885. Mr. Richardson is a member of the Masonic order and he and his wife are members of the Methodist Episcopal Church South. In 1881 he served as recorder of Tullahoma, and in 1882 and 1884 served on the board of aldermen of the same place. In politics he is a Republican.

Emmett Russell, one of the young business men of Tullahoma, was born in Bedford County, Tenn., November 26, 1866, and is the son of W. F. Russell. He was reared in his native county, near Shelbyville, and attended the common schools. In 1881 he came to Tullahoma and entered the store of Carroll Bros. as clerk, and remained with them for three years, when he accepted a similar position with R. Wilson. October 1, 1886, he engaged in business for himself, opening a fancy and family grocery store, is meeting with success, and has built up a splendid trade. In politics he is a Democrat.

James H. Rutledge, merchant, and a prominent young citizen of Tullahoma, Tenn., was born in Lincoln County, Tenn., November 13, 1855, and is the son of Samuel Rutledge, a native of North Carolina. Our subject was reared on the farm, receiving his education in the public schools. In 1876 he began farming in his native county, and continued until 1882, when he came to Tullahoma, and with his brother, R. F. Rutledge, engaged in the grocery business; they have since added clothing, furnishing goods, and a boot and shoe stock. Mr. Rutledge was married in 1876 to Ida Roughton, a daughter of J. M. Roughton of Moore County. To them have been born four children. He and his wife are members of the Primitive Baptist Church. He carries a policy of $2,000 in the New York Mutual Insurance Company. Politically he is a Democrat.

Col. H. S. Sheid, farmer in Coffee County, was born January 27, 1827, in this county. His father, James Sheid, born May 22, 1776, in South Carolina, was a pioneer of Tennessee, in 1803 settling on the present farm of our subject, where he died April 18, 1856. The grandfather of Col. Sheid served with distinction in the Revolution, while other ancestors were the first settlers in Maryland. His mother, Sibyl (Robertson) Sheid, was born November 26, 1779, and died in 1868; she was of Irish, and her husband of Scotch descent. At seventeen our subject left the farm, and after four years as salesman at Pelham, he began his career of farming and trading uninterruptedly, excepting a short service for the Louisville & Nashville Railway. As captain of his recruited company, he entered Confederate service in November, 1861; he was soon elected lieutenant-colonel of the Forty-fourth Tennessee Infantry. After a disabling wound at Shiloh, he was honorary member of Gen. Hardee's staff for a while. He was State senator for two years. In 1848 he married Mary E., daughter of Gen. R. E. Patton of Grundy County. Their children are Mary C., Cara C., Ella C., Jessie L., Will F., James H. and Kittie W. A self-made man, Col. Sheid is a member of the Baptist Church and the Masonic order at Pelham, and politically is a Democrat and advocate of the "Temperance Alliance." His brother, Col. James M., of Alabama, was a prominent politician in Tennessee before the war.

Joel B. Smith, a pioneer of Tullahoma, was born in Nashville, Tenn., September 12, 1829, and is the son of Joel M. and Charlotte (Bateman) Smith. The father was a native of North Carolina, born in 1797, and died in 1861. He was treasurer of Nashville, and United States pension agent, appointed to that office by President Van Buren. He was also proprietor of the Nashville *Union*, the pioneer newspaper of the capital city. The mother was also born in Nashville in 1805, the daughter of Henry Bateman, an early settler of Nashville; she died in 1876. Both were members of McKendree Methodist Episcopal Church, of Nashville. Our subject was reared in Nashville, and educated by Prof. Alfred Hume. When twenty-one years of age our subject entered the pension office of his father, buying and selling land warrants. In 1852 he was sent to Tullahoma as agent for the Nashville & Chattanooga Railway Company. After two years here he began speculating in wheat, and became proprietor of the Lincoln House and Tullahoma Hotel. During the war he was special aid-de-camp on Gov. Harris' staff, and for a while occupied a similar position on the staff of Gen. Bragg. After the war he continued the hotel business until 1872, when he engaged in business with James G. Aydelott for eight years. At present he is bookkeeper and financial agent of the Tullahoma planing and saw mills. Our subject was married to Bettie Yell, daughter of Gov. Archibald Yell, the first governor of Arkansas, who was killed at the battle of Buena Vista, Mexico. She was born in Fayetteville, Tenn., in July, 1832. They have had eight children: William H., Archibald Y., Joel M., Frank K., Clinton, Lawson M., Lotta R. and Anna V. Our subject was the last mayor of Tullahoma before the war, and the first elected after the conflict, and has served several terms as alderman. He is a member of the Masonic order, and he and his wife both are members of the Episcopal Church. His son, Archibald J. Smith, is agent of the Nashville, Chattanooga & St. Louis Railway at Tullahoma, a director of the First National Bank of the city, and is one of the progressive and enterprising young citizens.

I. C. Stone, is of English, Irish and Scotch descent. His ancestors settled in the colony of North Carolina. Their descendants mainly kept pace with the tide of immigration to the new States and Territories. The paternal grandfather, Thomas Stone, probably of English, and Scotch origin, married Miss Sally Corder, of Scotch family, about 1789 in North Carolina on the waters of the Yadkins River, and not long after settled in Tennessee, where the father, C. H. Stone, was born December 22, 1796. The maternal grandfather, Joseph Allison, supposed to be partly of English and known to be partly of Irish origin, married Jane Donaldson, a native of Ireland, and settled in Orange County, N. C., about twelve miles northwest of Hillsboro. Here the mother, the youngest child of her parents, was born about 1793. Here she lived until maturity and obtained an ordinary education. The grandfather Allison had settled in White County and grandfather Stone had settled in Jackson County, Tenn., before 1818. At the home of the former in White County, the father and mother were married in October, 1818. They had five children of whom our subject was the fourth and the only son. In 1826 our subject was taken to Smith County, two miles from the mouth of Hickman Creek, and there reared, and received a country school education. The father was an independent farmer of ordinary education for frontier life. In June, 1846, our subject was a volunteer in the Tennessee Mounted Rifles in the Mexican war. After marching from Memphis, by Little Rock, Ark., Washington and Victoria, Tex., he arrived at Matamoras late in the fall. He was attacked by a severe case of measles at

Washington but kept up with the regiment. In Mexico, although not recovered, he was given night duty by J. F. Gardner, and in a severe norther, after standing his time, convinced that he would die if he staid on duty, he told the officer his condition, returning to camp in the face of the officer's threats, but the next morning he was so sick he was sent to the hospital and afterward discharged. Reaching home almost dead, April 19, 1847, he has never fully recovered. Having earned his money he entered Irving College, March 11, 1848, and graduated in June, but remained until September 19, 1851. Returning home he taught ten consecutive months there, then the same at Granville Academy in Jackson County almost immediately after. Three days after the close of this he entered the Lebanon Law School, Tennessee, and thus paid his way, and after fifteen months graduated. Soon after he began to practice law at Smithville, Tenn. In 1861 he entered the Southern Army, and served as a private mostly. He was one of Jefferson Davis' escorts from Greensboro, N. C., to Washington, Ga. He heard the statesman speak and saw much of him, and says he appeared as the great man and statesman only. November 7, 1864, he married, in Merriwether County, Ga., the beautiful and accomplished Sarah E. Faulkner, at her grandmother, Mrs. Martha Allison's residence, and returned to his command in seven days, and saw her no more until after he was paroled in 1865. She died May 19, 1866, at Manchester, Tenn. February 28, 1876, he married Mrs. Dora Huggins a native of Hanover, Germany, and whose maiden name was Shroder. Their five children are Ada Flora, Ella Jane, Iraby Claiborn, Sally and Albert Marks. Late in the fall of 1865, he located at Manchester. January 19, 1866, at their instance, he formed a partnership at Winchester to practice law in Coffee County, with Cols. A. S. Colyer and A. S. Marks, continuing with the latter until he was elected chancellor, and resuming with him when his governorship expired. Treated kindly by these gentlemen, he expresses gratitude to them. His practice with them has been a fair proportion of Coffee County business, while before it was moderate. He is a member of the Disciples of Christ, and a Democrat.

B. S. Stroud, a prominent citizen of Manchester, and register of Coffee County, was born in Warren County, Tenn., February 14, 1854. He is the son of B. S. and Nancy (Winton) Stroud, the former born in 1825 in Warren County, and the latter February 2, 1826, in Coffee County. Their deaths occurred October 12, 1853, and June 4, 1869, respectively. After their marriage, about 1844, the elder Stroud was farming and shipping and trading in live stock. He was politically a Whig. Our subject, one of four children, was educated at Manchester College, under

Rev. W. D. Carnes. After four years' prospecting in Texas and Arkansas, he returned to Manchester and engaged in the printing business, and soon bought a half interest in the Manchester *Guardians*. In the fall of 1878 he was made deputy clerk of chancery court, Coffee County. A year later, finishing an unexpired term of register, he was afterward elected to the office, serving two terms. December 17, 1879, he was married to Fannie Powers, born September 13, 1860, in Manchester, and educated at the college there. Their son, Horace. was born March 20, 1881. Mr. Stroud is a Democrat.

F. M. Taylor, farmer in Coffee County, was born January 16, 1845, in Tennessee. He is the son of Daniel and Mary (Angel) Taylor, the former born about 1813, in Tennessee, and the latter about 1811, and is still living, while her husband died in 1846. His grandmother, also Mary Angel by name, a native of Virginia, died in 1885, about one hundred years old. Leaving the farm, our subject served a year in Company A, First Tennessee Infantry, Not yet eighteen, he was discharged on account of his years, and after two years' teaching, he began his life of farming, uninterrupted except from January 1, 1883, to October 1, 1885, in general merchandising at Manchester. Blowing Spring, a natural curiosity, is located near his land. December 17, 1863, he married Lucinda J., daughter of Anderson and Rebecca Lambert. Their nine children are Andrew J., William T., Robert E. L., Sarah E. (died September, 1878), Albert S., Eliza J., Roger S., Lulu F. and Josephus Z. Mr. Taylor served two terms as magistrate, is justice of the peace, a member of the Masonic order and of the Separate Baptist Church. He is a Democrat. Mill Cove is a remarkably finely watered land and well situated.

Hon. John F. Thomas, real estate agent and a prominent citizen of Tullahoma, Tenn., was born in Lincoln County, Tenn., April 17, 1828. His father, Joshua Thomas, a native of North-Carolina, died while our subject was a small boy. At the age of eleven years our subject was bound out to Joshua Gore, but ran away and returned to his mother. His advantages were limited, but through his own efforts he acquired a good education, and when twenty-three years of age began teaching school. In 1851 he removed to Coffee County and taught a school on Duck River, with his residence in Tullahoma. In 1859 he became a member of the firm of Holland & Thomas, general merchants, Tullahoma, continuing until the war, when he went to Shelbyville, Tenn. On the Federal occupation of Tullahoma he returned home to again engage in business. In 1862 he was appointed postmaster at Tullahoma and held his commission until he was elected to represent Coffee County in the lower house of the Legislature in 1865. He was one of the twenty-one members who resigned their seats rather than vote for the "Disfranchise Bill." His constituency endorsed his course by re-election to the same position, but he was denied his seat. He was the first constable of Tullahoma and served several times as alderman. In 1867 he was appointed assistant United States revenue assessor, and later deputy United States revenue collector. He served as superintendent of public instruction of Coffee County, and was next appointed as United States store-keeper, and soon after gauger, holding these until 1883. Elected magistrate in 1883 he holds that office, together with notary public at present. Mr. Thomas was married in 1854 to Mary J., daughter of Thomas Blanton, of Coffee County. Both are members of the Methodist Episcopal Church North. Politically he has been a Republican since the breaking out of the war.

J. W. Waggoner, Esq., of Coffee County, born October 8, 1836, is the son of J. A. and Rebecca Waggoner, the former, born in 1806, died in 1848, and the latter born in 1806, died in 1883. Our subject is of German and Scotch descent. After continuing on the farm to care for his mother, he entered the Confederate service in 1862. After six months in camp with Capt. McCutchen's company, he was made steward and bookkeeper of the hospital at Chattanooga, afterward farming and teaching; in 1869 he took his present office of magistrate. He began the successful practice of law in Manchester in 1878. November 5, 1875, he married Eliza, daughter of Alford B. and Nancy Cook. Their six children are James H., William H., Nannie R., Addie M., Alice G. and James N. Mr. Waggoner is worth about $2,000, is a member of I. O. O. F. Lodge, and is at present chairman of the Democratic executive committee of the county. In 1887 he was appointed county clerk.

James F. Ward, member of the livery firm of Ward Bros., of Tullahoma, was born in Moore County, Tenn., in 1859, and is the son of Noah Ward, a native of Moore County. Reared on the farm of his parents, near Lynchburg, Tenn., our subject attended the public schools of the neighborhood. At the age of eighteen he began for himself, and came to Tullahoma in 1880, where he worked at different occupations until 1885, when, with his brother, R. H. Ward, he purchased the livery stable which they are now conducting. Politically he is a Democrat, and is regarded as one of the progressive young citizens of his adopted city.

E. M. Whitworth, a farmer of Coffee County, was born August 3, 1840, in Bedford County. His father, Benjamin F., was born in Marshall County January 8, 1814, and died October 12, 1876. In the fourth generation back were three brothers who were among the famous Jamestown, Va., settlers, and the next generation came to Tennessee. His mother, Minerva L. (Morton) Whitworth, was born in 1820, in Tennessee, daughter of Jacob and Annie (Fisher) Morton; the former was in the war of 1812 under Gen. Jackson. Reared on his father's farm until of age he then began his present successful career as farmer. From 1862 until the surrender he was a Confederate soldier. He married Hattie Johnson, of Rutherford County, February 1, 1860. Six children— four living—were born to them. His wife died November 8, 1874. June 25, 1876, he married Virginia Thompson, daughter of George Thompson, of English blood and a descendant of Pocahontas, through his grandparents, Burwell and Nancy (Wafford) Thompson. A Democrat in political faith, he has been elder in the Cumberland Presbyterian Church for twenty-five years, a member of the Masonic order, and served as superintendent of public instruction for two terms.

J. C. Winton, a well known citizen of Manchester, was born in Coffee County, Tenn., July 16, 1856. He is the son of John and Martha (Layne) Winton, both natives of Tennessee, the latter born about 1830. Engaged in mercantile trade at Hillstore before marriage, the elder Winton then became a successful farmer. He was a Democrat. Our subject, after receiving a good education, was engaged in farming, when in 1880 he entered the firm of Wooton & Hickerson, Manchester, which two years later became Wooton & Winton, our subject owning a third interest. They do a business of about $45,000 annually. March 17, 1883, he married Blanche, born in 1863, in Coffee County, daughter of Mayor P. C. Isabell of Manchester. Their children, Clark, Wooton and Edwin, are four, three, and one year old respectively. Politically he is a Democrat, and his wife is a member of the Christian Church.

S. H. Wood, M. D., a physician of Hillsboro, was born in Rutherford County, Tenn., November 13, 1824. His parents, Thomas and Susan (Baldridge) Wood, are natives of Orange County, N. C., immigrating to Tennessee about 1806. A blacksmith by trade the elder Wood moved to Hickman County, Ky., in 1827, remaining there to the close of his life in 1837. Reared on the farm, our subject began the study of medicine in 1844, and before beginning to practice in Bradyville, Tenn., attended Louisville University. Since 1866 he has had successful practice at his present home. He married Elizabath Lyon, of Rutherford County, in 1849. Born to them were John, May 14, 1850, and Mary F., June 10, 1852. His wife died July 10, 1853. He next married Mary J. Lyon, by whom he had seven children. Her death occurred May 2, 1872, at Hillsboro. In 1874 he married Sarah C. Huffar. They have six children. He is a member of the Christian Church. In 1861 he was State representative, and is now justice of the peace. Politically he is a Democrat.

J. D. Wooton, M. D., a leading physician of Manchester, was born in Warren County, Tenn., April 5, 1840. He is the son of Jonathan and Nancy (Hampton) Wooton, the former born in 1792, in North Carolina, and died in Warren County, in 1877; the latter born in 1802, in Kentucky, and died in February, 1886. The elder Wooton was a farmer, a soldier of the Revolution, and a consistent member of the Christian Church, while in political faith he was a Whig. His wife, a near relative of Gen. Wade Hampton, was a member of the Baptist Church. Our subject, the youngest of six children, received, besides his early education, a course at Burritt College. He soon after sold goods for his brother-in-law, Dr. A. B. Davis, at what is now Viola. In 1859 he entered the medical department of the University of Nashville, and graduated before he reached his majority. He soon enlisted as second lieutenant in Company D, Thirty-fifth Tennessee Regiment Infantry, Confederate Army. He served as assistant surgeon, and acted as chief surgeon at various times. He acquired considerable reputation for skill in his long service, surrendering with Johnston at Greensboro, N. C. A hip-joint amputation of the leg of a comrade might be mentioned as an example of his skill and the confidence of his fellows. He located at Viola, and for fifteen years was one of the leading physicians of the county. Since 1880 he has been equally successful in Manchester, engaging also in merchandising with a stock of $10,000, the care of his two plantations of 1,500 and 450 acres in Coffee and Warren Counties, the latter of which feeds a stock of about 100 young mules. He owns a half interest in the Duck River Paper Mills, the largest south of the Ohio River, and the only ones in Tennessee, that make wood pulp. He is a self-made man. July 20, 1865, he married Fannie Hickerson, a cultured lady, daughter of Judge W. P. Hickerson. They have two children: Wade H., aged seventeen, and Lillie, aged twenty. Mr. Wooton is a believer in the Christian religion, though not a member of any church, while in political faith he is Democratic. Mrs. Wooton is a member of the Christian Church.

J. W. Yates, merchant and a prominent young citizen of Tullahoma, Tenn., was born in Cincinnati, Ohio, August 24, 1855, and is the son of James and Mary A. (Walters) Yates, natives of England. The parents came to America in 1855, and our subject was born three days after their arrival in Cincinnati. The parents are members of the Episcopal Church, and are citizens of Coffee County, Tenn. Our subject received a good education in the public schools, and followed it with several courses in bookkeeping. In 1882 he came to Tullahoma and engaged in business, and is at present carrying a stock of about $18,000, and meeting with success. In 1882 he married Ida, daughter of Cooper Grandberry, a native of South Carolina. They have two children: Wilton Earl (born in 1884) and Lillie May (born in 1886). Politically he is a Democrat. His wife is a member of the Methodist Episcopal Church South.

DE KALB COUNTY.

Hon. James M. Allen, one of the prominent citizens of the county, was born September 25, 1822, at Allen's Ferry on Caney Fork, seven miles from Smithville, the county seat of De Kalb County, Tenn. He is the youngest of eleven children born to Jesse and Nancy (Walker) Allen, both of whom were natives of Virginia. The father settled in what is now De Kalb County in 1801, being one of the oldest settlers. He died in 1857, and the mother in 1840. Both were members of the Baptist Church. Our subject was reared on the farm and became interested in agriculture. His education was acquired in the country schools and at the Fulton Academy in Smithville, his present home. He studied law, and in 1876 was licensed to practice. His public services began as a constable in the Ninth District of his native county, which position he held for twelve years. He was justice of the peace for twenty-two years, was engaged in the mercantile business in Smithville for five years, and also served as deputy sheriff. In 1884 he was elected to the State Legislature. The term was so satisfactory to his constituents that he was re-elected in 1886. October 22, 1846, he wedded Elizabeth M., daughter of Spencer and Araminta (Eddings) Talley, of Statesville, Wilson Co., Tenn., who was born January 2, 1830. To this union ten children were born, two of whom died in infancy. The others: Emma (born in August, 1850, married A. T. Phillips, and died in April, 1878), Ada (born in 1853, married J. A. Marks, and died in August, 1878), Nancy W. (born in 1856, married W. D. Carnes, and now resides in Texas), Elizabeth J. (born in 1858, is the wife of W. B. Carnes, a resident of Trousdale County, Tenn.), James M. (born in 1862 and died in 1881), Jesse T. (born in 1865), William G. (born in 1868), John S. (born in 1872). The mother was a consistent member of the Christian Church, and died in September, 1886. Our subject is also connected with the same church, and is a member of the Masonic fraternity. He is a Democrat, and one of the county's most enterprising and worthy citizens.

Alvin Avant, attorney at law, of Smithville, was born in De Kalb County in 1856, a son of William C. and Nancy (Williams) Avant. The father is of French descent, born in 1822 in De Kalb County. His father, Benjamin Avant, was a native of Virginia, who immigrated to De Kalb County at an early date. William C. married and settled in the Twelfth District of his native county, where he is a prosperous and respected farmer and possessor of 300 acres of valuable land. His wife was also born in De Kalb County, of English descent. She is now sixty-two years of age. Of their eleven children, Alvin is the fifth. His early education was received at Fulton Academy in Smithville. At the age of eighteen he commenced the study of medicine under the care of Dr. J. S. Harrison. In 1873 he entered the medical department of the university at Louisville, Ky., graduating in March of the next year as M. D. For one year he practiced in Smithville, at the expiration of which time he abandoned medicine and took up the study of law. His preceptor was M. D. Smallman, now judge of the Sixth Circuit of Tennessee. Mr. Avant was admitted to the bar in 1879. The same year he was elected county attorney, serving two years. January, 1881, he became superintendent of public instruction, holding the office four years, declining another re-election. Since that time he has given his attention to his profession. In 1881 he entered into partnership with Hon. B. M. Webb and Judge J. S. Gribble, the latter withdrawing in 1883, the firm being known as Webb & Avant. Our subject is a talented, able lawyer, enjoying a good practice. He is a gentleman in the full sense of the word, and highly esteemed by a large circle of friends. He is a member of the Christian Church, and a Democrat. His parents belong to the Methodist Episcopal Church South.

J. M. Baker, a well known farmer of the Fourteenth District, was born March 31, 1830, in White County, Tenn. His parents were William H. and Lucinda (Erwin) Baker. The father was born about 1800 in Virginia, of English descent, a son of James and Mary (Holmes) Baker. The father was a brave soldier in the war of 1812. He died at Norfolk. His widow immigrated to Tennessee with her children, five daughters and one son. They located in White County, where she died in 1856. William H. died November 14, 1872. His wife was of Irish origin, a daughter of William and Jane (Dildine) Erwin. His maternal grandfather held a prominent position in the Revolutionary war. The subject of this sketch was raised on a farm, and educated at the Union Institute, De Kalb County, in which county he engaged in farming when about twenty-three years of age. Shortly afterward he moved to White County, where, about 1870, he was elected magistrate, and served two terms. In 1883 he returned to De Kalb County, and in 1885 was elected magistrate. He was married, in March, 1854, to Barbary, daughter of William and Zelpha Robinson. This union resulted in the birth of Mary Viola (the widow of S. Simrell), Elizabeth C., William R., Susan M. (the wife of M.

Davis), James M., Sarah Lena, Emma Florence, Barbary L. and Charles R. Mr. Baker is a worthy citizen and self-made man. He has accumulated his possessions by economy and judicious management. He has been an elder in the Cumberland Presbyterian Church since 1883. He is a member of the Masonic order and K. of H., and a stanch Democrat.

Col. J. H. Blackburn, attorney at law and solicitor of claims, was born in 1842 near Liberty, Tenn. He is the third of eight living children of William and Ann (Hayes) Blackburn, the former born in 1808 in South Carolina, and the latter in 1820 in Wilson County, Tenn. The father, when a young man, located near the present college home, Wilson County, where he afterward married. In 1846 he came to Liberty, and continued farming on his farm lately bought, and since 1885 he has lived in Dowelltown, in feeble old age. For fourteen years before the war he was constable at Liberty and mail contractor for six years. The mother is also living. Our subject was educated at Liberty, and in 1861 enlisted in the Federal Army, Company A, Fifth Tennessee Cavalry, and, though but eighteen, immediately elected captain. In November, 1864, he resigned his captaincy, and by order of Gov. Johnson raised a regiment at Liberty, known as the Fourth Tennessee Mounted Infantry, and served as colonel of the same until the close of the war, and was honorably discharged in August, 1865. He was in several battles, the most important of which were Nashville, Chattanooga, Snow Hill and Milton, where he defeated Morgan. He also cleared of guerrillas the counties of White, Putnam, De Kalb and Jackson by capturing Camp Ferguson, after which even rebel sympathizers felt more secure. He is said to have been in 217 engagements, in all of which he was successful. He was wounded at Liberty in a charge by a rifle ball in the left shoulder, and ruptured at Big Harbor. From the former effects he receives $10 a month pension. Since the war he has practiced some at Dowelltown, and now owns 500 acres of land in De Kalb County, and a house and lot at Dowelltown, and lost $12,000 in real estate on securities. In 1861 he married Jennie, daughter of Samuel and Cynthia (David) Barger, and born in 1844 in De Kalb County. Their two children are Caledonia (wife of R. Griffith) and Ulysses (a civil officer at Dowelltown). He is a Republican, and is adjutant of the G. A. R. at Dowelltown. His children are both members of the Missionary Baptist Church, and he and wife are professors though members of no church.

Prof. J. L. Boon was born two and a half miles north of Alexandria, in Smith County, in 1855. He is the fifth of nine children of Jas. N. and Sarah (Barry) Boon. The father was of English descent, one of the same family as the Kentucky pioneer, Daniel Boone. Jas. N. was born in Wilson County in 1817. He was raised and educated mostly in Smith County. By close application to study, he was enabled to enter the teacher's profession, which he followed in connection with farming. He was one of the most efficient and successful educators of that day. He married about his twenty-seventh year. The latter portion of his life was entirely devoted to agricultural pursuits. He accumulated considerable property and means, although he began a poor man. He died in 1886. His wife was born in Smith County about 1826. Both were consistent and esteemed members of the Christian Church. Five of the children are living, all members of the same church, one of them a minister in the Christian Church at Joplin, Mo. Prof. James L. received his early education at Alexandria. After teaching several years, attended two years at the National Normal University at Lebanon, Ohio, graduating in 1879, in the literary and business courses. In 1880 he began teaching at Alexandria, where he has since been. He is an intelligent, cultivated and thorough instructor, and is universally popular with both patrons and pupils. May 29, 1885, he married Miss Mattie, daughter of Lun and Jales Wood, who was born in 1865, and educated at Alexandria, completing a musical course at Cincinnati, and now teaches music in the Masonic Normal School. The Professor is a Democrat. He and his wife are active and influential members of the Christian Church.

Hon. J. W. Botts, attorney at law, is the son of Aaron and Sarah (English) Botts, and born on Smith Fork, De Kalb County, in 1830, one of eight children, five of whom are living. The father, of English ancestry, was born in North Carolina, and died in 1860 about sixty years of age. Left an orphan when a child, he was reared and married in his native State, and soon after removed to Kingston, Tenn., and afterward to De Kalb County, as it is known now. He settled at the mouth of Helton Creek where he resumed his business of hatter, until about 1831, since when he lived in Alexandria until his death. He was tax collector one term and twice defeated as candidate for sheriff by only five and seven votes respectively. The mother, a native of North Carolina, died in Nashville about 1865. Our subject was educated at Alexandria, and at Gainesboro under Hon. William DeWitt, now of Chattanooga. In August, 1850, he married Cynthia, daughter of Dr. Thomas J. and Nancy Sneed, of Alexandria, where Mrs. Botts was born. Seven of their thirteen children are living: Robert A., undertaker at Alexandria; Lizzie, wife of Andrew Kersey; Sarah, wife of John Argo (deceased), of Nashville; John E., with the St. Louis Railway; Norman and Earnest, both at Dixon Springs, and Charley. Mrs. Botts died in August, 1883. February 23, 1884, he married Nora, daughter of Louis W. and Sarah Manning, of

Smith County. They have one child, Lena. A carpenter and cabinet-maker during his earlier years, our subject was for the fifteen years preceding the war, magistrate and mayor of Alexandria. In 1862 he entered Allison's squadron of cavalry and was in active service in Kentucky and Middle Tennessee until July, 1863, when he was captured near Alexandria and taken to Nashville, then Louisville, Camp Chase, Ohio, Philadelphia, and finally to Fort Delaware, where after seventeen months' imprisonment he was paroled, taken south and soon made his way home, mostly on foot, after nearly four years of service and suffering. In 1868 he was licensed to practice his present profession in which he has a large practice in Cannon, De Kalb, Smith and Wilson Counties, in the circuit, and also the federal courts. An ardent Prohibitionist, he refused the candidacy for the Legislature, because he was expected to work against submitting the question of prohibition to the people. Although reared a Whig, he has been a strong Democrat, first voting for Pierce. He is a member of the Y. M. C. A., and is the oldest male citizen of Alexandria.

W. G. Bratten, farmer, was born in 1823, in Smith County (now De Kalb), the oldest of two sons of Henry and Nancy (Givan) Bratton, the former of Irish origin, born in Maryland about 1798, and the latter of Scotch origin, born in the same State about the same year. The mother's parents came when she was a year old to Nashville by boat after reaching the Ohio River, and were three weeks in cutting a road to Liberty, which was named by her father in honor of their old home in Maryland, as he was something of a leader in the forty families which came there. The father's people were among the number, and about 1820 they were married, and in 1823 the father died. Joel Bratton, an ancestor, was one of the Mayflower Pilgrims. The mother afterward married Osburn Munlacks. Their three children were Mary, Sarah and Joseph. She died about 1831 near Liberty. Our subject, reared by his uncle, and with little education, married when twenty-two, Caroline, daughter of James and Lucretia Groom, of North Carolina, and began farming in Cannon County. After eight years he sold and bought his present farm near Liberty. Mrs. Bratton was born in 1826 on our subject's present farm and died in 1859. But one of their eight children is living, Thomas G. Our subject married Martha, daughter of James and Nancy (Branch) Young, in Wilson County, where she was born in 1832. Their four children are Annie, Nettie, Herschal A. (who has considerable artistic genius), Geneva and Minnie. Beginning life with but a horse, saddle and bridle, our subject now owns a fine residence on his two equally fine farms of 300 acres, and is in vigorous life even at sixty-four years of age. Formerly a Whig he is now a Democrat; has been a Mason since twenty-two years of age. His whole family are members of the Missionary Baptist Church.

N. M. Brown, of Brown & Donnell, millers, was born in De Kalb County in 1856, the youngest son of six children of Isaiah and Rachel A. (Wood) Brown, both natives of Virginia. The father, of Dutch origin, was born in 1818 and died in 1885. He was the son of John Brown, a tanner. Isaiah was reared and married in his native State, and in 1854 removed to De Kalb County, Tenn., where he worked at his trade as cooper. The mother, born in 1823, is still living with our subject and is a member of the Methodist Episcopal Church. Our subject was educated at Alexandria, and at the early age of thirteen began life as an engineer, to which he has since devoted most of his time. He has had a varied practice under different persons and is a skillful engineer. During 1881 he was a merchant, but since then he has been in charge of the Alexandria mills, in which he has an interest and which are doing a profitable business. He and his brother are also owners of a saw mill in Warren County. June 18, 1885, he was married to Julia, a daughter of John and Julia Rollings, of Alexandria, where Mrs. Brown was born in 1861. She is a member of the Methodist Episcopal Church. They have one child, Maud. Mr. Brown is a Republican, casting his first vote for Gen. Garfield.

J. L. Colvert, retired merchant, was born in 1828 in Culpeper County, Va., the son of William I. and Harriett (Weedon) Colvert. The father, born in the same county in 1791, was a farmer and a soldier in the war of 1812, on duty in his native State. In 1828 he came to Warren County, Tenn., thence to Alabama for a few years, and about 1840 returned to Cannon County, Tenn. He finally settled in De Kalb County in 1848 and bought a home of 150 acres, where he lived the greater part of his life. He died in Nashville in 1859. The mother, born in 1801 in Fairfax County, Va., is still living, receiving a pension for her husband's services in 1812. Our subject, one of seven children, came to Tennessee when an infant, and was reared and educated in Cannon County. At the age of sixteen he served a year's apprenticeship in a tannery, then farmed a year, and in 1848 sunk a tannery in De Kalb County with his brother as partner. In April, 1846, he married Johanna Matthews, born in Cannon County in 1830. Their two children are Mary E., wife of S. D. Blankenship, and Harriett. In 1852 he engaged in farming and merchandising besides tanning. In 1854 he sold his tanyard and store and established a store in Smith County. After six months here he bought 500 acres in District No. 14 and farmed for three years. He then moved to Nashville, where he ran a lumber and woodyard and as contractor built Carroll and Wharf Avenues, rebuilt Market Front and built a sewer from the river to the Maxwell House. He also owned a third interest in a wholesale and retail grocery on Market Street. In 1862 he returned to De Kalb County and in 1864 settled in Smithville, where the next year he began merchandising at which he was engaged until January, 1886. He then sold to his son-in-law, Blankenship. Mrs. Colvert died in 1855, and in January, 1858, he married Martha M. Tysee, born in De Kalb County in 1839. Mr. Colvert is the oldest continuous merchant in Smithville and a most successful one. In 1873, besides his Smithville business, he was in the grocery business in Nashville. In politics he is a Democrat, first voting for Fillmore. He is a Royal Arch Mason and a member of the Missionary Baptist Church, while his wife belongs to the Methodist Episcopal Church.

J. R. Corley, a well known farmer and stock raiser of the Fourth District, was born in De Kalb County in 1848. He is one of seven children of John and Elizabeth (Upton) Corley. The father was born in Virginia in 1802, and immigrated to De Kalb County when a young man. He was a farmer. His death occurred in 1875. His wife was born in Smith County in 1816 and died in 1880. Our subject received his education in the common schools of De Kalb and White Counties, and attended the Cumberland Institute. At the age of nineteen he began clerking in the dry goods store at Temperance Hall, where he remained five months. The next four years were spent in Putnam County in same business. He then returned to his native county and gave his attention to farming. He has been very successful, and owns 185 acres of highly cultivated and improved land. He is a stanch Democrat; cast his first presidential vote for Horace Greeley. He is a member of the Missionary Baptist Church, and respected, worthy citizen. In 1869 he married Sarah F., daughter of James A. and Eliza Scruggs. Mrs. Corley was born in Smith County in 1846. She is a member of the Methodist Episcopal Church. To their union have been born George S., James. R. (deceased), Carrie L., William M. and John R.

Maj. W. G. Crowley, an ex-judge and attorney at law of Smithville, was born in Smith (now De Kalb) County in 1830. His parents, John J. and Elizabeth Crowley, were both natives of Virginia. The father was of Scotch-Irish descent, a farmer by occupation. He married in his native State and in 1830 came to Tennessee by way of the Cumberland River. He died in Smith County in May of the same year, when but twenty-two years of age. His wife was born in 1810. Her second marriage was with Mr. Peter Adams, who is also dead. Mrs. Adams died in 1866. Our subject was the only child, and but one month old when his father died. When a mere lad he was ambitious to gain information, as his step-father was poor, and there being but little benefit derived from public schools, his advantages were indeed limited. He labored and saved a few dollars which enabled him to enter school. At the age of sixteen he began teaching in the neighborhood. He attended school at Alexandria as well as other schools at different places, and in this way obtained a good practical education. After his schooling was finished he was in debt $500 and taught school and paid it. In 1850 he commenced reading law under guidance of Col. S. H. Colms of Smithville. In March, 1851, he was admitted to the bar, and immediately entered the profession, buying his law books on a year's credit. He first formed a partnership with Samuel Turney in De Kalb County business, and at the same time a partnership with Col. S. H. Colms in the Cannon County practice. He soon had a lucrative practice. July 4, 1853, he married Rebecca, daughter of Martin and Polly Foutch, who was born in 1837 in De Kalb County. Their union resulted in the birth of ten children: Mary E., wife of Judge W. W. Wade; Martha E.; Martin A., who is clerk and master of the chancery court of De, Kalb County; John B., a farmer and miller; Jessie Frances, wife of John B. Tubb, a lawyer of Smithville; William L., a farmer; Kate, wife of W. B. Foster, a merchant of Smithville; Pleasant C.; Prudence and Leslie (deceased). In June, 1861, Mr. Crowley enlisted in the Twenty-third Tennessee Infantry (Confederate Army), and at the organization of the regiment he was appointed sergeant major. He was in the battle of Shiloh, in which he was severely wounded April 6, 1862, by a canister-shot, just above the left knee. He was taken to Corinth and afterward to Jackson, Miss., in a helpless condition. September 7, 1862, he reached home, greatly to the surprise of his family, who believed him to have been killed at Shiloh. In 1863 he moved to the western portion of De Kalb County and taught a subscription school until hostilities ceased. In 1866 he returned to Smithville and resumed his practice in partnership with Col. John H. Savage, afterward with Joseph Clark and M. D. Smallman, now circuit judge. In 1872 our subject was elected chancellor of the Fifth Division of Tennessee, Col. Colms being one of his competitors. In 1878 he was re-elected. Judge Crowley is now engaged in the law practice and has many friends. He is also one of the county's eldest native citizens. He has been unusually prosperous in life, considering his opportunities and will do well in his profession. His residence is a half mile east of Smithville on the Sligo Ferry Turnpike. He has been a member of the Christian Church since 1860. Previous to the war he was a Whig, voting the first time for Fillmore in 1852. He is now a Democrat.

Dr. Thos. P. Davis, one of Alexandria's most respected citizens, was born in Smith County, August 31, 1858. He is the youngest of ten children of Benjamin and Kittie (Whorley) Davis. The father was born in North Carolina about 1817, and moved to Tennessee when a young man; afterward married and settled in Smith County. He was one of the most substantial, enterprising and industrious farmers in the section. His death occurred about the close of the late war. His wife was a native of Virginia and came to Tennessee with her parents; she died when the Doctor was an infant. Of her children eight are living. Her mother lived to the unusual age of one hundred and two. Her father was a soldier in the Revolutionary war. Mr. and Mrs. Davis were members of the Methodist Episcopal Church South. Our subject was raised by the elder members of the family, receiving his literary education at the country schools and Alexandria. In 1876 and 1877 he read medicine with Dr. E. Tubb, and entered the medical department of the Vanderbilt University, graduating in 1879. He immediately returned to Alexandria and began to practice. He has received an extensive and liberal patronage, and is now recognized as one of the leading physicians of the county. April 29, 1880, he wedded Miss Lillie, daughter of John and Martha Luckey. To their union one son and two daughters have been born: Elsie, Lear and Tho. Vernon. The Doctor is enterprising and much esteemed. He is a stanch Democrat; gave his first presidential vote for Gen. Hancock. Dr. and Mrs. Davis are consistent and respected members of the Christian Church.

D. W. Dinges, a notary public, and a leading business man of Alexandria, was born in 1836, in Warren County, Va., the youngest of five children of Wm. M. and Clara P. E. (Lincoln) Dinges, both natives of Virginia. The father was born about 1810, of Scotch-Dutch descent, a son of Mortica Dinges. He was a blacksmith, and spent his entire life in his native State, where he died in 1837. His wife was born about 1814, and is living in White County. She moved to Tennessee soon after her husband's death. She has been three times married; is a consistent member of the Christian Church. Our subject received rather limited educational advantages at Sparta. He taught school about three years. In 1861 he enlisted in Company K, Sixteenth Tennessee Infantry, serving principally in Tennessee, West Virginia and South Carolina. In 1862 he took part in the battle of Perryville, and was captured near Barbersville, Ky.; in a few hours was paroled, returned home and about three months later joined the Eighth Tennessee Cavalry under Gen.

Dibrell. He participated in the battle at Sparta, was again captured and paroled, and returned home after serving his country gallantly for three and a half years. In 1865 he moved to Alexandria and began merchandising, in partnership with W. H. Lincoln, the firm being known as Dinges & Lincoln. They did a flourishing business. In 1872 he purchased Mr. Lincoln's interest, and in 1881 R. B. Floy became a partner. They discontinued their business about three years later. In 1885 he established the firm of D. W. Dinges & Co., which has an extensive trade. It is one of the best general merchandise houses in this place, carrying a stock valued at about $5,000. During his commercial career he sold as high as $40,000 worth of goods in a year. In 1883 he erected the first livery stable in the town; it is large, well stocked and prosperous. He began life with little or no capital, but by industry and good management has accumulated a considerable amount of this world's goods, being one of the wealthiest citizens of the county. He owns 450 acres besides other valuable property. He is a firm Democrat, casting his first presidential vote for John C. Breckinridge. In 1884 he represented the Fourth District, in the Democratic Convention at Chicago. He is one of the directors of the Bon-Air Coal, Lumber & Land Company; was formerly a member of the I. O. O. F. and is a strong advocate of general education. March, 1873, he married Miss Norah, daughter of John and Bettie Crutchfield, formerly of Wilson County. Mrs. Dinges was born in 1854. Of their seven children five are living: Dibrell, Paulean, Clara, E. Turner, and Donnell C. Mrs. Dinges is a member of the Methodist Episcopal Church South.

James A. Donnell, United States commissioner of internal revenue for the middle district of Tennessee, and an influential citizen of Alexandria, was born August 13, 1834, in Wilson County. He is the eldest of two children of Allan and Casandria H. (Britton) Donnell. The father was a native of Gifford County, N. C., born in 1806, of Irish ancestry, a son of Adlia Donnell, a native of North Carolina, whose father came from Ireland. Allan came to Tennessee about 1832, and a year later married and located in Lebanon, where for some time he taught school, afterward engaging in the mercantile business at the same place, then at Center Hill and finally at Commerce, where he died in 1838. He was a man of ability and influence, successful in all his undertakings. His wife was a daughter of Lanie Britton, a native of East Tennessee, and an early settler of Smith County. Mrs. Donnell was born in 1813 and died in 1876. Both were members of the Cumberland Presbyterian Church, highly respected by the entire community. The subject of this sketch was educated in the common schools in Wilson County. At the age of twenty he went to Missouri, where for two years he engaged in farming and stock raising. He returned to Wilson County. At the outbreak of the civil war, he enlisted in Company A, Seventh Tennessee Infantry, was in Virginia and all the great battles. He was captured at Gettysburg, Penn., July, 1863, and taken to Baltimore, then to Point Lookout. After seven months' imprisonment he was exchanged and joined the army in the Southwest. In the spring of 1864 he was sent to Tennessee to look after some absentees of the original command; he was again captured and took the oath of allegiance. In February, 1866, he married Mrs. Nannie M. Ward, a native of Alabama, by whom he had one child, Robert G. Mrs. Donnell died in 1867. The same year he wedded Miss M. E., daughter of William and Mary Swann, who was born in Wilson County in 1844. Four children were born to this union: Jane Annette, Minnie C., Mary E. and Ann Lou. After living in Smith County Mr. Donnell returned to Wilson County in 1872, and resumed his farming. In 1878 he removed to Alexandria and purchased a half interest in the flouring-mills, now owned by Brown & Donnell, and since that time has been engaged in his present business. For one year he served as constable of the Twelfth District of Wilson County, and in October, 1886, was appointed by Judge Howell E. Jackson to his present office. He is a strong advocate of general education, and is trustee of the Masonic Normal College. Previous to the war he was a Whig, casting his first presidential vote for M. Fillmore, in 1856. He is now of the Democrat party. For nearly twenty years he has been a Mason. He and his wife are esteemed and earnest members of the Methodist Episcopal Church South.

E. J. Evans, commercial traveler for Weel, Connell & Riddle, dry goods, shoes, clothing, etc., Nashville, was born in 1850 in the District of Columbia, and now resident of Smithville. He is the son of John G. and Lucinda (Vick) Evans. The father, born in 1819, in De Kalb County, Tenn., is the son of Joseph Evans, a native of Maryland, who, when a boy, came to Tennessee and settled where Liberty, De Kalb County, is located, among the very earliest white settlers. John G. had learned the carpenter trade under his father, and after his marriage in 1844, he settled in Liberty. In 1861 he moved to Dry Creek, and in 1881 to Smithville, where he was elected to his present position of register in 1866. His wife, born in 1822, in De Kalb County, is still living. Our subject, educated in Liberty, began reading law in 1872 under Hon. J. B. Robinson, and was admitted in 1873. The following year he was elected county clerk of De Kalb County, and served one term. In 1879 he established a dry goods store in Smithville, and after two years sold out and became traveling salesman for Settle & Kinnard, and two years later for Pigg, Manier & Co., then twelve months after for Tracy & Co., with whom he remained until he was employed by his present firm. In August, 1875, he married Virginia, daughter of Watson and Sarah Webb, and born in Warren County. Their children are Sherrell J., Herschel, and Sarah. Mr. Evans has two residences, three store buildings and a livery stable in Smithville. He is a fine salesman and business man. In politics he is a Republican, and is a member of the K. of H. order. His wife is a member of the Baptist Church.

Capt. J. T. Exum, merchant, was born December 4, 1842, in Smith County, Tenn. He is the son of Kinchen D. and Elizabeth (Allen) Exum, the former born in 1821, in Smith County, and the latter in 1821, in Wilson County. His grandfather, William, a native of North Carolina, was one of the earliest pioneers of Smith County, where he died. Reared on a farm, our subject was educated at Cumberland Institute, in White County, and soon enlisted in the Federal Army as private, then corporal, then second lieutenant and recruiting officer for the Fifth Tennessee Volunteer Cavalry. He was soon promoted to first lieutenant, and in 1862 was made captain at Nashville. In March, 1865, he resigned his commission and for about two years was engaged in merchandising at Laurel Hill, Tenn. Then after about seven years in Buffalo Valley, Putnam County, in the same business, he was made United States storekeeper and gauger for the Fifth Internal Revenue District. In 1881 he was deputy United States marshal, under Marshal Tillman, and a year later was appointed United States commissioner for the middle district of Tennessee, but resigned in 1883. For four years previous to 1884 he was chairman of the Republican Executive Committee of the Fourth Congressional District. After a year's travel in the West he returned to De Kalb in 1886 and engaged in merchandising for a short time. In 1868 he married M. S. Maddox, who died in 1876, in which year their two children, James R. and John D. died also. In 1882 he married Alice McDonald, who lived but about seven months after. She was a member of the Methodist Episcopal Church South. Mr. Exum is a Republican and a member of the I. O. O. F. Lodge.

T. W. Fitts, a farmer and stock dealer of the Tenth District, was born March 4, 1823, in Smith County. He is the youngest of six children of Wootson and Tabitha (Winfrey) Fitts. The father was born in 1787, near Halifax, Va. He was lieutenant of a company in the war of 1812, was under command of Gen. Jackson at New Orleans; he came to Tennessee about 1822, and died near Eddyville, Ky., about 1850. The mother was born about 1787 near Petersburg, Va., and came to Tennessee after her marriage. Our subject had but limited educational advantages, but is a man of good practical understanding and business qualifications. In 1840 he married Miss Isabell Foster, who was born about 1812. She is still active and robust. To this union eight children were born of whom six are still living: Sanford (deceased); Jasper Newton; Durinda, now Mrs. Taylor; Golden; Nancy, afterward Mrs. Winfrey (deceased); Delia, now Mrs. Williams; Sarah, now Mrs. Hayes, and Martin. Mr. Fitts and children are members of the Methodist Episcopal Church South. The first year after marriage Mr. Fitts rented; he then bought an old soldier's right to 640 acres; the following year he purchased 200 more, and finally became the owner of 1,300 acres of excellent land. Besides what he has given his family, he still has 1,000 acres, cultivated and improved, located in Cove Hollow, on the Smithsville and Temperance Hall road, three miles east of the latter place. He has always been a successful farmer and stock raiser, and made money rapidly, but has had security debts to settle, amounting to about $10,000. He has traveled quite extensively through thirteen States of the Union. He met with a severe accident before the war, which prevented him from entering the service. While riding a race horse, the animal fell, dashing Mr. Fitts' head against a rock. Thirteen pieces of bone were taken from his forehead by Dr. Gray of Nashville, who received $1,000 for the operation. Although Mr. Fitts is not a church member, no man in the community has contributed more liberally to religious institutions and charity. He built and donated one church, and has given two building sites for others. During the war he supported seven families besides his own. He lost considerable stock and $8,000 in Confederate money. He has owned some of the most famous horses in the country. He raised "Dock Alvin," "Tom Hal," "Elizabeth Hill," and partially raised "Queen Ariel." He paid $1,000 for "Elizabeth Johnson" in Utah. When only two years old she won a famous race in Mississippi.

Hon. J. J. Ford, attorney at law, was born in De Kalb (then Smith) County November 22, 1822. He is one of ten children of Daniel and Mary (Fite) Ford, the former of Irish origin. The father, born about 1794 in South Carolina, was the son of Daniel Ford, Sr., of Virginia, who became one of the earliest settlers of Tennessee, when Daniel, Jr., was but a small boy. He settled in Smith County near what is now Temperance Hall, where he remained until his death. With ordinary education in his youth, Daniel, Jr., married about 1818 and spent his life in Smith and De Kalb Counties. He was an able man and served as magistrate and constable several years. He died in 1864. The mother, a native of Tennessee and of Dutch descent, died in 1836. She was a daughter of Rev. J. Fite, an early Tennessee settler from New Jersey, who spent the early years of his settlement in a cane tent on Smith Fork, and who with his brother cut a road through the cane to Nashville. He made some money by dealing in the skin and flesh of bears. He was a Baptist minister for nearly sixty years and a historic character of early Tennessee. With no educational advantages our subject began the blacksmith trade when fifteen years old, and, when of age, purchased the property of his overseer and continued until 1859, having in the meantime served as magistrate six years. He was elected to the memorable General Assembly of 1859–60, in which he so distinguished himself that Judge R. Caruthers and other able jurists persuaded him to enter his present profession, in which he has since so well succeeded. He is the oldest practitioner in Alexandria. He again represented De Kalb County and in 1877–78 De Kalb, Wilson and Trousdale Counties, making in all seven sessions. He is one of the foremost criminal lawyers with a practice second to none, extending into all the adjacent counties, Nashville, Tuscumbia, Alabama and Cincinnati, Ohio. For eight years he was an equal partner with Judge Cottrell, of Lebanon, and is an able and honorable man. In March, 1846, he married Mary E., daughter of Aaron and Sarah M. Botts, natives of North Carolina and among the earliest settlers of Tennessee. Mrs. Ford was born in 1826 in what is now De Kalb County. They have one daughter, Adelia Jane, wife of J. H. Blackburn, of Alexandria. Mr. Ford, although sixty-five years of age, has the vigor of his earlier life, a fact which he attributes to his care of himself and abstinence from liquor and tobacco. Always an active Democrat, his first vote was for Clay. Of considerable wealth, he owns 500 acres, 100 of which are in Wilson County. Mrs. Ford is a member of the Cumberland Presbyterian Church.

H. D. Foust, of Foust & Jones, carriage manufacturers at Alexandria, was born in Wilson County in 1845, a son of William E. and Betsey (Luster) Foust. The father, born in Wilson County about 1818, was the son of William Foust, a native of Germany. William E. was married in 1844, and was all his life a blacksmith and carriage manufacturer in his native county. He was sheriff of the county four terms. The mother was born in the same county about 1829, and both were members of the Missionary Baptist Church. Educated at Lebanon, our subject at fifteen entered Company A, in the Forty-fifth Tennessee Infantry, and operated in the extreme South for about eighteen months, when, under the conscription act, he was rejected on account of age. He then returned home, and soon after joined Gen. Forrest's command and afterward Gen. Morgan's on his Indiana and Ohio raid, but was captured on reaching the Ohio River.

He was soon recaptured, however, and went home and south to join Gen. Wheeler at Dalton, Ga., with whom he remained until his surrender at Raleigh, N. C., and then returned home. In December, 1865, he married Catherine, daughter of W. A. Robinson of Lebanon, where she was born in 1844. Their six children are living: William E., Jr., Bettie, Henry D., Malinda, John L. and Etta. Mrs. Foust, died in 1880, and in 1881 he married Mary J. Lannon. They have one child, Lillian. Mr. Foust was a blacksmith and carriage-maker at Lebanon for several years, when after some time in Shop-Springs he removed to Alexandria and entered the present firm, which is the only large enterprise of the kind in the county. For seven years Mr. Foust was marshal of Lebanon. He is a firm Democrat, first voting for Seymour. He and wife are members of the Cumberland Presbyterian Church. His first wife and two children were members of the Missionary Baptist Church.

Hon. John A. Fuson, an eminent practicing physician and surgeon of the Fourth District, was born in 1815 in Champaign County, Ohio. He is the third of seven children (three living) of James and Martha (Sneed) Fuson, both of whom were natives of Patrick County, Va. The father was of English descent, born in 1792. Two years after marriage he moved to Champaign County, Ohio, where he engaged in farming, occasionally preaching. He died in 1863. The mother was of French origin, born about 1795, and died in 1885. The subject of this sketch received a limited education in the common schools of his native county, remaining with his parents until he was twenty-two, when he came to Tennessee, and settled at Alexandria, De Kalb County, where for three years he studied medicine under direction of Dr. Thomas J. Sneed, at the expiration of which time he began practicing at Liberty, in 1842. In 1847 he married Martha L., daughter of John W. and Lucy W. (Flowers) Allen, near Rome, Smith County. Mrs. Fuson was born in White County, in 1826, and became the mother of eleven children. The eight surviving ones are James; Lucy Jane, wife of Chas. McCaverty of West Virginia; John A.; Elizabeth, wife of Isaac N. Fite; George M.; Wm. Francis; Josephine, wife of Chas. Williams, and Joseph Benjamin. In 1856 the Doctor purchased a farm in the Fourth District of De Kalb County, and moved his family there. He has always had an extensive patronage; is one of the most skillful and popular practitioners in the section. He has accumulated considerable property and wealth, but has lost heavily by security debts. He owns 300 acres of well cultivated and improved land. His son, William Francis, is now taking a large portion of practice off the Doctor's hands, and has been successful and prosperous. In 1854 the Doctor was elected to represent De Kalb County, in the General Assembly of 1855-56. He was elected in 1865, for 1865-66. He was senator for De Kalb and Wilson Counties one term. His official career was satisfactory and highly creditable. He was the author of the Small Offense law. Previous to the war he was a Whig, casting his first presidential vote for Wm. H. Harrison in 1840. He was a stanch Union man, and now a Republican. He and his wife are members of the Missionary Baptist Church, and the five eldest children are Methodists.

Pat Geraty, a merchant of Dowelltown, was born in 1832 at Castle Bar, County Mio, Ireland. He is one of six surviving children of a family of nine born to John and Catherine (Conway) Geraghty. The father was born in 1795, same place where Pat first saw the light. Early in life he was a carpenter, afterward a farmer. He died about 1880, in the vicinity in which he had always lived. The mother was born about 1798, in the same county, at Clare, and died in 1883. Our subject was educated in the common schools of his childhood's home. After attaining his majority he came to America, landing in New York, where for six or eight months he lived in the suburbs. He then went to Canada; for six months he was engaged in farming. He moved to Rock Island, Ill., in 1857, and became a United States soldier, serving as such eight years. In the late civil war he was in Company G, Fourth United States Cavalry. He took part in the famous battles of Perryville, Murfreesboro, Lookout Mountain, Kennesaw Mountain, Atlanta and in numerous skirmishes. He was honorably discharged at Gravely Springs, Ala., March 13, 1865, from the army in which he had so bravely fought for the preservation of the stars and stripes. He was very much enfeebled in health, from the hardships and exposures common to a soldier's life, and remained delicate several years. Immediately after the restoration of peace, he established himself in the mercantile business in Clear Forks, Cannon County, Tenn., where he remained fourteen years, when he sold out and moved to Donelltown, again embarking in the same business. About 1870 he married Sallie Melissa, daughter of John and Julia (Knights) Hale, of Cannon County. Mrs. Geraty was born in 1842, where her marriage took place. This union has resulted in the birth of Catherine, Julia Ann and John. Mr. Geraty is a self-made man; he landed in New York without a penny, but a stout heart and firm determination. He now owns a valuable farm of sixty acres Dowelltown, and his store has a first-class stock, valued at about $3,500. He is a worthy citizen, and much respected. He is a Republican, and cast his first presidential vote for A. Lincoln, in 1864. He is a member of the G. A. R., Floyd Post, No. 16. He is a Roman Catholic, and his wife a Missionary Baptist.

Prof. H. L. W. Gross, principal of the Masonic Normal School, Alexandria, and the associate principal, Prof. James L. Boon, are well and favorably known throughout the country. Prof. Gross is the son of Milton and Clara P. C. (Lincoln) Gross, and a native of White County. The father was of German descent, born in Sullivan County, Tenn., and a son of Jacob Gross, a native of North Carolina and pioneer settler of Sullivan County, where he was engaged in farming and gunsmithing. He died about 1880. His widow, who is ninety-five years of age, enjoys the best of health, is robust and vigorous as a young woman, and never had a serious illness in her life. Milton went to Sparta when about eighteen years of age, and engaged in the saddler's trade. He married about 1838, and died about 1854. His wife was born in Hardy County (now West), Va., in 1815; is still living at Sparta. Her father was of English ancestry, and a cousin to Abraham Lincoln. Prof. Gross was raised on a farm near Sparta, where he received his early education. After attending Burritt College at Spencer, lacking only a term of five months, finishing the course, and two years' teaching in Alexandria, he entered the Vanderbilt University in 1877; took the first collegiate course, finishing the university course in English. He returned to Alexandria and entered upon the duties of his present position, which he has discharged to the satisfaction of all, winning the confidence and esteem of the community. In 1886 he made an extended tour through the North for mental improvement. He attended the two weeks' session of the eminent Dr. Parker's, and visited the Cincinnati schools. He is a Democrat, and for fourteen years has been a faithful member of the Christian Church.

William T. Hale. This gentleman is a merchant, lawyer and *litterateur* of Liberty; was born in 1857 at Liberty, De Kalb Co., Tenn., and is one of three boys of C. W. L. and Malissa (Overall) Hale. He received his education at the Masonic Academy, at Liberty, and has been a close student at home. At the age of seventeen he began business life as a partner with his father in the mercantile firm of Hale & Son, and has continued in the same business, in connnection with his profession, which he entered in 1884, having at the same time found leisure enough to indulge his literary tastes. In 1876 he married Lula Lewis, who was born in 1860, and who was the daughter of G. W. and Sophie (Allen) Lewis, of Lebanon, Tenn. He has two children: Charles and Herbert. Since finishing his studies under James A. Nesmith he has built up a flattering practice in De Kalb and adjoining counties. He is best known as an author, being the author of "Vernon Wild," a novelette, which had a considerable local reputation, and of the two poetical volumes, "Violets," and "Swallow Flights"; while his ephemeral pennings for the press would fill volumes. His poems are dainty, finished and full of feeling, and have been praised by Joaquin Miller and Gerald Massey. Below are given a few quotations, taken at random from his poems:

"I think this thing as proper quite
　As anything e'er writ or spoken—
No golden calf should loom unbroken,
　When overshadowing prostrate Right!

"And I think the prettiest thought God had
　When he made all of earth but the human,
Was that which led him to brighten the world
　With woman, beautiful woman."

"Am I not one who know's Love's worth?
　Lo! my hands are empty, although my days
Were spent in search of the joys that seemed
　Far in the front and hidden from gaze.
"While smiles of Luna from realms aloft—
　Gleams they seemed from the land of bliss—
Settled down over the scene as soft
　As mouth over mouth in a kiss."

In 1886 Wm. Hale was a candidate to represent his county in the General Assembly, but was defeated on account of his prohibition principles. He is a Democrat politically, and cast his first vote for W. S. Hancock for President.

D. T. Harrison, druggist, was born in 1856 in De Kalb County, the son of John and Mary (Kelley) Harrison. The father, born in Ireland, came to America with his parents when eight years old, and when eleven left home and in some way settled in White County, Ill. He married in White County and learned the tanner's trade. He was in the late war about one year, and in 1865 came to Smithville and bought a tanyard of W. H. Magness, at which he continued until 1880, when he was elected register. He served four years and in 1886 moved to his present residence near Temperance Hall. His wife was born in White County, and died in 1881. Their six children were James B., in Harrison, Ark., a merchant; our subject, Cora, John H. (deceased), Robert S., and William (deceased.) Our subject was educated in Fulton Academy and Pure Fountain College, Smithville. In 1879 he and his brother, J. B., established a tobacco factory at Smithville, and since 1882 when his brother withdrew, he has been running it independently. He manufactures about 15,000 pounds annually. In March, 1886, he bought a drug store of his brother and has since carried on both lines of business, and is a promising young business man. Politically he is a Democrat and is a member of the I. O. O. F., Pure Fountain Lodge, No. 217, Smithville, and a member of the Cumberland Presbyterian Church.

Isaac Hayes, an enterprising farmer of the Fifteenth District, was born November 3, 1810, in Georgia, and brought when an infant to De Kalb County by his father. He is the third of nine children born to John and Martha (Young) Hayes. The father was born in South Carolina. He was for some time a resident of Georgia, then Alabama, and finally came to Tennessee, locating where De Kalb County now is. He died when Isaac was a mere boy. Our subject was educated in the subscription schools of the county. He remained with his widowed mother until his marriage. In 1832 he wedded Miss Elizabeth McGinniss, who bore him seven children: Mary, Lucinda, Richard, Elizabeth, Isaac, and twins, all of whom are dead. The mother departed this life January 29, 1852. He married Miss Eliza Helen Robinson, December 23, 1852. This union resulted in the birth of eight children, of whom are living John R., Richard, Kizzie, Rebecca, Mary, Isaac and Eliza. After farming on rented land for some time, Mr. Hayes purchased fifty acres on Holmes Creek, and now owns 500 acres of valuable land, well cultivated, located on the Lancaster and Smithville road, eleven miles from the latter place. His property was greatly damaged by the late war, almost ruined, but he now has it in fine condition, and is one of the healthiest localities in the county. Mr. Hayes is a stanch Democrat, and a worthy, respected citizen. He is interested in the advancement of educational affairs, and a generous contributor to all charitable and beneficial enterprises.

R. F. Jones, merchant, was born in 1857, in Alexandria, De Kalb County, Tenn., one of three children of Jas. and Martha P. (West) Jones, the former, probably of English origin, and born near Alexandria about 1825, and the latter of like ancestry, and born in the same vicinity about 1835. The father was engaged in merchandising the most of his married life at Alexandria. At the battle of Chickamauga he received a shot from which he died in a few hours. The mother died near Alexandria in 1884. Educated at Alexandria and Liberty our subject began clerking in 1874 for William Vick, at Liberty. After nine years here, he established himself in his present business at Dowelltown in which he has been most successful. In 1878 he married Eliza, daughter of Isaac and Nancy Whaley, of Liberty, where she was born in 1857. Their two children are Mattie and Frank. Our subject is a Democrat, first voting for Hancock. He and his wife are members of the Methodist Episcopal Church.

Prof. T. B. Kelly, A. M., LL. B., president of Pure Fountain College, Smithville, was born in Columbia, Maury Co., Tenn., in 1852. His parents were Thomas J. and Elizabeth (Hardwicke) Kelly. The father was of Irish descent, born March 9, 1810, in Dickson County,

Tenn., where his father, Thomas Kelly, located after emigrating from Ireland, about 1800. Thomas J. married in 1838, and about 1844 moved to Columbia, where he established a queensware store which he managed successfully until the year of his death, 1861. His first wife was of French extraction, born in 1817, in Buckingham County, Va. She died in January, 1854. There were eleven children, only two of whom are living: George M., a farmer of Maury County, and our subject. Prof. Kelly received his early education in his native county, at Jones' academy. In 1873 he entered the University of Tennessee at Knoxville, remaining five months. In the winter of 1873 he began the study of law at Nashville, his preceptor being Hon. F. C. Dunnington. He also assisted in the office of the clerk of the supreme court. In the fall of 1874 he entered the law department of Cumberland University at Lebanon, graduating the following June. He located in his native town. In September, 1876, he commenced teaching in the Lewisburg Institute. For fifteen months he was assistant principal, at the end of which time he entered upon the practice of his profession in Lewisburg. Later he became principal of the institute. In 1881 he was called to serve in same capacity in the high school at Columbia, remaining two years. In 1883 he took charge of the college of which he is now president. The attendance is an average of 150 a year. In June, 1886, Cumberland University conferred upon him the degree of A. M. He is one of the most thorough, intelligent and respected instructors in the county. He is highly esteemed by both patrons and pupils. January 4, 1876, he married Miss Ella Steele, daughter of Prof. P. W. Dodson, the efficient teacher at Dover, Stewart County. Mrs. Kelly was born in 1855 in Williamson County, Tenn., and is the mother of three living children: Pauline, Thomas B. and Inez. Prof. Kelly is a K. of H. and an F. & A. M. He and his wife belong to the Methodist Episcopal Church South. His wife is a lady of superior culture and is considered one of the best pianists in the South.

Rev. Ira W. King, pastor of the Cumberland Presbyterian Church, and a prominent citizen of Alexandria, was born December 3, 1819, in North Carolina. He is the fourth of eight children born to Prof. Tho. H. and Ann (Harris) King. The father was a native of Virginia, born about 1790, of Scotch-Irish descent, a son of Henry King, also a native of Virginia. Tho. H. was reared and liberally educated in his native State. He went to Rockingham County, N. C., when a young man, where he married about 1810. In 1820 he moved to Williamson County, Tenn., and in 1832 located in Smith County. A few years prior to his death he went to Jackson County. He died in 1865. Many years of his early life were spent as a school teacher in North Carolina and Tennessee. He served as deputy sheriff and captain of militia for several years. The latter portion of his life was devoted to agricultural pursuits. His wife was born in North Carolina about the same year of his birth and died in 1873, a member of the Cumberland Presbyterian Church. Our subject was mostly educated at Castalian Springs, Sumner County, and at Lebanon, where he married in June, 1843, Miss Deborah, daughter of Jackson N. and Elizabeth (Whitson) Brown. Of the ten children born to this union, four are living: Dr. Robt. W., of Gordonsville, Smith County; James D., a merchant of Wilson County; Emily C. (wife of John A. Gwaltney, of Smith County), and Mary J. (wife of A. J. Sullivan, a merchant and farmer, of Wilson County). Mrs. King was born in Wilson County in 1819 and died in 1874. February 16, 1876, our subject married Miss Tobitha L. Roundtree, who was born and reared in Rome, Smith County. Mr. King first settled in Wilson County as a teacher, two years later moved to Granville, Jackson County, where he taught about three years, after which he began farming. In 1850 he located at Gordonsville, Smith County. He spent two years in traveling for the American Tract Society, and since that time has been engaged in ministerial work and looking after his farm. In 1856 he was elected trustee of Smith, serving with so much satisfaction, that he was twice re-elected, making six years in all, and though strongly solicited to continue, declined. In 1866 he became superintendent of public instruction, which office he held two years. From 1856 to 1864 he had charge of Ebeneezer and Union Hill Churches. In 1864 he was appointed by Gov. Johnson as sheriff of Smith County to reorganize civil government. Judge McCleain appointed him clerk of circuit court but he declined to serve. All of his political positions were filled with credit and distinction. In 1875 he sold his farm and moved to Wilson County, purchasing property in the Fourth District. In 1884 he sold out and located at Alexandria. December, 1885, he assumed the pastorate of the Cumberland Presbyterian Church, and still holds it. For many years he has worked faithfully in this noble cause. He is greatly beloved by his entire flock. For thirteen years he had charge of a congregation in Wilson County. Since August, 1886, he has been connected with the drug business, in partnership with his nephew, Ira W. King, the firm being known as Ira W. King & Co. He owns a commodious dwelling in Alexandria, with pleasant surroundings. He is a total prohibitionist, an old and prominent member of the Masonic order, and a strong advocate of general education. His wife and three children are members of the Cumberland Presbyterian Church.

James H. Kitching, a prosperous farmer and stock dealer of Alexandria, was born May 28, 1840, in Smith County. He is the fourth of fourteen children of Thomas and Mary (Davis) Kitching. The father was born in Smith County in 1809, a son of James Kitching who was a native of North Carolina. He immigrated to Tennessee at an early date stopping first at the top of Bledsoe's Lick, Sumner County, afterward located in Smith County, near the head of Kitching Creek which was named for him. He was one of the first settlers in that section, where his life was passed. Thomas was reared in his native county, where he married about 1831. He is a substantial farmer, well and favorably known. His wife was born in North Carolina about five years later than her husband. Both are faithful members of the Methodist Episcopal Church South. They raised a large and intelligent family; all lived to maturity. There are now three sons and four daughters. The subject of this sketch was educated in the common schools. In September, 1862, he enlisted in the United States Army, in Company B, Fifth Tennessee Cavalry. He took part in the battle of Stone River and many skirmishes. In August, 1863, he was discharged on account of disability, but in the fall of 1864 enlisted in Company G, Fourth Tennessee Mounted Infantry, as a private, but soon became second lieutenant and was detailed to take command of a force to restore order and enforce civil law in Smith County, in which capacity he served until the close of the war, when he resumed farming. February, 1870, he married Mattie E., daughter of Robert and L. D. Dowell, of Alexandria. Of their seven children, two sons and three daughters are living: Robert D., Jesse, Ella, Hallie, and Edith. Mr. Kitching remained in Smith County until 1879, when he moved to Alexandria. Farming and trading has always been his occupation. He owns a farm, and a comfortable house in town. For some time he has been trustee of the Masonic Normal School. He served one year as constable of the First District of DeKalb County. He is a Republican; rather conservative. He cast his first presidential vote for A. Lincoln in 1864. Since 1868 he has been connected with the Masonic fraternity, and a consistent member of the Methodist Episcopal Church since his seventeenth year, of which church Mrs. Kitching is also a member.

John M. Mason, a well known farmer of the Fifteenth District, was born October 22, 1819, in North Carolina, and came to Smith (now De Kalb) County in 1827. He was the seventh of thirteen children born to Wiley and Nancy (Bénsy) Mason. The father was born January 31, 1785, in Virginia. He served in the war of 1812, and was mustered out at the close of the war at Norfolk, Va. He moved to Caswell County, N. C., and from there to Smith County in 1827. He was a man of considerable intelligence, well versed in the Bible, in which he took a deep interest. He was also thoroughly posted on all political subjects. His death occurred in 1840. His father was a native of Wales. Mrs. Nancy Mason was born October 4, 1783, and died in North Carolina. Our subject had but limited educational advantages until after his majority. He attended the common schools of the county. He worked as an overseer and manager for several years. He then farmed on rented land until he was able to purchase forty-two acres near Riddleton, Smith County. From time to time he has added to his place, and now owns 400 acres, well cultivated and improved, and a house and lot in Smithville. For nine years he has been magistrate, and trustee of the Earl Academy two years. From 1859 to 1880 he was engaged in the tanning business, also in general merchandising, always meeting with success. He is a life-long Democrat; cast his first presidential vote for Martin Van Buren. In 1849 he married Miss Eliza, the youngest of six children of Nicholas and Sarah (Compton) Smith. Mrs. Mason was born September 4, 1833, in Wilson County. This union resulted in the birth of Mary E., afterward Mrs. James Turner (deceased); Robert Wiley and Adelia (deceased). Mr. and Mrs. Mason are respected and earnest members of the Missionary Baptist Church.

R. C. Nesmith, attorney at law of Smithville, was born in De Kalb County in 1837, a son of William A. and Elizabeth M. (McDowell) Nesmith. The father is of Scotch-Irish descent, born in 1799, in York District, South Carolina. In 1809 with his father, William Nesmith, immigrated to Blount County, E. Tenn. A year later they went to northern Alabama, where for a number of years they lived among the Cherokee Indians. In 1824 he came to De Kalb County, and three years later married. He settled in the Nineteenth District, where he engaged in wagon making and farming. There were but two wagons in the county when he settled there. He has lived in various portions of the county, but for past few years has made his home in Smithville. From 1859 to 1862 he was county tax collector. He is the oldest living man in the county, and until the last seven years was unusually vigorous and active. He is rather eccentric, witty and humorous. He is now quite feeble. His wife was born in Wilson County in 1803, and died April, 1885. She was the mother of eleven children, of whom nine are living, our subject being the seventh. He attended the common schools but a short time. At the age of seventeen he began teaching, continuing four sessions. In 1862 he enlisted in Company G, Forty-fifth Tennessee Infantry. He was engaged in the battle of Murfreesboro, was captured and made prisoner of war. He was retained at Camp Douglas three months, then exchanged at City Point and rejoined his command at Tullahoma. In August, 1863, he returned home. After the war he farmed. In January, 1867, he began the study of law, under direction of his brother J. A., and April of the same year was admitted to the bar. In partnership with the above mentioned he began to practice. In 1870 he became a partner of Judge Robert Cantrell, now of Lebanon; the firm existed two years and changed to Nesmith & Smallman, who is now Judge M. D. Smallman, of McMinnville; the past two years he has had no partner. He is one of De Kalb County's most talented and eminent lawyers, and has a fine chancery practice. He is a stanch Democrat, and a Master Mason. In 1865 he married Miss Mary J., daughter of James and Mary McDearmon, who was born in Wilson County in 1839. Mrs. Nesmith is an earnest and active member of the Methodist Episcopal Church South.

W. W. Patterson, one of the leading business men of Alexandria, was born in Smith County in 1843, the second of eight children of Samuel F. and Catherine (Smith) Patterson. The father was of Scotch-Irish descent, born in Wilson County in 1801, and the son of Samuel Patterson, a native of Ireland who immigrated to America at about the age of sixteen. He settled in Wilson County, where he married and spent the remainder of his life as a tiller of the soil. Samuel F. was first married to Miss Lucy Waters, by whom he had two children, one living. His second union was with Mrs Compton, *nee* Coe; to them one child was born. About 1835 he wedded the mother of our subject, who was born in Wilson County about 1812, and died in 1876. In 1832 Mr. Patterson moved to Smith County, where he was a prosperous farmer. He served several years as constable and magistrate. He died in 1884. Both were members of the Cumberland Presbyterian Church. Six of their children are living. Our subject was educated in the country schools. In 1861 at the age of seventeen he entered the Confederate Army, Company F, Twenty-fourth Tennessee Infantry. He took part in the battle of Shiloh, and was the only one of nine guards who escaped uninjured. After twelve months' faithful service he was discharged on account of ill health. In 1863 he married Miss J. E., daughter of Willis and Martha Dowell, of Smith County, where Mrs. Patterson was born in 1844. Of their five children, one son died in infancy, and one son and three daughters are now living: Etta J., wife of R. M. Bone, postmaster at Alexandria, Nora, Mattie C. and Robert W. With the exception of one year spent in Arkansas, our subject remained with his father until 1875. He then located at his present place of residence. The farm contains 250 acres of cultivated and improved land, pleasantly situated near Alexandria. He has for several years been engaged in mercantile business; four years ago became interested in a drug house, the firm name being R. M. Bone & Co. Mr. Patterson is a man of enterprise and ability, to which the accumulation of most of his possessions are due. He is a charitable and worthy citizen and an ardent Democrat, casting his first presidential vote for H. Greeley in 1872. He is a Mason. Himself and family, with the exception of one child, are consistent members of the Cumberland Presbyterian Church.

S. B. Prichard, a respected agriculturist of the Nineteenth District, was born in Wilson County in 1820. He is the third of eight children of Benjamin and Mary A. (Campbell) Prichard. The father was born April 16, 1792, in Virginia, and came to the portion of Tennessee now known as De Kalb County in 1808. He was in Col. James Tubb's regiment, under command of Gen. Jackson, at New Orleans. His death was caused by rheumatism, which he contracted during the war. The exposure was very great. He made his way home from New Orleans on foot, his only provision until he reached the first settlement being one quart of parched meal; after that was consumed he happened to come across a squirrel, which he brought down with his gun. He and his companion endured all sorts of hardships and privations. He died August 3, 1872. His grandfather Prichard came from England to Virginia at an early day. Mrs. Mary (Campbell) Prichard was born March 10, 1796, in Wilson County, and died December 5, 1867. Her grandfather was a native of Ireland; he settled in Wilson County not far from Statesville when the country was an unbroken canebrake. He ran away from Ireland, agreeing to let the captain hire him out, when he reached America, to pay his passage, and accordingly he was engaged by a Mr. Campbell. The young Irishman had never seen a negro. One evening he was sent to a room by himself; soon afterward a colored female servant was sent in with a small bellows to start the fire and scare the boy. With many grimaces and gestures she began her work. The lad, thinking she was his satanic majesty in female form, seized the bellows and dealt her a severe blow on the head. He died about 1826, and Mr. Prichard's father died in 1830, both of whom our subject remembers. S. B. Prichard received a somewhat limited education in Wilson and De Kalb Counties. July 10, 1845, he married Miss Matilda Robinson, who died December 31, 1876. They had six children: Columbus, James, Thomas J., Jorden Lee, Nancy J. (now Mrs. Bass), Elizabeth (now Mrs. Fite). March 5, 1878, he married Miss Malissa Ann Dunnaway, who was born August 4, 1845. Three children have blessed this union: Lucretia Eller, Lucinda Della and Martha Jane. Mr. Prichard commenced life with no capital, but by energy and good management, has accumulated considerable means and property. He first worked at the carpenter trade, and was soon able to buy his present place of residence. His farm consists of 225 acres, all productive and cultivated, located on Disma Branch, eleven miles from Smithville and seven miles southeast of Alexandria. He was a Whig, but since the war has been a Democrat. For many years he has been an earnest member of the Methodist Episcopal Church South, having professed religion when only fourteen years of age.

James T. Quarels was born in Wilson County in 1836, the fourth of seven children of William and Eliza (Hopkins) Quarels, both of whom were natives of Virginia, where they were married about 1835. They came to Tennessee, locating in Wilson County, where the remainder of their lives was spent in farming. The father died about 1844, the mother in 1881, both esteemed members of the Methodist Episcopal Church South. Our subject was educated in the country schools of his native county. About his twentieth year he married a native of De Kalb County, Miss Caroline, daughter of Jonathan and Priscilla Doss, who died about a year and a half after her marriage. In 1860 Mr. Quarels married his sister-in-law, Miss Darthula, by whom he had six children. Those living are Nora (wife of T. C. Peck, of Wilson County), James D., Zora and Maud. In 1861 Mr. Quarels entered the Confederate Army under command of Capt. Bass, and served about one year, when he was discharged on account of disability, and returned home. In 1863 he again enlisted under Capt. Reese. He was engaged in the battles of Murfreesboro and Briston; after six months' service he again went home. In 1864 he sold his property in Wilson County and purchased a portion of his present farm in De Kalb County, where he moved. The farm now contains over 100 acres of cultivated and improved land. He has always been an industrious man; had it not been for misfortunes through generosity, he would be worth more than double his present possessions. He is a firm Democrat, and cast his first presidential vote for John C. Breckinridge. He has been a Mason twenty years. His wife is an earnest member of the Missionary Baptist Church.

Hon. John B. Robinson, attorney at law of Smithville, is a native of De Kalb County; was born in 1835. His parents were Alexander and Rachel (Barnes) Robinson. The father was of English descent, born in Cumberland County, Va., about 1804. He came to Tennessee in 1824, locating in Smith (now De Kalb) County. Two years later he settled in the Fourth District. He taught school several sessions and then married. He was surveyor of the county a number of years. He owned 150 acres of fine land at the time of his death in 1867. His wife was born in

De Kalb County, in 1804. Her parents, George and Bridget Barnes, were among the pioneers, settling in the county before 1800. Mr. and Mrs. Robinson had nine children, six of whom are living, our subject being the fourth. He was educated in the common schools. There were no public schools and his parents were unable to send him to college. After he attained his majority he began teaching, which he followed for several years. The last sessions he was in Illinois. In 1855 he commenced the study of law on his own responsibility, but advising with Judge Robert Cantrell, now of Lebanon. In 1858 he was admitted to the bar. When the war broke out he became one of the boys in blue. In June, 1862, he enlisted in Company I, Sixty-ninth Illinois Volunteer Infantry, for ninety days. After serving his time he returned home. He went to Jefferson County, Ill., at Mt. Vernon, and returned to Smithville in 1864. After the restoration of peace he resumed his practice and in 1867 was elected attorney-general of the circuit of Tennessee, and served two and a half years. At two different periods T. W. Wade was his partner; for twelve months he was with Nesmith. For twenty years our subject has been one of the leading and most prominent lawyers in the county. His honor has never once been questioned. His forte is in chancery practice. He is a Republican; previous to the war he was a Whig, casting his first presidential vote for Millard Fillmore, in 1856. He belongs to the I. O. O. F. Lodge, No. 217, Pure Fountain, of Smithville. In February, 1869, he married Miss Julia, daughter of H. B. and Julia G. McDonald, of Smith County, where Mrs. Robinson was born in 1849. Their union was blessed with six children: Mary, Alice, Harry, John, David, and William Loyd Garrett. Mrs. Robinson is an earnest member of the Methodist Episcopal Church South.

J. E. Robinson, a farmer living near Temperance Hall, was born October 31, 1832, in Smith (now De Kalb) County. He is the fifth of seven children of John and Eliza (Harris) Robinson. The father was born about 1799, near Nashville, and was brought when an infant, by his father, to the farm where his son now resides. The country at that time was an unbroken canebrake, and infested by many Indians, who were treacherous and troublesome. There were also great quantities of wild animals, the bears often coming about the place which Stephen Robinson purchased. He was one of the most extensive stock raisers in the country, especially blooded horses. Our subject was educated in the common schools of De Kalb County, and attended one session of Irwin College, Warren County. December 14, 1854, he married Miss Margaret E., daughter of Nicholas and Sarah (Compton) Smith. Mrs. Robinson was born November 8, 1831. Their union resulted in the birth of nine children: Charley E., John Morgan, Sallie E. (now Mrs. Martin), Willie, Sidney, Mattie. Those deceased are Lillie Dale, Lizzie and Henrietta. Mr. Robinson, at the time of his marriage, was in such close pecuniary circumstances that he had to borrow the money with which the license was bought. He farmed on rented land and finally purchased. He accumulated considerable property, but it was mostly destroyed by the war, with the exception of a house and lot near Temperance Hall. A few years since he inherited some property from his wife, and by hard work he has become the owner of 254 acres, all of which is well cultivated and improved. He was trustee of his church about six years, and superintendent of the Sunday-school. He was a Whig, but since the war has gone with the Democratic party. He has given his children good educational advantages, and is deeply interested in all school matters, and the advancement of all beneficial enterprises. He is a liberal contributor to religious and charitable institutions. Four of his children belong to the Methodist Episcopal Church South and Mrs. Robinson to the Missionary Baptist.

Louis E. Simpson was born in 1840, in Smith County, and was the son of Thos. and Atlanta (Ellison) Simpson, and one of seven children, five living. The father was born near Frankfort, Ky., in 1806, was a son of Jas. Simpson, an early pioneer of Kentucky, and of Irish ancestry. Thomas lost his father when a boy, and at about fifteen years of age came with his mother to Smith County, where he remained until his death in 1862, one of the wealthiest farmers in Smith County. His wife, to whom he was married in about his twenty-fourth year, was born in West Virginia, about 1804, and died in 1868, a member of the Missionary Baptist Church. At nineteen he left home and school, and entered Company F, Twenty-fourth Tennessee Infantry, under Col. Ellison, and was in all Gen. Bragg's engagements from Shiloh to Mission Ridge, where he was captured and taken to Rock Island, Ill. In 1865, by the earnest petition of his mother to Vice-President Johnson, he was paroled by President Lincoln, and returned home in a feeble condition from rheumatism, and after his recovery resumed work on the farm. In January, 1867, he married Nancy J., daughter of Willis and Martha Dowell, of Smith County, where she was born in 1846. Their eight children are William T., Mattie, Charles W., James L., Eddie, Della B., Robt. D. and Horace L. Mrs. Simpson died in June, 1885, a member of the Cumberland Presbyterian Church. He has remained on the old homestead almost entirely, until 1884, when he bought a farm near Alexandria, where he moved for the purpose of educating his children. Since 1886 he has lived in Alexandria, one of her wealthiest citizens, owning about 540 acres of land, part of which in Smith County has been in the family for several generations, and but a very small part of his wealth has been inherited. He is an active Democrat, and first voted for Seymour. He is a member of the Cumberland Presbyterian Church.

J. J. and W. R. Smith, of the firm of Smith Bros., the well known proprietors of a general store of Smithville, established their house in the fall of 1877. They are the sons of William S. and Catherine J. (Tippitt) Smith. The father was of English-Irish descent, born in Wilson County, Tenn., in 1823. His father, John Y. Smith, was a native of Virginia, and located in Wilson County when a small boy. He died in 1865. William S. married in 1842, and settled in the Eleventh District, where he became the possessor of 175 acres of land. He was a farmer and stock raiser. In 1876 he moved to Trousdale County, near Hunter's Point, where he now owns 250 acres. His wife was also born in Wilson County in 1826, of English-Dutch origin. They had eight children, seven of whom are living, our subjects being the second and third. J. J. was born in 1845, and was educated at the New Middleton Academy, under the management of Profs. J. P. Hamilton and N. J. Finney. At his majority he began teaching, first near Statesville, Wilson County. In 1873 the two brothers took charge of the Fulton Academy, at Smithville, remaining two years. They commenced with twenty pupils, and closed with one hundred and thirty; the average was eighty-six, which is the largest average of any school ever taught in the county. It was the only time that the county ever received the Peabody fund. In January the brothers went to Sparta, where for fifteen months they had charge of the Nourse Academy, at the end of which time J. J. returned to Smithville, resuming his professional duties in the institute. After another fifteen months, each teaching in a different place, they formed a partnership in Smithville, in the mercantile business, in which they have since been engaged. J. J., while teaching in Smithville, August 26, 1873, married Lollie, daughter of James T. Hayes. Mrs. Smith was born in De Kalb County in 1854. They have one child, Effie. W. R. Smith was born October, 1848, in Wilson County, and educated at Shop Springs. At the age of twenty-one he began teaching at Round Top, in his native county. In 1873 he joined his brother, as above mentioned. At Sparta, August 25, 1875, he wedded Miss Cannie Hayes, a sister of Mrs. J. J. Smith. To their union Aubery has been born. As instructors these gentlemen were all that could be desired. As merchants they have been successful, receiving an extensive and liberal patronage, which has been gained by their honorable transactions and courtesy. In politics, both are Democrats. J. J. is a Royal Arch Mason, and W. R. has taken the first degree. Both families are members of the Missionary Baptist Church.

A. P. Smith, attorney at law and farmer, of Temperance Hall, was born March 23, 1855, where he now resides. He is the youngest of nine children of Nicholas and Penelope (Summers) Smith. His father was born December 2, 1801, in North Carolina, and when a small boy moved to Wilson County, Tenn. He purchased the farm where our subject now resides in 1844, which then included the land now covered by the town. The only cultivated spot of this extensive tract was a small orchard. He soon built a two-story house, in the upper story of which the "Sons of Temperance" held their meetings, and from that fact the town got its name. Mr. Smith was a strong advocate of temperance and an influential man, and possessed a wonderful constitution. While clearing his land he built fences and worked nights by the light from brush piles which he laid during the day. A great deal of his property was destroyed during the war. He and another old gentleman were captured and compelled to walk to Murfreesboro, where they were imprisoned about two months. He began life a poor man, but by enterprise and industry, was worth a large sum at his death. He was a director and large stockholder of the Sparta & Lebanon Turnpike Company. He gave his children the benefit of the best schools, and was always deeply interested in all educational matters. Mrs. Smith was born March 8, 1810, in Tennessee. She was a model housekeeper and a most industrious, estimable woman. Her death occurred in September, 1886. She and her husband were consistent and active members of the Missionary Baptist Church. The grandfather, Daniel Smith, was of Welsh descent; his father came from Wales at an early day. Our subject received his education in the New Middleton Institute, Smith County. He studied law under Col. Stokes, and was admitted to the bar in 1878. He is a talented lawyer, and has met with great success. His practice lies in De Kalb and the adjoining counties. In 1883 he was elected justice of the peace, which office he still holds. His judicial decisions have always given satisfaction. He is a Democrat and cast his first vote for Samuel J. Tilden. He inherited some property which he has added to considerably. He is a bright, genial man, with a host of friends. In 1875 he married Miss Alice P., daughter of Wm. T. and Malissa (Stokes) Hoskins. Mrs. Smith was born March 23, 1858. Their union resulted in the birth of six children: Edith May, Eula Leath, Linnie Mason, Wm. Nicholas, Olive Ione and Alfred.

Gen. Wm. B. Stokes, one of the leading attorneys and best known citizens of Alexandria, was born in 1814 in Chatham County, N. C. He is the second and only surviving one of three children of Sylvanus and Mary (Christian) Stokes. The father was of English descent, born in Chatham County, N. C., in 1783, a son of Thos. Stokes who was a native of Virginia and a cousin of ex-Gov. Munford Stokes, of North Carolina. Sylvanus was married in North Carolina about 1810, and in 1818 started for Tennessee, where his father owned large tracts of land. While *en route* his team ran away and he was killed by the wagon running over him. The family proceeded on their journey and located in Smith County near Temperance Hall, where the widow remained until her death in 1853. She was a native of the same State and county, and also same age as her husband. The subject of our sketch was educated in the best schools of Smith (now De Kalb) County. In January, 1832, he married Miss Parilee A., daughter of Abraham and Hannah Overall, of De Kalb County, where Mrs. Stokes was born in May, 1815. Thirteen children came to this union, of whom one son and six daughters are now living: Melissia J., wife of W. T. Hoskins, of De Kalb County; Hannah L., wife of Jas. L. Calhoun, of Davidson County; Harriet A., wife of Hon. W. A. Bryan, of Nashville; Fannie, wife of Dr. Elial Tubb (deceased); W. Jordan, of Texas; Sallie, wife of Geo. McNelly, and Norah Stokes. Mrs. Stokes died in May, 1880. She was a devoted wife and mother, a woman of rare accomplishments and a consistent member of the Methodist Episcopal Church. For several years Col. Stokes was one of the county's most practical and successful farmers. He owned herds of fine blooded stock, the celebrated racer "Ariel" being one of the number, and with which he traveled and won some of the best races ever made. His political career began in 1849, when he represented De Kalb County in the Lower House of the General Assembly, also in 1851. In 1855-56 he represented Wilson and De Kalb Counties in the State Senate, serving two years. In 1859 he was brought forward by the Whigs as candidate for Congress of the Third Congressional District. His opponent was Hon. J. H. Savage, who had served the eight years previous, having been elected by a majority of 1,400. Col. Stokes was elected and served during the stormy session just previous to the civil war. He was one of the brave "Little Spartan Band." Although one of the youngest members of the House, he was soon recognized as the champion and leader of the Union cause, and in defense of which he delivered one of the most able and effective speeches made during the term, and one which was universally applauded in the North. Upon his return home he discovered how unsafe it was for him to remain there. When the Union forces arrived in Nashville, he went there and requested to enter the service. He organized the Fifth Tennessee Cavalry, better known as Stokes' Cavalry, of which he was commander until the downfall of the Confederacy. He opened the battle of Stone River on the morning of December 30, 1862, and fired the last shot on the Manchester Turnpike after the surrender at Murfreesboro. For his gallant and faithful services during the war he was breveted brigadier-general by President Andrew Johnson. In 1865 he was again elected to Congress and re-elected, his term expiring in 1871. He was verbally commissioned by Johnson to represent him (Johnson) in the Conservative Peace Convention at Nashville, of which he was made spokesman. During 1871 he served as supervisor of the internal revenue, since which time he has been engaged in the practice of law with the same activity and energy that so characterized his past. He is now one of the leading practitioners of the State, a man of intellect and indomitable will. He was formerly a Whig, casting his first presidential vote for Hugh L. White in 1836, but since the dissolution of that party has affiliated with the Republicans. He has repeatedly served as one of the presidential electors and has done more practical work as canvasser than any man in the State. He has raised and finely educated a large family of children. He is a generous contributor to all laudable enterprises. He and his family are members of the Methodist Episcopal Church. The Colonel has been a Mason since 1849, and a resident of Alexandria since 1868, but still owns the old farm, which contains 250 acres of valuable improved land on the Smith Fork. He also owns property in town.

J. G. Squires, M. D., was born in 1839, near Middleton, Smith County, one of eight children, four living, of John and Maria (Gulick) Squires, the former of Scotch-Irish origin, born in Virginia about 1795, and the mother of like ancestry, born about 1804 in Smith County, Tenn. The father's parents settled at the head of Plunkett Creek in Smith County about 1800, when he was a boy. He was a farmer and a soldier of the Mexican war, the long service in which, during its whole course, left him in such feeble health that he died in a few years after its close. The mother died in 1843 at the birthplace of our subject. Trained a tanner, and educated at New Middleton Academy (coeducational). Our subject worked at his trade until twenty-two years of age, when he began attending school and studying medicine. In 1869-70 he attended lectures in the medical department of the University of Nashville, at the close of which lectures he began practice at Liberty. In 1873 he married Sarah C., daughter of Eli and Eliza (More) Vick, and born near Liberty in 1851. Their four children were Mattie F., Cecil H., Pearl and Jonathan G., besides whom they are also rearing and educating four orphan children. Our subject has an excellent practice, and owns property, including 276 acres and fine town property, all the result of his own efforts. Formerly a Whig, and first voting for John Bell, he has since become a Democrat. He is a Mason and a stanch temperance man. He and his wife are members of the Methodist Episcopal Church South.

Will a Vick, editor of Liberty *Herald*, born in 1864, at Liberty, is the eldest of three surviving children of William and Sarah A. (West) Vick. The father was born in 1824 in Smith (now De Kalb) County. He has been a merchant of Liberty since the age of nineteen. The mother was born in 1829 at Liberty, where she died in 1881. Our subject received his early education at the Masonic Academy of his native place, and later attended the Vanderbilt University, of Nashville. At the age of twenty he became a member of the firm of William Vick & Son. In connection with his mercantile business he established the *Herald* in April, 1886. He began with a fair number of subscriptions, and the circulation is now quite extensive. The secret of his success has been in making the paper strictly non-partisan. It strongly advocates prohibition. By the time the *Herald* is one year old there will be a second story added to the office, and a steam cylinder press used. Mr. Vick is an intelligent, energetic and rising young man, who has a bright, and we trust, successful future. He is a stanch Prohibitionist, and a consistent member of the Methodist Episcopal Church South.

Hon. W. W. Wade, judge of the Fifth Chancery Division of Tennessee, is a native of De Kalb County, born in Smithville in 1848, a son of Wm. M. and Caroline (Eastham) Wade. The father was of Scotch-Irish descent, born in Virginia in 1826. His father (grandfather of our subject), Wm. H., was also a native of Virginia. He was a hatter by trade. After residing in Wilson County for a few years he located, in 1840, in Smithville, De Kalb County, where he passed the remainder of his days. Wm. M. studied law when a young man with Judge M. M. Brien, who afterward became his partner. About 1855 he entered into partnership with Judge Robert Cantrell, now of Lebanon, continuing until his death in 1858. His wife was born in Wilson County, Tenn., in 1828. After Mr. Wade's demise she went to Nashville, in 1869, where she now resides. Of her five children three are living: Timothy W., a lawyer of Smithville; Louella, wife of Winfield Graves, a resident of Nashville, a produce dealer, and our subject who is the eldest living. He received his literary education in the Fulton Academy at Smithville, and at the age of nineteen began the study of law, under John B. Robinson. In December, 1867, he was admitted to the bar and immediately entered upon his practice. In 1873 he formed a partnership with Hon. Joseph Clark which continued until 1877, when Mr. Wade was appointed clerk and master of the chancery court, by Judge W. G. Crowley. For six years he filled this office, making an efficient and able officer. In

1885 he entered into partnership with his brother, T. W. Wade. In August, 1886, he was elected to his present position, commencing the discharge of his duties in September. His election was very complimentary. He had six opponents, and his plurality was upward of 1,500. He was one of the first aldermen, after the incorporation of Smithville. He is a member of the Methodist Episcopal Church South; of the I. O. O. F., Pure Fountain Lodge, No. 217, Smithville, is also connected with the K. of H. and K. of G. R. He is an eminent and esteemed professional man and citizen. In March, 1875, he married Miss Mary E., daughter of Judge W. G. Crowley. Mrs. Wade is a native of De Kalb County, and the mother of two children: Wm. M. and Ida Belle. Mrs. Wade is an estimable lady and member of the Christian Church.

Samuel Walker, a prominent physician of the Tenth District, was born February 8, 1848, in De Kalb County. He is the fourth of seven children of Hampton and Mary (Hicks) Walker, both of whom were also natives of De Kalb County. The father was born in 1811. He served two years in the late war, at the expiration of which time he was discharged on account of disabilities. His death occurred in November, 1886. The mother was born in 1813. Our subject received his literary education in the common schools of Missouri, attending later two terms at the Kirksville branch of the State Normal School in the same State. At the age of thirteen he became a member of Company C, Second Tennessee Cavalry. He was orderly sergeant. The first six months, on account of his youth, he was excused from carrying arms by Gen. Forrest. He took part in the battles Tissue Mingo Creek, Harrisburg, Miss., Abbyville, also in the famous raid of Memphis, Nashville, Franklin and Murfreesboro, and numerous skirmishes and expeditions in which Gen. Forrest participated. The command surrendered May 8, 1865, at Gainesville, Ala. He then returned home. After his father's death he went to Missouri, where two of his brothers preceded him. In partnership with Dr. Myers, of Queen City, Mo., he dealt in stock two years; they were so successful that our subject was enabled to educate himself for his chosen profession. After studying medicine in Dr. Myers' office, in 1874, he attended the Missouri Medical College, after which he engaged in the drug business with Dr. Myers. The winter of 1874–75 he took a course of lectures at the Physicians and Surgeons College, at Keokuk, Iowa, where he graduated in the spring of 1875, with high honors. He began his practice with Dr. Myers, who gave him a share in an extensive and lucrative patronage. The spring of 1878 Dr. Myers died, and owing to a severe illness Dr. Walker was forced for a time to give up his practice. He came to Middle Tennessee to regain his health.

In August, 1878, he established himself in his present location, and is now one of the leading and most popular physicians of the county. He is a comparatively young man, talented and highly esteemed both in professional and private life. His possessions are the fruits of his own labors and industry. He is a stanch Republican, casting his first presidential vote for Gen. Grant. February 8, 1880, he wedded Miss Sarah H., daughter of John and Jane (Mauldon) Glenn. Mrs. Walker was born March 14, 1861. Five children were born to their union: Laura, an infant, deceased; Claude, Mary Jane and Samuel Rosco.

Hon. Bethel Magness Webb, attorney at law, Smithville, Tenn., was born in Warren County, Tenn., September 21, 1847. He is the sixth of thirteen children born to D. W. and Sarah (Magness) Webb. His father was of English descent, born in Warren County in 1815, a son of Julius Webb, who was a native of North Carolina and came to Middle Tennessee in his youth and settled in what is now Warren County. He was one of the pioneers of that section. After marriage D. W. Webb located in the northern part of Warren County, where he lived till his death in 1866. He was a prosperous merchant and a large slave and land holder up to the late civil war. He was a Democrat and went with the South in that unfortunate struggle, and sustained heavy losses during the war. At his death there were eight of his children single and living with him, of whom Bethel was the oldest, and some of them were quite young, and owing to the ravages of the war, they and their widowed mother were left with meager resources for support. Mrs. Webb was of Scotch-Irish descent and was born in 1820 in what is now De Kalb County, Tenn. Her father, P. G. Magness, Sr., was one of the pioneer settlers of that section. He was a strong Democrat and an active influential man in politics and did much in shaping the politics of his section in *ante bellum* days. He was a prosperous farmer and live stock dealer, and then a prominent merchant in Smithville; and Jacob-like had a long line of respectable descendants, many of whom attained to considerable prominence in financial and intellectual spheres. Bethel, the subject of this sketch, had but limited educational advantages, owing to delicate health before the late war, and the interruption by the war, and the consequences of the war. Because of delicate health, at the age of eleven he was taken from school at Middleton Seminary and placed in his father's store, where he was salesman and bookkeeper for two years, when the war broke out and mercantile business was suspended. During the war he worked on the farm in crop time and taught the children of the neighborhood during the fall and winter, and the proceeds of his labor were used to assist in supporting the family. At different times several crippled and discharged Confederate and Union soldiers, were his pupils. He was a boy of seventeen when the war ended, and when he taught his last, about seven sessions as assistant or principal, yet by his inherent executiveness, his well balanced head and heart, and his untiring energy and industry, he achieved victories in his youthful employments that would have been a credit to one of mature years with superior advantages. He never went to school but about five months in all after he was eleven years of age, but he applied himself closely and by dint of effort in the judicious use of valuable time, by the firelight and with borrowed books, he succeeded in acquiring a good English and Latin course. While reading law he earned a living for himself and family, and aided his mother's family in acquiring a support and education, at first by peddling on "barter" with hired wagon and team, and then by farming, trading in live stock, selling goods, etc. He was married January 11, 1867, to Miss Helen Ware, who was born in De Kalb County, in 1852. Their union resulted in the birth of five children: Hallie, Carrie, Mattie, Robert Bethel, and Nora; the first mentioned is dead. His wife is an amiable good woman, and his children are quite brilliant and well favored. He, with his family, ranks with the first of his town in the social circle and otherwise. Mr. Webb commenced the study of law at the age of eighteen, and in connection with other business devoted as much time as possible to his studies for about six years and was admitted to the bar in 1872, and became the law partner of Hon. Holland Denton, of Cookeville, Tenn., in January, 1873. In 1873 he was elected superintendent of public instruction for Putnam County, Tenn., and in connection with his law practice, he filled this office for one term, when he declined a re-election. In January, 1876, he located at Woodberry, Tenn., where he was associated as a partner in the practice of law with Judges Robert Cantrell and J. S. Gribble, of Lebanon, Tenn. In 1880 he located in Smithville, Tenn., and associated with him Alvin Avant, under the firm name of Webb & Avant. In the latter part of 1886 Mr. Avant retired from the firm, and J. B. Moore, Esq., took his place. In 1886 Mr. Webb was a candidate for chancellor for the Fifth Chancery Division of Tennessee, entering the canvass with but limited acquaintances in the division; yet he ran a good race, made a fine impression, and many substantial friends, who would delight at his promotion. There were six Democratic candidates, however, and only one Republican candidate in the division, where about one-third of the voters were Republicans and the vote was so much divided that the Republican was elected. During the campaign Mr. Webb was the recipient of many complimentary letters, press notices and testimonials from his numerous friends, and from prominent jurists, judges and officials of the State, which speak in strong terms of his many moral and intellectual qualities. On different occasions Mr. Webb has presided as special judge of the circuit and chancery courts, has served as attorney-general *pro tempore*, and served as chairman and delegate in different political conventions and other representative bodies, and on each occasion dispatched the business before him with efficiency and honesty. Judge Webb is one of the most brilliant and able lawyers in the State. He is a profound jurist and an able advocate. He commands an extensive and lucrative practice, and ranks high as a lawyer in both the inferior and supreme courts. He is earnest and zealous in his pursuits, firm in his convictions, yet social and affable, with good address and a good talker. He is a devoted husband and father, a true friend and a good citizen, and a liberal, charitable, devoted Christian, with temperate habits. He is a Royal Arch Mason and with his wife and two children members of the Methodist Episcopal Church South.

CANNON COUNTY.

Hon. J. H. Cumings, of Woodbury, attorney at law, is a native of Warren County, Tenn., and was born in 1839. His parents were Warren and Orlend Cumings, both natives of Warren County, the former having been born in 1814, is a farmer by occupation and held the office of sheriff of Cannon County six years. He was a member of the constitutional convention of 1870, and now resides at Woodbury, Tenn. The subject of this sketch received his literary education at Woodbury, and in 1872 began the study of the law with T. B. Murry of McMinnville, Tenn., and afterward attended the law department of the Cumberland University at Lebanon, Tenn. He was admitted to the bar in 1873 and has since been engaged in the practice of the law at Woodbury. In November, 1885, he was elected to the Legislature. He enjoys an extensive and lucrative practice, and in politics he is an ardent Democrat. In May, 1861, he enlisted in Company D, Eighteenth Tennessee (Confederate) Infantry, under Capt. H. J. St. John. He was with the company three years and engaged in some of the heavy battles of the war. During the last year of the war he was with the Fourth Tennessee Cavalry, commanded by Col. Baxter Smith of Nashville. H. A. Wiley of Woodville was his captain. He participated in numerous engagements, was captured once but soon paroled, and returned home in 1865.

J. A. Dement, an enterprising farmer of the First District, was born in Rutherford County, Tenn., in 1823. He is the only son of Cader and Mary (Andrews) Dement. The father was born in Tennessee in 1777. He took part in the war of 1812 under Gen. Jackson. He was a farmer by occupation, but filled some minor political offices. He was well known and universally respected. He was three times married and raised thirteen children. His death occurred in 1849. The subject of this sketch received his education in the schools of his native county. In 1847 he married Margaret, daughter of Alexander Lockey of Rutherford County. She died in 1851. A few years later our subject wedded Miss Jane J., daughter of Rev. E. McMillian of Gallatin, Tenn. By this union there are three children living: Mattie (widow of D. Hogwood), Albert M. and Wilson M. In 1847 Mr. Dement located where he now resides. He has always been an energetic, worthy citizen and a generous supporter of all laudable enterprises. He has been a member of the Presbyterian Church for fifty years; his wife belongs to the same church. He is a Democrat, but was a Whig previous to the war.

Josephus Finley, clerk of the circuit court of Cannon County, is a native of the county, and was born in 1825. He was the first of a family of nine children, six of whom are still living. His parents were Isaac and Eleanor Finley, the former a native of Tennessee, born in 1799, and was a farmer, and had held the office of magistrate and county register, holding the latter at the time of his death. The mother of our subject was born in Kentucky in 1796, and is now living at the old homestead near Woodbury. The subject of this sketch received his education in the schools of the county. In 1848 he was married to Louisa Simpson, by whom he has two children living, and who died in August, 1860. He has followed farming most of his life. In 1865 he was elected clerk of the county court, and was twice re-elected. He has held the office of magistrate for the past twenty-four years, and in 1886 he was elected to his present office. In 1861 he was married to Zenobia Foster, who was born in Cannon County in 1834. They have six children, all of whom are living. Mr. Finley is an independent in politics, voting for principles rather than for party. Both he and his wife are consistent members of the church, and both are widely known and highly esteemed.

D. D. Hare, a prominent farmer of the First District, was born in Williamson County in 1833. He is one of four surviving children of a family of eleven born to John P. and Nancy Hare. The father was born in North Carolina in 1809, and came to Tennessee with his parents when a child. He has been a farmer and resident of Cannon County since 1840. The mother was born in Tennessee in 1809, and died in 1855. Our subject received his education in the county schools, and at Irwin College. In 1855 he located where he now resides. In 1859 he married Miss Martha L., daughter of Rev. E. McMillan, of Carlinville, Ill. Their union resulted in the birth of B. B., Minnie and Fannie. In September, 1862, Mr. Hare enlisted in the Confederate Army, Company E, Fourth Tennessee Cavalry, under command of Col. Baxter Smith, and Capt. H. A. Wiley. He took active part in the battles of Perryville, Murfreesboro, and Chickamauga, and many minor engagements. He was captured shortly after the battle of Chickamauga. He was confined a few days at Carthage, Gallatin and Nashville, and finally taken to the Federal prison at Indianapolis and retained nineteen months. He returned home in March, 1865. Previous to the war he was a Whig, but is now a Democrat and a Mason. He is a useful and respected citizen, deeply interested in the advancement of educational and beneficial enterprises. He and his wife are members of the Presbyterian Church.

Hon. W. C. Houston, of the firm of Jones & Houston, attorneys at law, residing at Woodbury, Tenn., is a native of Bedford County, having been born there March 17, 1852. He is the son of William and Elizabeth Clay (Morgan) Houston. The former was a native of Iredell County, N. C., born in 1821, and came to Tennessee about 1835. He located in Bedford County, where he lived the rest of his days. He was a planter and a very successful business man. His death occurred in March, 1853. His wife was born in Rutherford County, March 10, 1822. She was first married to Newton Clark, of Bedford County, whom she survived; afterward married William Houston, and some time after his death she married Benjamin Fugett, of Cannon County, who is now deceased. The subject of this sketch received his education mostly at Woodbury. At the age of twenty-two he took charge of the *Woodbury Press,* and continued editor and proprietor two years. In 1876 he was chosen representative in the Legislature from Cannon and Coffee Counties. On his retirement from this position he devoted himself to his farm and to the study of the law until 1879, when he was admitted to the bar. In 1880 he was again elected to the Legislature, and in 1882 he was again re-elected. At the session which convened in 1883 he was appointed chairman of the committee on finance. While occupying his seat in the Legislature he took a very active and prominent part in the settlement of the State debt question. From 1882 to 1884 he was a member of the State Democratic executive committee. In November, 1878, he was married to Miss Lura Kittrell, daughter of Maj. M. B. Kittrell, of Rutherford County. She is a native of Wilson County, and was born March 22, 1859. By their marriage they have two sons: Frank, born July 4, 1882, and William, born March 19, 1884. Mr. Houston has a half-sister, formerly Hattie Clark, now wife of the Hon. William Barton; and also a half-brother, Simpson Fugitt, both of whom are residents of Cannon County. The law firm of Jones & Houston was formed in 1886, and is universally considered the strongest in the county, both members being men of high honor and marked ability. Mr. Houston is an ardent and enthusiastic Democrat, and both himself and wife are members of the Christian Church.

Hon. James A. Jones, of the firm of Jones & Houston, Woodbury, Tenn., is a native of Alabama, born in 1838. His parents were Joseph and E. A. Jones, the former a native of North Carolina, a dentist, a planter and a very successful business man, dying in December, 1857; the latter born in Butler County, Ala., in 1818, and dying in 1853. The subject of this sketch completed his literary education at the Brownwood Institute, La Grange, Ga., in 1858, and shortly afterward began the study of law with Judge John K. Henry, of Greenville, Ala., where he remained until April, 1861, when he enlisted in the Confederate Army, becoming sergeant of Company A, Eighteenth Tennessee Infantry, under Capt. M. P. Rushing. He served as sergeant about four months, and was then transferred to the Twenty-third Tennessee Infantry, and elected captain of the company just before the battle of Shiloh, after which he returned home. He then served as quartermaster in the Fourth Tennessee Cavalry, and at the close of the war was on the coast defenses in Florida, as lieutenant of his company. After the close of the war he returned to Alabama, and was engaged in the real estate business until about 1870, and in 1871 he moved to Woodbury, where he has since been engaged in the practice of the law. In 1874 he was elected to the State Senate from Cannon, Warren, Coffee and De Kalb Counties, and was in the Legislature that elected ex-President Johnson to the United States Senate. In 1859 he was married to Miss Harriett Morton, of Warren County, by whom he has nine children. Mr. Jones has always been an active man, and was for some time engaged in the newspaper business. He is a Democrat in politics, is widely known and as a lawyer stands very high. He is an elder in the Presbyterian Church, and both a Mason and an Odd Fellow.

L. L. Melton, an enterprising and prominent resident of the Tenth District, was born in Cannon County, in 1845. He was one of eleven children born to John and Catherine Melton. The parents are natives of North Carolina, and now reside in the Seventh District of Cannon County. The father was born in 1800. He is a farmer. The mother was born in 1804. The subject of our sketch received his education partly in the county schools and by private instruction. In 1859 he married

Miss Pairlee, daughter of William Powell. By this union there are five children living. For many years our subject was successfully engaged in agricultural pursuits. In 1884 he purchased a saw mill, and since then has done an extensive manufacturing business, and has also been engaged in merchandising with G. G. Melton. They have a liberal patronage. In August, 1879, Mr. Melton was elected magistrate, and has since held the office. He is a stanch Democrat and a Mason. He has always been an active and able business man, widely known and esteemed and ever interested in the improvement and welfare of the community. He and his wife are earnest members of the Christian Church.

W. T. Mingle, editor and proprietor of the *Cannon Courier*, was born in Cannon County, August 25, 1857, one of seven children of William J. and Alice G. (Cathey) Mingle, both natives of Cannon County. The father was born in 1828. He is a farmer of the Eleventh District, and served as deputy sheriff some time. The mother was born in 1826. The subject of this sketch received his education in the county schools. In 1873 he went to Alexandria, where he and his brother, R. A., had charge of the *Alexandria Enterprise* for a year. He then located at Woodbury. November, 1884, he took his present position and has been very successful. He is an ardent Democrat and wide-awake business man, and an able editor. July, 1880, he married Miss M. A., daughter of J. A. and N. L. Bryson, of Cannon County. Four children have been born to the union: Clingman T., Eliza J. (deceased), Hugh L. and Lemuel B.

J. G. Moore, clerk of the county court of Cannon County, is a native of the county, having been born in 1837 and is the eldest of a family of ten children, nine of whom are still living. His parents were William and Elizabeth (Warren) Moore, both natives of Virginia, the former having been born in 1813, and having come to this country in about 1843. The latter was born in 1816. The subject of this sketch received his education mainly in the Mountain Creek Institute, Warren County. In 1866 he was married to Miss Elizabeth Taylor, daughter of N. M. Taylor. To this marriage were born six children. Mr. Moore is a carpenter and builder by trade and also a farmer, though he follows his trade most of the time. In 1872 he was elected register of the county, and filled the position for one term. In August, 1886, he was elected to his present position. He served as magistrate of the district ten years. He is a man well known and highly esteemed by all, and has always given encouragement to every laudable public enterprise. Politically he is a Democrat, and he is a member of both the Odd Fellow and Masonic fraternities. Both himself and wife are members of the Missionary Baptist Church. In 1861 he joined the Confederate Army, becoming a mem-

ber of Company H, Eighteenth Tennessee Infantry, of which J. H
Palmer was at the time colonel. He was in many of the hard-fough
battles of the war, was wounded at Fort Donelson, and was captured a
Missionary Ridge, whence he was taken to Indianapolis, Ind., wher.
was held as prisoner until the close of the war.

Index
Compiled By:
Colleen Morse Elliott
&
Lois Mashburn Ott
Ft. Worth, Tx.

Adams, J. P. 840
  Mitchell 835
  Peter 958
Adcock, B. G. 849
  David 847
  John 829
  Perry 850
  William 847
Adkins, Joshua 815
Adrian, ___ 936
Akeman, John 820
Akins, Flora C. 861
  Lewis 861
Albritton, Janie 919
Alexander, ___ 852
  J. D. 844
  M. A. (Miss) 927
  Abigail 941
  Silas 814
Allen, ___ 810
  H. K. 850
  J. M. 851
  O. H. 831
  W. T. 843
  Ada 951
  Benjamin 854
  "Billy" 926
  Elizabeth 962
  Elizabeth J. 951
  Elizabeth M. 951
  Emma 951
  George 846
  James M. 951
  Jesse 846, 847, 951
  Jesse T. 951
  John 846
  John S. 951
  John W. 965
  Lucy W. 965
  Martha L. 965
  Nancy 951
  Nancy W. 951
  Samuel H. 846
  Sarah 926
  Sophie 967
  Thomas 815, 848
  William G. 951
Allison, R. D. 850
  Carter 877
  Jane 945
  Joseph 945
  Margaret 877
  Martha 946
  Mary 877
  Thomas 829
Alwood, ___ 840 [Allwood]
  Delilah 921
  Ella 921
  Levi S. 921
  William 921
Ames, David 804, 807
Anderson, M. 811
  P. W. 813
  W. M. 860
  Alice 861
  Betsy 879, 881
  Church 852
  Hannah 941
  Hannah B. 941
  Isaac 799
  John 799
  John B. 811
  John H. 804
  John W. 834, 835
  Martha M. 879
  Matthias 800

Anderson, Cont.
  Matthis 799
  Nancy 865
  Nancy A. 860
  Pierce B. 835, 842
  Rebecca 860, 861
  Sallie 881
  Samuel 833, 835
  Thomas 829, 842, 941
  Thos. R. 907
  Wm. 799, 810, 819, 858, 861, 879, 881
  Zachariah 860
Andrews, Mary 988
Angel, Mary 947
Anthony, ___ 806
Arant, A. 849
  Benjamin 854
Argo, John 954
  Sarah 954
Armstrong, John 817, 821
  William 818, 819
Arnold, James W. 832
  John 835
Arrington, George 829, 833, 840
Ashley, W. F. 922
  Alfred 832
  Ellender J. 922
  Freelin H. 922
  John H. 834, 922
  Lidia A. 922
  Mamie 922
  Mary 921
  Mattie E. 922
  Simeon 834, 921
  William 921
Ashly, Nancy 905
Astlay, W. F. 937
  Leona 937
Atkinson, Elizabeth P. 886
Attwell, J. B. 850
Austell, Amelia 927
  Amos 829, 927
  Lucy 927
  Mary E. 931
  Samuel 829
Austin, E. D. 810
  Catherine 861
  Frank P. 861
  Flora C. 861
  James Mc. 861
  John 861
  John W. 861
  Mary E. 861
  Pleasant 861
  Robert S. 861
  Sarah Alice 861
  William Bluford 861
Avant, Alvin 951, 952, 986
  Benjamin 952
  Nancy 951
  William C. 951, 952
Aydelott, ___ 842
Aydelott, Davidson & Co. 923
Aydelott & Stevens 923
Aydelott, George Cortner 924
  James G. 835, 837, 844, 923, 945
  Jesse Mai 924
  John D. 923
  John Doak 924
  Sallie 924
  Sarah 923
Bailett, ___ 843
Bailey, Eli 857

Bailey, Cont.
  James E. 907
Bain, John K. 850
Baird, ___ 843
  Napoleon 819
Baker, J. M. 952
  R. P. 811, 826
  T. H. 835
  Barbary 952
  Barbary L. 953
  Charles R. 953
  Elizabeth C. 952
  Emma Florence 953
  James 952
  James M. 953
  Lucinda 952
  Mary 952
  Mary Viola 952
  Sarah Lena 953
  Susan M. 952
  William H. 952
  William R. 952
Baldridge, Susan 949
Baldwin, Elizabeth 895
Ball, Lettice 907
  Thomas 907
Banks, David 829
  Joseph 848
Banton, Wm. 813
Barbour, Richard 799
Barclay, John 815
Barger, Cynthia 953
  Jennie 953
  Samuel 953
Barklay, James 854, 855
  John 854
Barnes, ___ 841, 851, 860
  J. M. 807
  Bridget 977
  George 977
  Jesse 826
  Rachel 976
  Ricy O. 863
Barrett, Ruth 914
Barry, Sarah 953
Barton, ___ 859, 860
  C. 836
  C. L. 852
  J. S. 858
  Hattie 990
  James S. 819
  Joshua 854
  William 829, 990
Bashan, B. P. 830
Bashaw, J. E. 836, 841
  P. B. 835
Bass, ___ 825, 976
  E. W. 850
  John 814
  Nancy J. 975
Bassom, Wm. 800
Basson, Wm. 800
Bateman, Charlotte 944
  Henry 944
Bates, ___ 859, 879
  Elijah 799
  Wm. 857
Batey, James 849
Batts, ___ 852
  J. W. 849
Baxter, Joseph 836
Bean, C. H. 924
  Ella 924
  Robert 829
Beard, J. D. 852
  J. M. 852

Beard, Cont.
  John 830
  William 830
Beardon, Walter S. 819
Beatie, James 857
Beckman, ___ 830
Beckwith, George 851
Bell, ___ 824, 825
  A. E. 915
  B. F. 852
  W. E. 822
  David M. 915
  John 833, 834, 840, 982
  Mary J. 915
  Thomas 829
Bennett, John 835
  John P. 923
Bensy, Nancy 972
Berry, ___ 842
  James 829
  Josiah 829, 830, 832
Bethell, Tilman 855
Beulah, Maria 930
Bickford, G. W. 800
Biddleman, ___ 890
Biles, ___ 825
  J. C. 819, 883
  R. P. 810
  T. B. 810
  Eliza J. 900
  Jane 885
  Nancy 884
  Robert 814
  Robert B. 884
  Willaim 899
Black, ___ 851
Black & Mercer 905
Black, C. G. 825
  Alexander 885, 903
  Emma J. 886
  Jane 928
  John 824
  Mary A. 885
  Thomas 821, 826, 885
  William 824
Blackburn, J. H. 850, 953, 964
  Adelia Jane 964
  Ann 953
  Caledonia 953
  Daniel 835
  Jennie 953
  Ulysses 953
  William 953
Blackman, Harvard 829
  John 835
  Pleasant 815
Blackmore, Howard 830 (843)
Blackwell, Carroll 836
Blair, Thomas 830
Blake, J. R. 842
  Alexander 905
Blakely, Alexander 831
Blakemore, ___ 843
Blankenship, G. W. 800
  S. D. 851, 956
  Mary E. 956
  Tabitha H. 937
Blanton, ___ 840
  Coleman 829
  Laura 936
  Mary J. 948
  Thomas 948
  William 936
  Willis 834
Blodes, Benjamin 855
Blood, Wm. 840
Blount, ___ 806
Bloyds, Benjamin 853
Blythe, John 829
  Richard 852
  William 852
Bobo, F. M. 835
  Lecil 829, 830, 831, 834

Bobo, Cont.
  Minerva 934
  Wm. 935
Bolin, Jeremiah 814
Bond, ___ 851
Bone, ___ 852
  R. M. 974, 975
  Etta J. 974
  John 847
Bonner, Miles 814
Boon, J. L. 953
  James L. 954, 967
  Jas. N. 953
  Mattie 954
  Sarah 953
Boone, Daniel 875, 898, 953
Booth, A. W. 843, 924
  J. B. 924
  Elizabeth 924
  Ella 924
Borin, Thomas 814
Bosson, J. R. 861
  Amanda 861
  Caroline B. 862
  Carter T. 862
  Charles T. 861
  Edward E. 862
  Francis M. 862
  James R. 862
  Sarah (B)ell 861, 862
  Sue M. 862
Botts, J. W. 954
  Aaron 954, 964
  Charley 954
  Cynthia 954
  Earnest 954
  John E. 954
  Lena 955
  Lizzie 954
  Mary E. 964
  Nora 954
  Norman 954
  Robert A. 954
  Sarah 954
  Sarah M. 964
Bounds, Thomas 799, 801
Bowen, J. H. 799
Bowers, Hezekiah 847
Bowden, G. W. 843
  Travis 830
  William 829, 830
Bowmen, Glaphrey 916
Boyacin, Annie 887
Boyd, Francis M. 834
  Frank 871
  George C. 907
  Louisa 871
  Malvine 871
  William 847
  Wm. H. 804
Bozarth, Joseph 851
  Levi 846
Bradford, T. J. 805
Bradley, ___ 874
  Alfred 829
  Jonathan T. 803
Bradshaw, William 831
Bragg, John 830
Brainard, ___ 842
Braly, G. 919
Branch, Nancy 955
Brandon, John 829
Brantley, James A. 830, 834
  Samuel 830
Brantly, James A. 833
Bratten, W. G. 955 (Bratton)
  Annie 955
  Caroline 955
  Geneva 955
  Henry 955
  Herschal A. 955
  Martha 955
  Minnie 955

Bratten (Bratton), Cont.
  Nancy 955
  Nettie 955
Bratton, Elijah 853
  James 846
  Joel 955
  Joshua 853
  Thomas G. 955
  William 846
Brawley, Columbus 834
Breckenridge, ___ 907
Brerard, W. F. 856
Brevard, Zebediah 858
Brewer, C. C. 834, 836
  Russell 814
  William 860
Brewster, ___ 893
Bridges, ___ 852
Bridleman, Henry 815, 826
Brien, M. M. 849, 983
Brin, M. M. 859
Bristow, Catharine H. 893
  James 893
  Nancy 893
Britain, Washington 819
Brittan, W. C. 810
Britton, Casandria H. 960
  Lannie 960
Brixey, John O. 835
  Walter 829
Brockett, ___ 811
Bronson, ___ 811
  Chas. V. 862
  Mary A. 862
  Robt. L. 862
Brookstein, Mannering 799
Broom, C. C. 860
  C. P. 860
Brown, ___ 798, 825, 847, 961
  A. G. 858
  D. L. 825
  D. T. 806
  H. L. 820
  I. M. 857
  N. M. 956
  T. J. 927
  Aaron V. 887
  Alexander 799, 815
  Bettie 927
  Deborah 971
  Elizabeth 971
  Isabella 871
  Isaiah 956
  Jackson N. 971
  James M. 855, 858
  John 956
  Joseph 804, 824, 829, 840
  Julia 956
  Loirja 876
  Maud 956
  Rachel 956
Bruce, Robert 837
Bruster, J. F. 862
  Amanda 862
  Kittie 862
  William 862
Bryan, W. A. 981
  Andrew 799
  Harriet A. 981
  John S. 848
Bryant, ___ 840, 856
  John A. 831
Bryson, J. A. 991
  M. A. (Miss) 991
  N. L. 991
Buchanan, Andrew 815
  Tommie 822
Buck, Dexter 852
Buckaloo, James 835
Buckley, J. C. 851
Buckner, David 836
Bundrant, ___ 816
Vurger, ___ 826, 840

Burger, Cont.
  J. H. 921
  S. N. 833
  Abraham, Jr. 858
Burgess, Charles 862
  Margaret 862
  Ricy O. 863
  William S. 862
  Winfield 863
Burgie, ___ 841
Burgis, W. S. 800
Burke, Smith 829
  Willis 829
Burks, R. P. 819
Burnett, Nancy Ann 911
Burney, M. 826
Burnham, Larkin 829, 830, 832
Burroughs, ___ 825
  Elizabeth P. 886
  James M. 886
  John S. 886
  Mattie E. 886
  Nancy A. 886
  Peter 886
  Thomas F. 886
Burton, Henry 846, 849
  John W. 819, 833
  Nettie C. 884
  William 799, 810
Busby, Thomas 830
Butcher, Richard 813
Butler, David 830
  James 835
Butterworth, A. 841
Byard, Christianna 881
Byars, H. 917
  J. 917
  Mary 917
Byers, Harrel 815
Bynum, Pumphrey 855
Cain, John 903
Caldwell, Thomas 824
Calhoun, Hannah L. 981
  Jas. L. 981
Call, E. A. 831, 924
  Daniel H. 924
  Francis E. 924
  Lizzie 924
  Nancy 924
  Susan 924
Calley, ___ 830
Calms, ___ 879
Camden, John W. 830, 832, 834
Cameron, W. M. 811
  Elijah 799
  Henry 846
Campaign, Joseph 814
Campbell, ___ 842, 904
  M. R. 843
  James N. 834
  John 815
  Mary A. 975
  Wm. B. 804
Campton, ___ 974
Cane, ___ 824, 825
  J. M. 825
  R. B. 824
  John J. 824
Cannon, ___ 856
Cantrell, ___ 826
  B. M. 850
  C. A. 918
  Martha C. 890
  Mary 890, 902
  Robert 849, 850, 890, 891, 974, 977, 983, 986
  Watson 848, 849
Carden, ___ 837
  J. A. 834
  M. A. 834
  W. L. 834
  Catherine 925
  Dora 925

Carden, Cont.
  Emily P. 925
  Eva C. 925
  James 925
  John A. 925
  Joseph S. 925
  Lewis 925
  Louis 829
  Mary L. 925
  Minnie O. 925
  Peter R. 925
  Pharaba 925
  Reuben 829
  Robert L. 925
  Sarah E. 925
  Thomas F. 925
  William A. 925
  William L. 829
Cardwell, H. J. 886, 887
  Francis 886
  Judy 886
  Louisa 887
Carlee, Calvin 854
Carnes, W. B. 951
  W. D. 947, 951
  Elizabeth J. 951
  Nancy W. 951
Carney, Smith 830
Carrick, H. L. 804, 807
  S. & H. 810
  John M. 803
  Montgomery 799
Carroll, ___ 842, 943
  H. W. 834, 925
  Aaron 835
  Eldora E. 925
  Felix 830
  Goldie O. 926
  James K. P. 834
  John B. 843, 925
  Joseph 835
  Mary 925
  Norma E. 926
  Timothy 829, 837
  William 830
Carson, ___ 825
  D. B. 906
  Florence M. 906
  Robert 855
Carter, W. F. 876
  George N. 843, 925
  James 925
  Joseph 819, 833
  Mildred 866
  Wm. F. 803
Cartwright, W. J. 889
  Joshua 814, 815
  Julia A. 889
  Malinda 889
Caruthers, R. 964
  Abraham 804
  Robert L. 907
Casey, R. W. 834
Castleman, J. M. 820
  Alice J. 940
Cathey, Alice G. 991
Cate, Ephram 829
Catron, John 804, 805, 865
Cellers, Elizabeth 912
Chandler, Jack 836
  Marion 836
  Samuel 851
Chapman, ___ 825
Charles, W. C. 829
  John 829, 832
  Oliver 815
Chasteen, W. T. 816
Cheatham, Joel 849, 857
Cherry, W. P. 836
  Daniel 814
  Isham 854
Childress, John 829
  Moses B. 830

Chilton, Elizabeth 935
Chisem, Elijah 799
Christian, T. M. 850
  W. T. 820
  Mary 980
Clardy, Martha 930
Clark, I. M. 926
  J. A. 926
  J. P. 822
  M. L. 800
  R. S. 926
  W. A. 926
  Absalom 814
  Anthony 926
  Elizabeth 926
  Elizabeth Clay 989
  Ellen 926
  Hattie 990
  James 926
  John 926
  John D. 926
  Joseph 848, 849, 855, 958, 983
  Joshua 835, 926
  Mack 835
  Millie 926
  Newton 989
  Rachel 931
  Robert H. 926
  Rufus 926
  Sallie 926
  Sarah 926
  William E. 926
  Willie D. 926
Clay, Wm. H. 840
Cleburne, P. R. 821
Clemmons, ___ 810
Cleveland, S. W. (Miss) 929
Clift, W. J. 819, 833
  Annie 822
Coatney, F. S. 803
Coe, ___ 974
Coffee, C. 825
  H. C. 824
  P. H. 819, 820
  Chatham 837
  Joshua 852
Coggin, Daniel 850
Cole, E. W. 797
  Hattie E. 879
  Mattie 869
  Nancy N. 869
  William 869
Collier, A. S. 840
  James 814
  Wm. 814
Collins, ___ 842
  John 852
  Joseph 799
  William 830
Colms, S. H. 958
Colston, Charles 829
Colvert, J. L. 956
  Harriett 956
  Johanna 956
  Martha M. 957
  Mary E. 956
  William I. 956
Colville, J. F. 825
  S. 824
  S. L. 825
  Joseph 814, 817, 818, 821, 914
  Martha 914
  Peggie 914
  Sam. T. 825
Colwell, Liddie 939
Colyer, A. S. 946
Conley, A. B. 843, 926
  A. W. 926
  Mattie J. 927
Connell, ___ 961
Connelly, David 799

Conway, Catherine 966
Conwell, Milly 938
Cook, Alford B. 948
  Eliza 948
  Nancy 948
Combs, ___ 806
  S. H. 805
Comer, James 799
Compton, Sarah 973, 977
Coombs, Jeremiah 815
Cooper, Amanda 864
  Belle 864
  Benjamin 799
  D'elma 864
  Lyla 864
  James W. 864
  John S. 864
  Margret 863, 864
  Mary Jane 864
  Vernon 864
  Willie Landis 864
  Wm. 800, 863, 864
Cope, W. B. 881
  Ann 881
  James 805, 815
  Jane 881
  John S. 804
  Joseph 814
Copher, Joseph 810
Corder, Sally 945
Corey, W. G. 835
Corlee, Cullin 855
Corley, J. R. 957
  Carrie L. 957
  Elizabeth 957
  George S. 957
  James R. 957
  John 957
  John R. 957
  Sarah F. 957
  William M. 957
Cortner, Delilah 924
  George 924
Corzelius, F. 843
Cottrell, ___ 964
Couch, Bell 928
  Elijah 928
  Robt. 835
  Wm. 835
Coulson, B. M. 887
  David 887
  James 887
  Mary 887
  Sarah 887
Cox, ___ 811
  E. N. (Miss) 918
  J. C. 851
  M. T. 824, 825
  Dorcas 935
  Sarah 887
Cowan, J. B. 843
  Mary 927
  Robert 817
  Stewart 829
Cowen, James 799
Cram, J. 810
Crane & Witherby 923
Crane, G. R. 927
  M. A. 927
  George R. 843
  Mary E. 927
  William 927
  Wm. 842
Crawford, R. N. 810
Crisp, Jesse 814
Crocker, S. G. 836
  Wm. 836
Crockett, J. T. 829
  S. G. 835
  S. J. 829, 927
  Amelia 927
  Archia W. 927
  Bettie 927

Crockett, Cont.
  Cynthia E. 927
  Eliza 927
  Jno. G. 927
  John 829, 927
  Mary 927
  Samuel A. 927
  Sarah 927
Crompton, Thomas 852
Cross, G. W. 835
  Beulah 928
  George W. 928
  Jane 928
  Samuel 840
  William 829, 928
Crowder, Florence 875
Crowell, ___ 843
Crowley, M. A. 850
  W. G. 804, 847, 957, 983, 984
  Elizabeth 957
  Jessie Frances 958
  John B. 958
  John J. 957
  Kate 958
  Leslie 958
  Martha E. 958
  Martin A. 958
  Mary E. 958, 984
  Pleasant C. 958
  Prudence 958
  Rebecca 958
  William L. 958
Crutchfield, Bettie 960
  John 960
  Norah 960
Cumings, J. H. 987
  Orlend 987
  Warren 987
Cummin, James 799
Cummings, J. H. 858
  J. J. 810
  M. A. 805
  W. B. 864, 865
  W. H. 858
  Ann 876
  Benjamin 855
  Joseph 864
  Maggie 871
  Malachi A. 864, 865
  Warren 855, 858
  Wm. 815, 855
Cummins, Joseph 876
Cunnegan, James 829
Cunningham, F. E. 928
  L. D. 865
  M. T. 928
  S. E. 805
  Amanda 888
  America 865
  Bell 928
  Edmond 865
  Fannie 919
  George W. 887, 888
  James 829
  John 887, 888
  Mamie 928
  Martha 865
  Nancy 865
  Richard 829
  Sarah 887
  Sarah A. 888
  Vester 928
Curl, A. J. 819
Dale, Adam 846, 847
  John 846
  Judson 850
  William 846
Daniel, Henrietta B. 937
Daniels, Catherine 898
  Elizabeth 898
  James 842
  Thomas 898

Darnell, Dave 816
  James 829, 834
Darwin, Lucinda C. 938
  Robert 938
Daugherty, F. H. 806
Davenport, Reuben 814
David, Cynthia 953
Davidson, S. W. 929
  Abraham L. 929
  Elizabeth 928
  Ellis 831
  George W. 835, 844, 928
  Hugh 830, 831, 829
  Joan 929
  Joel 928
  John W. 844
  Maud 929
  Ransom 835
  Robert H. 929
  William J. 929
Davis, ___ 816, 830, 919
  A. B. 950
  A. L. 811
  M. 952, 953
  Benjamin 959
  Caleb B. 858
  Ella M. 881
  Elsie 959
  James 846, 876, 881
  Jefferson 910
  John 814
  Joshua 799
  Kittie 959
  Lear 959
  Lillie 959
  Loirja 876
  Margaret 881
  Mary 972
  Nat 810
  Nathaniel 799
  Nettie 876
  Susan M. 952
  Thomas 852
  Thos. P. 959
  Tho. Vernon 959
Deakins, G. S. 929
  Fredrick T. 929
  Mary 929
  Mary A. 929
  Sarah 929
  Vernie S. 929
  William 929
Dean, ___ 843
Dearing, W. L. S. 897
  Mary T. 897
  Virginia A. 897
Dearman, John L. 851
  John W. 850
Debard, ___ 816
DeBerry, Michael 814
Deckard, Benjamin 829, 842
Dement, J. A. 987
  Albert M. 988
  Cader 988
  Jane J. 988
  Margaret 988
  Mary 988
  Mattie 988
  Wilson M. 988
De Montfort, Simon 906
Denny, Ann 876
Denton, Holland 986
  Samuel 800
Dergan, John 799, 803, 804
Dewey, ___ 843
  H. P. 930
  Cyrus J. 930
  Eddie L. 930
  Lillie E. 930
  Maria 930
  Minnie E. 930
DeWitt, William 954
Dibrell, ___ 799, 807, 810, 960

Dibrell, Cont.
  G. G. 798, 803, 805, 810, 811, 865, 877
  M. & C. 810
  M. C. 797, 804
  W. C. 797
  W. L. 804
  Anthony 799, 804, 805, 866
  George G. 805, 806, 866
  Mary E. 866
  Mildred 866
Dikes, Isham 814
Dildine, Jane 952
Dillahunty, Edmund 858
Dillard, Catherine 936
  James 936
Dillon, Amanda 861
  Caroline 861
  Carter 861
  E. T. 858
  Thomas 799
  Z. 860
Dinges, ___ 852
  D. W. 959, 960
  Clara 960
  Clara P. E. 959
  Dibrell 960
  Donnell C. 960
  E. Turner 960
  Mortica 959
  Norah 960
  Paulean 960
  Wm. 803
  Wm. M. 959
Dingess, D. W. 852
Doak, John 814
Dodson, J. 865
  P. W. 970
  America 865
  Ella Steele 970
  Felix 800
  Jesse 814, 865
  John 815
Donaldson, Jane 945
Donnell, ___ 847, 956
  D. M. 820, 885
  M. E. 961
  Adlia 960
  Allan 960
  Ann Lou 961
  Casandria H. 960
  James A. 960
  Jane Annette 961
  Levi 830, 834
  Mary E. 961
  Minnie C. 961
  Nannie M. 961
  Robert G. 961
Dorse, Jonathan 847
  Stewart 847
Dorton, J. W. 873
Doss, M. F. 850, 852
  Caroline 976
  Darthula 976
  Jonathan 976
  Jonathan C. 849
  Priscilla 976
Dougherty, ___ 852
Douglas, G. W. 868
Douglass, Thomas 829
Dowell, J. W. (Miss) 974
  L. D. 972
  Martha 974, 978
  Mattie E. 972
  Nancy J. 978
  Robert 972
  Willis 974, 978
Downey, (Alex)ander 829, 832
Doyle, Jos. 862
Drake, Elijah 815
  Elizabeth 898
  Jacob 799
  James 830

Drake, Cont.
  John 815
  John M. 819
Draper, Elizabeth 882
  Thomas 882
Driver, Giles 846
  Reddick 847
Drummond, ___ 879
Dryer, ___ 884
Dubray, Christopher 866
Duncan, ___ 853
  D. W. 835
  G. W. 855
  J. H. L. 834, 836
  Ambrose 829
  Douglas 829
  Hamilton 829
  John J. 804
  Josiah 846
  Thomas 847
Dunkerson, ___ 859
Dunlap, Jesse 815
  Sallie 926
Dunnaway, Malissa Ann 975
Dunnington, F. C. 970
Dunny, William 864
Durham, James 815
  Thomas 847, 848
Earls, P. H. 869
  Carrie E. 869
  Ella E. 869
  Martin 869
  May L. 869
  Nancy N. 869
  Titia 869
Eastham, G. W. 850, 851
  Caroline 983
Eastland, ___ 828, 841
  Thomas 799
Eaton, P. W. 851
Eddings, Araminta 951
Edge, ___ 814
Edmondson, Wm. 818
Edwards, ___ 842
  Arthur 836
  George 814
  George W. 835
  Jesse R. 814
Elam, Sarah 814
Elan, ___ 843
  Reuben 815
Elledge, Clint 858
Eledge, Isaac W. 857, 858
Elkins, ___ 842
  D. L. 858
  Gabriel 855
  James 814
  Ralph 815
Ellison, Atlanta 978
  Timothy 859
Emack, G. M. 841
Emerson, G. D. 834
  H. S. 835
  Burr H. 834
  Elizabeth A. 939
Emmerson, ___ 840
  H. S. 830
  Hiram S. 834
England, E. M. 876
  J. P. 810
  Aaron 801
  Francis 877
  John 815, 877
  Mary 877
  Rebecca 860
English, Aaron 799
  James 817
  Sarah 954
Enoch, ___ 842
  R. R. 835
Ensey, J. H. 836
Eoff, Eldora E. 925
  Narcissa 925

Eoff, Cont.
  Narcissa 925
  William 925
Epley, Daniel 829
Eppes, Lucretia T. 915
Epps, Frances 878
Ervin, Andrew 829
  James 851
Erwin, Jane 952
  Lucinda 952
  William 952
Espy, Charles 855
Essary, James L. 857
Estell, Liley T. 903
Estes, Micajah 815
Estill, Wallace 930
Etter, G. H. 888
  H. R. 889
  W. G. 820, 889
  Charlotte 889
  Charlotte B. 889
  Cleopatra 888
  E. Bruce 889
  Electra 889
  George 888, 904
  Georgia 888
  Harriet 888
  Harriet B. 888
  Jane 889
  Lemma 889
  Lillie L. 888
  Mary J. 889
  Mary M. 888
  Myrtle 888
Evans, ___ 810
  E. J. 851, 850, 961
  Charles 855
  Charles C. 857
  John G. 850, 961
  George 852
  Herschel 962
  James 831
  Joseph 961
  Lucinda 961
  Reuben 847, 849, 854, 857
  Sarah 962
  Sherrell J. 962
  Virginia 962
Evart, T. F. 852
Ewell, David 830
Ewing, Juanita B. 822
Exum, J. T. 962
  M. S. 962
  Alice 962
  Elizabeth 962
  James R. 962
  John D. 962
  Kinchen D. 962
  William 962
Fain, ___ 842, 844
Fairbank, Andrew J. 890
  Arminta M. 890
  David 889
  Emery L. 890
  John 889
  John P. 890
  Julia A. 889
  Levy L. 890
  Nancy A. 890
  Sarah 889
  Sarah L. 890
  William W. 890
Fairbanks, W. W. 819
Fancher, J. A. P. 869
  Jane 870
  Levina T. 870
  Susan A. 869
  Thomas H. 804, 869
Fariss, W. M. 843
  Amanda M. 931
  Martha 930
  William M. 930
Farmer, ___ 811

Farr, Jonathan 858
Farrar, Jonathan L. 849
Farras, Samuel J. 837
Farren, William 829
Farrington, ___ 847
Farris, J. K. 931
  W. J. 873
  Annas A. 931
  Ellen K. 931
  John K. 931
  Mahaley 931
  Mary E. 931
  Samuel J. 931
  Sophia C. 931
  Sue J. 931
  William C. 931
  William R. 931
Faucher, J. A. P. 800
Faulkner, H. H. 825
  J. J. 891
  T. H. 816, 826
  W. P. 825
  Anne 890,891
  Anis 890
  Archibald 814, 815
  Asa 814, 815, 890, 891
  Carrie L. 890
  Charles H. 890
  Clay 816, 826, 890, 891
  Daisy 891
  Herschel C. 891
  Kate C. 890
  Margie 891
  Mary 890
  Maryetta 890
  Mary K. 891
  Mattie L. 890
  Robert A. 890
  Sarah E. 946
  Thomas H. 890, 891
  William F. 890
Ferguson, Wm. 840
Ferrell, James 855
  Leighton 857
Ferrill, ___ 829
  R. R. 834
Finch, Nannie M. 919
Findley, W. S. 811
Fingers, C. M. 816
Finley, A. 858
  Eleanor 988
  George 858
  Isaac 857, 988
  John 855
  Josephus 858, 988
  Kittie 862
  Louisa 988
  Nathan 855
  Thomas 858
  Zenobia 988
Finney, N. J. 821, 979
Fisher, W. H. 836
  Annie 949
  David 849
Fish, ___ 811
Fite, ___ 853
  J. 964
  L. D. 852
  David 850
  Elizabeth 965, 975
  Isaac N. 965
  Jacob 852
  Leonard 847
  Mary 963
  Samuel M. 804
Fitts, ___ 816
  T. W.962
  Delia 963
  Durinda 963
  Golden 963
  Isabell 963
  Jasper Newton 963
  Martin 963

Fitts, Cont.
  Nancy 963
  Sanford 963
  Sarah 963
  Tabitha 962
  Wootson 962
Fitzgerald, Joben 799
Flemming, W. H. 825
  John 815
  Joseph 799
Fletcher, ___ 810
  Elijah 815
Fletcher, Greenville 834
  James 831
  Lewis 799
Flipp, Henry 830
Flippin, H. C. 852
Flippo, Wm. 835
Flowers, ___ 860
  Lucy W. 965
Floy, R. B. 960
Floyd, C. S. 913
  Jane 896
  John W. 810
  Mattie S.913
  Porter 913
  William 847, 852
Ford, ___ 852
  J. J. 849, 963
  Abraham 806
  Adelia Jane 964
  Daniel 963
  Henry 854
  John W. 811, 818
  Martha 937
  Mary 963
  Mary E. 964
  Wm. 826
Forest, James 815
Forester, Robin 846
  William 799
Forrest, C. M. 894
  N. B. 807, 867
  Annie 894
  Chas. M. 819
  Charles W. 820
  Jeffrey 806
  Mary E. 893
  Sallie 911
Forrester, John B. 819
Fortner, John 815
Foster, A. L. 851
  W. B. 851, 958
  Isabell 963
  Kate 958
  Wm. B. 857
  Zenobia 988
Foust, H. D. 964
  Betsey 964
  Bettie 965
  Catherine 965
  Etta 965
  Henry D. 965
  John L. 965
  Lillian 965
  Malinda 965
  Mary J. 965
  William E. 964, 965
Foutch, Martin 958
  Polly 958
  Rebecca 958
Fowler, Rezin 858
  Thomas 855
Fraley, Caleb 799
Franklin, J. P.810
Franks, Joseph 814
  Nancy 895
  Wm. 800
Frazier, C. S. 850
  John 846, 849, 857
  Mary 929
Freeman, ___ 842
French, ___ 825

French, Cont.
  S. W. 842
  W. R. 843, 844
  Hughes 815
  Mason 814
Fruit, ___ 846
Fugett, Benjamin 989
  Elizabeth Clay 989
  Simpson 990 (Fugitt)
Fulkerson, James 799, 801
Fuller, Adam 858
Fulton, Elizabeth 937
Fuson, Elizabeth 965
  George M. 965
  James 965
  Jonathan 857
  John A. 965
  Joseph Benjamin 965
  Josephine 965
  Lucy Jane 965
  Martha 965
  Martha L. 965
  Wm. Francis 965
Fuston, W. J. 891
  Arthur 892
  Bell D. 892
  Catherine 892
  Hamilton T. 892
  Jonathan 849
  Mary E. 892
  Nancy 891
  Samuel 891, 892
  William N. 892
Gabe, John 799
Gains, James 799
Gales, J. W. 818
Galloway, ___ 842
Gambill, Andrew 814
Gamble, Andrew J. 803
Gannaway, R. P. 940
  Mary A. C. 940
Gardner, J. F. 946
  J. P. 826
  Mary E. 910
  Minnie E. 930
  Nathaniel 930
  William Rose 910
Garner, Liley T. 903
Garrett, Johnson 830, 832
Garrison, ___ 859
  Andrew J. 851
  Benjamin 847
  John 852
  Samuel 858
Gartner, Alline 892
  Anna 892
  Florence 892
  Henry 892
  John P. 892
  John W. 892
  Leonhardt 892
  Leonhardt P. 892
  Misouri Polk 892
Gay, ___ 853
Geltford, William 852
Genthner, ___ 842
George, John A. 858
  Reuben 829
Gentry, Charles 830
  Joseph 830
Geraghty, Catherine 966
  John 966
Geraty, Catherine 966
  John 966
  Julia Ann 966
  Pat 966
  Sallie Melissa 966
Gibble, J. S. 849
Gibbs, J. B. 850
  George W. 799, 804, 805, 866
  Jesse 814, 815
Gibson, W. F. 834
  Randolph 829

Gifford, ___ 942
Gilbert, W. H. 843
Gilliland, Mollie 873
Gill, H. S. 850
Gillam, J. 927
  Sarah 927
Gillentine, Cary 873
  Nicholas 799, 801
  Sarah 873
  Susan 873
Gilliam, L. S. 854
Gillins, G. W. 800
  George 800
Gillis, ___ 825
Gissom, J. J. 873
  Sallie E. 873
Gist, ___ 810
  D. R. 811
  Joseph 870
  Margaret 870
  Melcena 870
  Norman 861
  Sarah Alice 861
Givan, T. S. 844, 932
  W. D. 931, 933
  Ellen 932
  Harry M. 932
  James Archer 933
  James M. 931
  John F. 933
  Mellona 931
  Minnie M. 933
  Nancy 955
  Rachael 931
  Timothy S. 931
  Walter T. 933
Given, Thomas 847
  William J. 850
Givens, George 846
  William 846, 853
Glasscock, ___ 825
Glenn, Jane 985
  John 985
  Leeann 872
  Sarah H. 985
  Wm. 799, 810
Goff, J. D. 803
Gooch, W. W. 870
  Addelia M. 870
  Dora A. 870
  Everett B. 870
  Haden E. 870
  Henry L. 870
  James W. 870
  Joseph 870
  Joseph J. 870
  Lavinia 870
  Martha 878
  Melcena 870
  Wade H. 870
  Wyman D. 870
Good, E. 829
Goodall, John L. 804, 805
Goodbar, Jane 911
  Murray (Mary) 911
  William P. 911
  Wm. 811
Goodlow, Thomas 836
Goodner, T. C. 836
  James 847, 849, 852
  John F. 850
  Thomas C. 835
Goodpasture, W. W. 804
Goodson, A. J. 816
Goodwin, James 857
Gordon, F. H. 896
  Robert 814
Gore, Joshua 947
Gossett, Johnson 829
Gould, T. A. 852
Gowan, ___ 842, 860
Gracey, W. H. 870
  Ann 870

Gracey, Cont.
  Franklin 871
  Hugh 870
  Lillie 871
  Malvine 871
  Quillie 871
Grady, Clara B. 916
Graft, Jacob 843
Graham, J. R. 842
Grandberry, Cooper 950
  Ida 950
Grandstaff, Wm. 847
Grant, James 836
Grass, Adam 837
Graves, ___ 825
  Louella 983
  Winfield 983
Gray, ___ 963
  E. 834
  George 852
  Wylie 858
Green, B. B. 820
  I. J. 840
  S. W. D. 816
  W. M. 840
  Gardner 803
  James 815
Gribble, ___ 860
  A. J. 892
  J. S. 952, 986
  Catharine H. 893
  Handerson C. 893
  Hannah 892
  Hannah P. 893
  James B. 893
  John T. 893
  Lovia T. 893
  Mary P. 892
  Robert L. 893
  Thomas 814, 892
Griffith, R. 953
  Caledonia 953
Grimer, ___ 840
Griswald, N. W. 899
Grizzard, James 842, 923
  Sarah 923
Grizzle, J. 816
  George 858
Groom, Caroline 955
  James 955
  Lucretia 955
Gross, ___ 825
  A. H. 818
  H. L. W. 967
  Clara P. C. 967
  Jacob 967
  John 814
  Milton 967
  Ruthea J. 939
Grove, Albert 894
  Charles F. 894
  Flora J. 894
  George D. 894
  Joseph R. 893
  Mary E. 893
  Minnie 893
  Peggy 893
  William 894
  Wm. 819
  Wm. M. 893
Grundy, Felix 903
  Mary E. 903
Guest, Moses 799
Gulick, Maria 982
Gunn, ___ 829
  T. S. 831
Gunter, August 799
Gurley, ___ 837
Gwaltney, Emily C. 971
  John A. 971
Gwyn & Ramsey 913
Gwyn, C. R. 913
  Ransom 814

Hackett, W. S. 820
  Elizabeth 915
  Wright S. 819
Haggard, G. W. 830
  Nathaniel 804
Hale, ___ 847
  C. W. L. 967
  Charles 967
  Fate 853
  Herbert 967
  John 966
  Julia 966
  Lula 967
  Malissa 967
  Martin Van Buren 844
  Sallie Melissa 966
  Will T. 849
  William T. 967
Haley, Allen 857
  Carroll 836
  Hattie 914
Hall, ___ 811
Hallin, J. T. 850
Hallum, John 850
Halsell, Nannie G. 822
Hamilton, J. P. 979
Hammer, A. R. 818
Hammond, Leroy 814, 821
Hammons, Leroy 887
  Mary 887
  Susan 911
Hampton, ___ 868
  Mary 887
  Nancy 950
  Reuben 815
  Wade 950
Hancock, E. D. 819, 833
  W. A. 815
  John 799
  Jubal 810
Hanford, Fred A. 833
Hardee, W. I. 867
Hardwicke, Elizabeth 969
Hare, B. B. 989
  D. D. 988
  Fannie 989
  John P. 988
  Martha L. 989
  Minnie 989
  Nancy 988
Hargess, Mary 874
Harmon, ___ 840
Harper, Claiborne 829
Harpole, Hiram 829
  Samuel 799
Harris, ___ 820
  C. S. 842
  W. W. 831
  Ann 970
  Edward 799
  Eliza 977
  Howell 815
  Thomas K. 799, 805, 819, 865
Harrison, ___ 826
  D. S. 851
  D. T. 968
  J. S. 894, 952
  Cora 968
  Edmond R. 894
  Horace H. 819
  James B. 968
  John 850, 968
  John H. 968
  Joseph 854
  Julia E. 894
  Mary 968
  Rebecca M. 894
  Robert S. 968
  William 968
Hart, Moses 830
  Samuel 836
  Seth 843

Harty, Jacob 799
Harvey, William P. 851
Harwell, M. B. 825
Hash, J. W. 895
  Charles M. 896
  Drucilla 895
  Elizabeth 895
  Ella D. 896
  George H. 895
  George W. Henry 895
  James H. 895
  Jane L. 896
  Jefferson D. 895
  John W. 895
  Lean 895
  Margaret L. 895
  Mary 895
  Nancy 895
  Monroe G. (Hash) 895
  Sophia 896
  Tabitha 895
  Thomas 895
  Victor H. 896
  William 895
  William H. 895
Haskins, W. T. 850
Haston, E. S. 871
  Catherine 861
  David 871
  Elizabeth 871
  Fred Dexter 871
  Isaac T. 871
  Maggie 871
  Walter Eugene 871
  Willie Burt 871
Hathaway, W. L. 850
  William L. 851
Hauks, David 799
Hawkins, ___ 843
  Angeline 916
  James 855
  Rebecca M. 894
Hayes, H. L. 820
  I. H. 846
  J. A. 800
  Ann 953
  Cannie 979
  Eliza 969
  Eliza Helen 969
  Elizabeth 969
  Isaac 969
  James T. 979
  John 969
  John R. 969
  Kizzie 969
  Lollie 979
  Lucinda 969
  Martha 969
  Mary 969
  Rebecca 969
  Richard 969
  Sarah 963
Haynes, J. H. 850
  Andrew 831
Heathcock, William 829
Heed, Abraham 912
  Mary 912
Henderson, ___ 825
  B. H. 799
  Pleasant 819
  Samuel 818
Heneger, Elizabeth T. 900
  Geo. W. 900
Hennegun, G. W. 819
Hennessee, A. W. 888
  Jennie 888
  Sarah A. 888
Henry, Elizabeth 928
  John K. 990
Hepp, David 835
Herald, Whitley 829
Herd, Joseph 803
Hern, H. M. 860

Herriford, John 830, 832
Hess, Joel 800
Hickerson, ___ 842, 949
  L. D. 830, 843, 933
  W. A. 834
  W. P. 835, 928, 933, 934, 950
  Beulah 928
  Chisum R. 933
  David 829
  Ella 933
  Fannie 950
  Georgie M. 933
  John 829, 831, 933
  Joseph 828, 830, 831, 841
  Joshua 815
  Leander 840
  Mary S. 933
  Nasion W. 933
  William 933
  Wm. P. 833
  Wylie 833
Hicks, ___ 942
  Archibald 819, 855
  Mary 984
Higgenbotham, J. E. 819
Higginbotham, Aaron 814
Higgins, Ella 921
  Harris 921
High, Belle 864
  Elizabeth 864
  James 864
Hightower, Mattie E. 922
Hildebrand, ___ 830
Hiles, Daisy D. 934
  Frank K. 934
  Gracie T. 934
  James W. 934
  Joseph 934
  Joseph E. 934
  Lena M. 934
  Mary E. 934
  Minerva 934
  Walter S. 934
  W. Evan 934
  Wilburn 934
Hill, ___ 811, 842, 859, 874
  B. J. 825, 920
  C. 850
  H. L. W. 816, 819, 896, 897
  I. P. 897
  J. W. 889
  L. D. 805, 883
  M. 826
  Adia G. 898
  Alexander 854, 856
  Andrew P. Melchisedec 898
  Athelia 897
  Beatrice 897
  Ben 890
  Benjamin J. 820
  Bertha 897
  Bettie C. 883
  Charlotte 889
  Dearing 897
  E. Elizabeth 898
  Eliza 897
  Ella M. 898
  Franklin 897
  George M. 803
  Henry 815
  Henry J. A. 814, 896
  Irwin 815
  Isaac 897, 898
  Isabella 871
  James 820
  James A. 878
  Leanora 897
  Lillian L. 898
  Livingston 897
  Martha J. 872
  Mary 889
  Mary D. 897

Hill, Cont.
  Mertie 872
  Octa 897
  Richard 799, 811, 871
  Robert L. 872
  Susan 897
  Susannah 896
  Virginia 897
  Virginia A. 897
  Walter 897
  William 871
Hillis, ___ 814
  Charles M. 898
  Elizabeth 898
  Isaac 898
  Isaac H. 898
  Isaiah T. 898
  Marandie J. 898
  Mary M. 898
  Ransom M. 898
Hinkle, Nancy 924
Hitchcock, Ann 870
Hoas, Philip 854
Hobson, R. V. 872
  Mary Ann 872
  Richard 872
  Samuel 872
Hodge, William (Wm.) 829, 832
Hodges, ___ 800
Hodgkins, Frank 843
Hoffman, Christopher 811
Hogan, J. E. 842
  Edward 814
Hogue, Edward 814
Hogwood, D. 988
  Mattie 988
Holder, J. D. 872
  Allie May 873
  Charley 873
  Elizabeth 872
  John 873
  Johnnie E. 873
  Josie 873
  Martha M. 873
  Sallie E. 873
  Spencer 872
  Spencer S. T. 873
  Susan 873
Holdman, D. W. 893
Holeford, Cynthia 874
Holland, ___ 947
  William 829
Hollander, M. 842
Hollandsworth, Susan 901
Hollis, J. T. 849, 850
  Wm. 854
Holman, J. H. 833
Holmes, Mary 952
  William (Wm.) 830, 833
Holt, A. M. 842, 843
  Joseph 842, 843
Holter, Wm. 803
Honn, Samuel 814
Hoodenpyle, ___ 825
Hoodenpyl, G. W. 899
  Hyxsy 892
  Mary 903
  Misouri Polk 892
  Philip 818, 892
Hooper, ___ 851
  Edward 847
Hooster, Samuel 815
Hoover, ___ 860
Hopkins, Edward 814
  Eliza 976
  Elizabeth 872
  Thomas 814
Hoppes, ___ 814
Hord, Annie E. 905
Hoskins, W. T. 981
  Alice P. 980
  Malissa 980
  Melissia J. 981

Hoskins, Cont.
  Wm. T. 980
Houchin, William 899
Houchins, ___ 825
Hough, E. S. 840
  J. E. 931
Houston, W. C. 989
  Elizabeth Clay 989
  Frank 989
  Lura 989
  William 816, 989
Howard, Abraham 829
Howell, Drucilla 895
Howard, James 831
  John 799
  William 829
  William J. 829
Howell, Laura 822
  Lewis 815
Hubbard, James 814
Hudgens, Kittie 874
Hudson, Lavenia 880
Huffar, Sarah C. 949
Huffer, ___ 831
  P. A. 924
  Ellen 924
  Lizzie 924
Hughes, ___ 825, 872
  J. C. 899
  J. H. 886
  W. D. 899
  Elizabeth 899
  Nicholas 815
Huggins, Dora 946
Hulfish, ___ 841
Hume, ___ 859
  Alfred 944
Hunt, ___ 842
  E. F. 836
Hurbert, ___ 825
Hurd, ___ 852
Hurst, Gillam 815
Huston, W. C. 858
  Peter 799
Ingle, L. W. 842
Irwin, Andrew 829
Isaacs, Jacob C. 804
Isabell, P. C. 949
  Blanche 949
Isbell, P. C. 835, 841, 934
  W. I. 850
  Washington 850
Jackson, ___ 841
  D. C. 935
  G. W. 840
  J. B. 935
  J. E. 840
  Andrew 804, 827
  Dorcas 935
  Edna 935
  Elizabeth 935
  Howell E. 961
Jacobs, Jeremiah 936
Jackson, John T. 935
  Mary F. 935
Jaco, Annie 887
  Jeremiah 814, 887
  Louisa 887
Jacobs, A. 936
  Catherine 936
  Laura 936
  Rebecca 936
  Stokely 936
  Wm. 815
James, Joseph 855
Jarrett, ___ 807
  Higdon R. 858
Jarvis, E. 805
  Eliphalet 873
  Lewis 815
  Margaret 873
  Mollie 873
  Reziah 873

Jeanmire, L. F. 825
Jenkins, Benjamin 829
  James A. 824
  James H. 810
  John 799
Jernigan, J. M. 937
  Alexander 937
  Elizabeth 937
  Louisa 937
  Martha 937
  Mary 937
Jett, John 803, 811
Jetton, Louis 855
Jinkens, D. O. 825
Johnson, S. J. 874
  W. C. 874
  Allan 846
  Andrew 878
  Britton 846
  Fannie 874
  John O. 831
  Hattie 949
  Joseph 874
  Martin 815
  Mary 874
  Samuel 800
  William 830
Johnston, Albert Sidney 821, 909, 910
  David 814
  Joseph E. 909
  Wm. 814
Jones, ___ 852, 964
Jones & Houston 990
Jones, E. A. 990
  E. J. 899
  H. L. 800
  I. N. 840
  J. L. 843
  R. F. 969
  T. E. 831
  W. E. B. 819
  W. J. 825
  Cecilia 899
  Eliza 969
  Eliza J. 900
  Elizabeth T. 900
  Ezekiel 837
  Frank 969
  Gabrial 829, 830, 832
  Hannah 911
  Harriett 990
  Hinton 835
  Isaac 847
  Jas. 969
  James 837, 847, 899
  James A. 858, 990
  James C. 907
  James E. 900
  Jonathan 855
  John 814
  Joseph 990
  Martha P. 969
  Mattie 969
  Rees 841
  Stephen 815
  Zachariah B. 900
Jordan, ___ 842
Jost, John 852
Justice, J. B. 816
Kane, James 814, 815
Keaton, L. M. 901
  Allen D. 901
  Charles L. 901
  Harriett A. 901
  Louisa 901
  Mary M. 901
  Parthenia C. 901
  Phoeba P. 901
  Robert 900
  Sarah A. 901
  Susan 901
  William 901

Keaton, Cont.
  William T. 901
Keel, John 829
Keeling, J. L. 830
Keith, Samuel J. 797
Kelley, ___ 890
  T. B. 851
  Mary 968
  Spencer 847
Kelly, T. B. 969
  Elizabeth 969
  Ella 970
  George M. 970
  Inez 970
  Pauline 970
  Thomas 970
  Thomas B. 970
  Thomas J. 969, 970
Kelton, ___ 840
  James 847
Kennedy, J. C. 850
  John C. 846
Kennerly, J. P. 931
  Mahaley 931
Kersey, Andrew 954
  Lizzie 954
Key, S. A. 833
Keys, ___ 810
Kincannon, L. A. 824, 825
King, E. W. 912
  H. J. 814
  J. W. 852
  W. C. N. 814
  Ann 970
  Deborah 971
  Elizabeth 912
  Emily C. 971
  Henry 970
  Ira W. 970, 971
  James D. 971
  Mary J. 971
  Robert 799
  Robrt. W. 971
  Tho. H. 970
  Tobitha L. 971
  Wilson 912
Kinnard, ___ 962
Kinzie & Butler 979
Kirby, John 814
  Philip 799
  William (Wm.) 814, 847
Kirk, ___ 843
Kitching, Edith 972
  Ella 972
  Hallie 972
  James 972
  James H. 972
  Jesse 972
  Mary 972
  Mattie E. 972
  Robert D. 972
  Thomas 972
Kittrell, M. B. 989
  Lura 989
Knights, Julia 966
Knowles, John 799
Kome, Jacob A. 814
Lackey, Robert 829
  William 829
Lafever, Zachariah 846
Lambert, Anderson 947
  Lucinda J. 947
  Mary E. 927
  Rebecca 947
Lamberth, J. G. 820
Lampton, Benjamin 799
Lance, Samuel 857
Lane, Alexander 804
  George (Geo.) 815, 799
  Jacob A. 799, 800, 803, 810
  Mary A. 862
  Turner 801, 804
Lannon, Mary J. 965

Lanse, James 814
Lasater, ___ 842
  R. E. 829, 833, 835, 840
  Richard B. 835
Lassater, Brinkley 858
Lausden, James K. 870
  Jane 870
  Jane S. 870
  Levina T. 870
Lawrence, ___ 852, 896
  E. 904
  J. P. 826
  T. M. 852
  W. T. 937
  John H. 937
  Leona 937
  Tabitha H. 937
  William 849
  Wm. P. 814
Lawson, ___ 811, 843
Laxon, James 799
  Thomas 799
Layne, B. P. 834
  Martha 949
League, D. 846
Leboe, Judy 886
LeCroy, ___ 840
Ledbetter, Wm. 799
Lee, ___ 866
  Z. P. 850
Leech, ___ 872
Leftwick, Jefferson 807
  Mary E. 866
  Waymond 810
LeGrand, ___ 826
Leichleucher, S. J. 842
Lester, B. F. 860
Lewis, G. W. 967
  J. A. 932
  T. L. 803
  Elijah 799
  Lula 967
  Samuel 854
  Sophie 967
  Wm. 799
Lick, James 847
Lilly, Noel 854
Lincoln, ___ 852
  W. H. 960
  Abraham 967
  Clara P. C. 967
  Clara P. E. 959
  Jesse 799, 810
Lindsley, Phillip 896
Lisk, Wm. 814
Little, Bryce 797
  Harmon 861
  Mary 861
  Nancy A. 860
  Wm. 803, 810
Lively, ___ 825
Livingston, Mrs. Joseph 825
Lochmiller, F. A. 929
  Mary A. 929
Lockey, Alexander 988
  Margaret 988
Lockhart, Benjamin 817
  James 846
Longstreet, ___ 867
Looney, John 814
Lott, Luthrell 814
Lowe, Isaiah 858
Lowery, J. J. 837
Lowrey, Alexander 799, 801, 802
  Charles 874
  David C. 874
  John J. 819
  Kittie 874
  Maggie 875
  Thomas 814
  Wm. 835
Lowry, W. 889
Lucas, John 815

Luckey, John 959
  Lillie 959
  Martha 959
Lumpton, ___ 810
Lunley, William 829
Lurk, Martha 920
Lusk, A. E. (Miss) 906
  J. A. 831
  J. D. 906
  John 830, 832, 833
  Pauline 906
  Wm. 814, 818
Lust, ___ 824, 825
  W. L. 819
Luster, Betsey 964
Lyda, Ann 880
Lydie, Louisa 871
Lyles, ___ 810
Lynd, Thomas 819
Lyon, Mrs. C. J. 937
  T. B. 937, 938
  Elizabeth 949
  Mary J. 949
McBee, Wm. 835
McBeel, Mathias 835
McBride, P. H. 836, 938
  Burr H. 939
  Demillion E. 939
  Elizabeth A. 939
  Margaret 862
  Milly 938
  Mollie C. 939
  Pleasant H. 939
  Thomas M. 939
  William H. 939
  William S. 938
McBroom, Alexander 855
  Henry D. 854, 857, 859
  Isaac 856
  Jack 858
McBrown, ___ 858
  Henry 836
McCall, ___ 825
McCaverty, Chas. 965
  Lucy Jane 965
McClain, John 855
McCleain, ___ 971
McClarty, C. 825
McClelland, S. W. 852
McConnell, W. W. 804
McCorkle, ___ 907
McCoy, ___ 843
McCreary, L. B. 860
  Robert 829
McCrury, C. 840
McCullough, Garrison 816
McCutchen, ___ 948
McCutcheon, Gordon 835
McDaniel, Joseph 799
McDearmon, James 974
  Mary 974
  Mary J. 974
McDonald, H. B. 977
  Alice 962
  Julia 977
  Julia G. 977
McDowell, Elizabeth M. 973
McDonald, Wm. P. 834
McEwin, R. 821
McFaddin, William 829
McFerrin, ___ 860
  A. F. 858
  Alexander 858
  Wm. 854
McGee, John 814
  Samuel 814
McGinn, Elizabeth S. 926
McGinniss, Elizabeth 969
McGregor, Ezekial 814
  Richard 818
McGrew, G. W. 830
McGuire, Charles 804
  James 850

McGuire, Cont.
  Robert 836
  Wm. 799
McHarner, M. H. 850
McKinney, Jane 911
McKnight, M. W. 858
  W. M. 859
McLain, Daniel 830, 833, 834, 837
McLean, Daniel 834
McLemore, ___ 842
  S. J. 843, 939
  W. H. 837
  Henrietta 939
  John C. 939
  Lamyra 939
  Laura 939
  Margaret J. 939
  Martha 939
  Ruthea J. 939
  William H. 939
McMahan, Jonathan 815
McManus. S. V. 803
McMillan, E. 989
  Martha L. 989
McMillian, E. 988
  Jane J. 988
McMirtle, Alexander 829
  James 829
  William 829
McNelly, Geo. 981
  Sallie 981
McQuillin, Delilah 921
McWhister, J. A. 800
Mabry, Joel 824
  Thomas 818
Mackey, Wm. 799
Mackleroy, Jacob 855
Macon, Harry 815
  John 821
Madding, Wm. 799
Maddox, M. S. (Miss) 962
Madison, ___ 811
Magness, Mrs. E. J. 902
  P. G. 846, 850, 902, 985
  P. W. H. 825
  R. M. 849
  W. H. 875, 810, 902, 968
  Cordelia 902
  Edgar 902
  Ella 902
  Florence 875
  Harriett 912
  Martha J. 875
  Perry G. 851, 875
  Sarah 985
  William H. 851, 902
Manier, ___ 962
Mankin, Lidia A. 922
Manning, Louis W. 954
  Nora 954
  Sarah 954
Mansfield, T. J. 816
Marbry, Allie 942
  Leonard 942
Marbury, ___ 842
  L. W. 834
  M. P. 842
  Benjamin 903
  Liley T. 903
  Mary 903
  Mary E. 903
  Phillip H. 903
  Rebecca 903
Marcell, ___ 840, 843
Marchbanks, ___ 810
  A. J. 833, 849
  C. 805, 862
  Andrew J. 819
  George 820
Markim, Arthur 799
Marks, A. S. 819, 833, 946
  J. A. 951

Marks, Cont.
  Ada 951
Marmaduke, John S. 867
Marshall, ___ 816, 842, 907
  J. D. 899
  J. W. 842, 938
  W. A. 843, 938
  Daisy L. 938
  Daniel 835
  Emma C. 938
  Harry L. 938
  Josiah M. 938
  Lottie L. 938
  Lucinda C. 938
  Mary L. 938
  Minnie V. 938
  Nancy T. 938
  William R. 938
Martin, ___ 860
  A. E. 915
  C. R. 889
  F. B. 858
  J. C. 825
  M. T. 850
  R. 825
  Alex. 846
  Jacob 814
  James 815
  John 846, 849, 857
  Margaret 882
  Mary S. 933
  Rock 814
  Sallie E. 978
  Tobe 846
Mashen, Fanny 822
Mason, ___ 816, 860
  C. J. (Miss) 937
  R. H. 819, 825
  Adelia 973
  Eliza 973
  Hal. 836
  James 937
  Jane 937
  John M. 972
  Mary 916
  Mary E. 973
  Nancy 972, 973
  Robert Wiley 973
  Wiley 972
Massey, Gerald 968
Matthews, Johanna 956
  Sarah 876
  Thomas 799, 817
Matthewson, George 814
Mauldon, Jane 985
Mauzy, Jane 896
  Sophia 896
  Thomas 896
Maxwell, H. P. 819
  S. P. 850
  Andrew 829
May, David 799
  Thomas 799
Mayberry, Joel 815
Mayes, Abraham 799
Maynard, H. P. 938
  I. F. 842, 938
  Charles 938
Maynor, John 846
Mead, ___ 825
  D. E. 939
  E. G. 903
  W. R. 939
  Adolphus 939
  Carlton E. 940
  Climena 903
  Cora L. 940
  David 903
  David E. 940
  Ethea L. 940
  George 816
  James W. 940
  Liddie 939

Mead, Cont.
  Lydia 940
  Mary A. C. 940
Meadows, E. 904
  J. J. 889, 904
  L. H. 820
  W. 889
  W. H. 825
  Augustus F. 904
  Aubrey D. 904
  Deborah 904
  E. Carlie 904
  Electra 889
  Francis M. 904
  Ida E. 904
  Minnie L. 904
  Parazaide 904
  Sarah J. 889, 904
  Thulah B. 904
  Virginia A. 904
  William D. 904
  William M. 904
  Wm. 835
Mears, Wm. 854
Meed, ___ 816
Meeks, Charles 803
Melton, G. G. 991
  L. L. 990
  Andrew 855
  Catherine 990
  John 990
  Pairlee 991
Mercer, ___ 824, 825
  L. D. 904
  Annie E. 905
  Fenton 903
  Foss H. 905
  Mary 904
  Rebecca 903
  Richard 904
Meredith, Maggie 875
Merritt, B. M. 850
  J. T. 917
  M. B. (Miss) 917
  Jack 858
  Sarah 917
Metcalf, Eva 883
Meyers, J. C. 818
  John 814
  John S. 818
  Thomas S. 818
Middleton, Wm. 854
Miles, James 855
Milican, Elizabeth 877
Miller, ___ 841, 843
  F. N. 841, 940
  J. L. 818
  Albert 940
  Alice J. 940
  Delilah 940
  Joaquin 968
  Wm. 815
Milton, John 857
Mingle, M. A. 991
  R. A. 991
  W. T. 860, 991
  Alice G. 991
  Clingman T. 991
  Eliza J. 991
  Hugh L. 991
  Lemuel B. 991
  William J. 991
Mintor, ___ 807
Mitchel, Mary 882
Mitchell, D. L. 803
  J. F. 875
  J. G. 811
  J. M. 800
  T. L. 800
  Bertha E. 876
  Denny 876
  Hannah 865, 875
  James H. 858

Mitchell, Cont.
  James W. 876
  John 865
  John W. 875
  Joseph 815
  Joseph A. 876
  Joseph G. 811
  Lyon 814
  Martha 865
  Mattie J. 927
  Nancy !. 876
  Nettie 876
  Sallie J. 876
  Tobitha 876
  Washington 927
  Willie 876
  Wm. 810
Moat, Margret 863, 864
Moffitt, Aaron 804
  Harriet 904
  Sarah J. 904
Mahler, J. G. 833
Monger, D. S. 842
Montfort, ___ 906
Montgomery, ___ 829
  J. M. 803
  William 830
  Wm. 832
Moddy, W. A. 858
Mooney, W. W. 820
Moore, ___ 840
  H. L. C. 811
  J. B. 986
  J. G. 858, 991
  J. S. 940
  M. N. 843
  T. W. 905
  V. J. 905
  W. H. 905
  W. M. 810
  W. T. 922
  Alexander 898
  Alfred M. 940
  Elizabeth 991
  Elizabeth P. 940
  Hannah 865, 875
  Hannah B. 941
  James 829
  James B. 896
  Jesse G. 855
  John A. 834
  John F. 852
  John S. 833
  Lemuel 849, 857
  Leonard 853
  Lillie 905
  Marandie J. 898
  Mary 898
  Nancy 905
  Nannie 941
  Ores 905
  William 829, 991
  Willie A. 888
  Wm. 842
Moorhead, Nathaniel 856
More, Eliza 982
Morford, ___ 825
  C. M. 906
  J. F. 818, 819, 905
  Charles R. 885
  Florence M. 906
  Jane 885
  Jane B. 905
  Josiah J. 906
Morgan, ___ 842
  H. 829
  L. B. 835
  Abigail 941
  Barclay 941
  Calladonia D. 941
  Cassandria V. 941
  Elizabeth Clay 989
  Frank A. 941

Morgan, Cont.
  George 836
  Grace M. 941
  Hannah 941
  Harvard 840
  John H. 877
  Lewis B. 834, 941
  Percy A. 941
  Smith 941
Morrison, F. M. 811
Morton, Annie 949
  Harriett 990
  Jacob 949
  Minerva L. 949
Mott, W. H. 853
Moulton, G. A. 843
Mouser, Philip 854
Mullican, Nancy 891
Mulligan, Anderson 815
  Solomon 815
Munford, E. W. 819
  Amelia A. 908
  Ed W. 906
  Edward 907
  George Wythe 906
  James 907
  Lettice 907
  Mary E. 910
  Richard 907
  Thomas 907
  Thomas Bolling 906, 907
  William 906, 907, 910
  William T. 907
Munlacks, Joseph 955
  Mary 955
  Osburn 955
  Sarah 955
Murray, W. T. 910
  Thomas (Thos.) 805, 820, 910
Murry, ___ 806
  T. B. 987
  W. T. 819
  Fannie L. 911
  Mary 911
  Samuel 829, 840
  Thomas V. 819
  William 829
  Wm. 840
Musgrove, Wm. 810
Myers, ___ 984
  J. N. 897
  N. 897
  Josie P. 921
  Leanora 897
  Martha J. 921
  Thomas S. 921
Nash, ___ 830
Neal, H. P. 826
  I. B. 818
  O. D. 911
  P. L. 911
  Alexander 830
  Catherine 892
  Duncan 829
  Elizabeth 911
  Hamilton 892, 911
  Hannah 911
  James 840
  Jennie 888, 911
  Jesse E. 911
  John M. 911
  Joseph B. 911
  Katherine 911
  Lula 911
  Martha 911
  Mary Martha 911
  Nancy Ann 911
  Nancy T. 938
  Robert L. 911
  Sallie 892
  Samuel T. O. 819
  William 911

Neals, Wm. 814
Needham, Mellona 931
Neeley, Nathan 859
Neely, Jane 905
Nelson, ___ 807
  W. E. 804
  Charles H. 799
  James 829, 837
  John 829
  Richard 804
Nesmith, ___ 977
  J. A. 974
  R. B. 973
  Elizabeth M. 973
  James A. 849, 967
  Mary J. 974
  Robt. C. 849
  William A. 973
New, ___ 860
  J. E. 858
Newman, ___ 852
  J. W. 853
Newton, H. P. 914
Nichols, J. W. 859
Nicholson, David 799
North, Wm. 814
Northcup, ___ 820
  James 814
  John A. 814
Northcut, A. 911
  E. W. 912
  James 911
  Sanford 912
  Susan 911
  Susan A. 912
Northcuts, ___ 904
Norton, ___ 842
  J. M. 943
  Allie 942
  Earl L. 942
  Ellen 943
  Glyndon Pearl 942
  James 842
  Mary 943
  Norman 829
  William 941
  William L. 941
Nourse, ___ 811
Norville, A. 905
Norwood, J. W. 810
  S. C. 818, 819
Oakley, James 847
O'Connor, Lavinia W. 870
Officer, J. C. 810
  J. H. 874
  Cynthia 874
  James C. 872
  Leeann 872
  Martha J. 872
  Robert H. 804
  Susan A. 869
  William 874
Ogle, Hercules 799
Ohlemacher, Charles 841
Ohlenmacher, Charles 886
Oldfield, Charles 830
Oldham, Nicholas 803
Oliver, Adam 830
  Anderson 830
  James 830
  John 835
  Sherrill 830
O'Neal, Hugh 829
Orr, Alexander 854
Osborn, Daniel 912
  Mary 912
Overall, D. D. 853
  G. W. 900
  J. H. 847
  Abraham 846, 981
  Cecilia 899
  Hannah 981
  John 852

Overall, Cont.
  Malissa 967
  Parilee A. 981
Overton, Archibald 799
  Archibald W. 804
Owen, M. 821
  Climena 903
Owens, John 835
Paine, Alford 826
  Bird 826
  John R. 826
Palmer, J. B. 992
Parker, ___ 816, 825, 967
  C. 851
  W. E. 937
  John R. 818
  Rachel 943
Parks, James M. 820
Paschal, J. M. 821
Patterson, J. E. 974
  N. A. 833
  W. W. 974
  Catherine 974
  Etta J. 974
  Lucy 974
  Mattie C. 974
  Nora 974
  Robert W. 974
  Samuel F. 974
Patton, R. E. 944
  Daniel 828
  John 828
  Mary E. 944
  Neeley 828
  Thomas 829
Paty, James P. 851
Payne, ___ 824
  T. H. 799
Pea, Thomas 816
Pearce, S. W. 852
  Frank 872
  Mary Ann 872
Pearson, ___ 800
  E. W. 942
  J. E. 842
  Charles 942
  Charles L. 942
  Fanny 942
  James P. 942
  Mary J. 942
  Meredith P. 842
Peck, T. C. 976
  John 850
  Nora 976
Pendleton, ___ 824, 825
  John 857
Penn, Joshua 835
  William 879
Pennington, Edmund 807
Pepper, Elisha 814
Perkins, Isham 819
Perry, ___ 815
Perryman, Alexander 821
Pettit, J. A. 803
Petty, Ambrose 855
  George 854
Phillips, A. T. 951
  H. A. 834
  J. W. 843
  M. C. 829
  Emma 951
  James F. 829
  Martin 846, 849, 857
  William 803
  Wm. 799
Pickett, Anderson 847
Pigg, ___ 962
Pittman, J. J. 833
Pocohontas 949
Polk, James K. 922
Pollard, Edward 800
Pollock, Benjamin 799
Porter, Archibald 815

Potter, ___ 825
　F. 918
　P. G. 912
　T. B. 851
　Arthur 913
　Clyde 913
　Elizabeth 918
　Ella 913
　Fannie 900
　Harriett 912
　James 913
　Melvina 913
　Minnie 913
　Osee 913
　Samantha 900
　Thomas 900, 918
　Watson 912
Potts, A. L. 800
　E. M. 876
　Andrew L. 876
　Catherine 876
　Patrick 876
Powell, James 847
　Lewis 836
　Pairlee 991
　Thomas 857, 858
　William 991
Powers, ___ 842
　Anderson 840
　Effie 941
　Fannie 947
　Henry 829, 941
　Nannie 941
　Thomas 831
Prater, Archibald 814, 856
Preston, E. C. 858
　H. L. 858
　R. H. 860
　Wm., Sr. 855
Price, ___ 840, 853
　C. E. 841
　R. R. 829
　Catherine 876
　Fanny 942
　James 833, 834
Prichard, S. B. 975
　Benjamin 975
　Columbus 975
　Elizabeth 975
　James 975
　Jorden Lee 975
　Lucinda Della 975
　Lucretia Eller 975
　Malissa Ann 975
　Martha Jane 975
　Mary A. 975
　Matilda 975
　Nancy J. 975
　Thomas J. 975
Prier, James 829
Pritchett, James 853
Pyburn, Kit 855
　Wm. 855
Quarels, Caroline 976
　Darthula 976
　Eliza 976
　James D. 976
　James T. 976
　Maud 976
　Nora 976
　Zora 976
　William 976
Quarles, ___ 941
　J. L. 810
　J. T. 810
Quinn, Martin E. 851
Ragon, Robert 829
Ragsdale, Frank 834
　Frank H. 836
Raines, Baden 858
Rains, ___ 814
　J. G. 820
　Isaac 829

Rainwater, C. 830
Ramsey, J. C. 816
　J. R. 913
　O. 919
　S. M. 919
　W. 942
　Ella 933
　Ellen 943
　James C. 933
　Joseph 859
　Lulillian 919
　Mary 913
　Mattie S. 913
　Nancy 884
　Pollie 942
　Rachel 943
　Samuel 942
　William 913
Randals, ___ 806
Randolph, John 893
　Mary P. 893
　Polly 893
Ratan, ___ 806
Rathbone, ___ 842
　D. P. 840
Ray, ___ 852
Rayburn, Adam 829, 832, 834
　Robert S. 829, 832, 834
Read, ___ 825
　E. C. 820
Ready, Charles L. 933
　Chas. 856
Reams, R. M. 826, 914
　Hattie 914
　Joshua M. 914
Reece, ___ 852
Reider, Louisa 901
Renshaw, ___ 811
Reynolds, Elisha 814
　Jack 847
　Jesse 829
　Peter 849, 857
　Wash. 847
　Wylie 852
Rice, T. B. 798, 799, 800, 810
Richards, Sarah 929
Richardson, D. D. 943
　R. H. 842, 943
　T. H. W. 847
　Bernard 848, 849, 847, 851
　George W. 833, 834
　Isaiah 835
　Linda M. 943
　Robert 835
　Thomas E. 943
　Warren W. 943
　William (Wm.) 814, 829
Richmond, Caroline 914
　Cyrus 914
　Job 914
　Ruth 914
Ridley, B. L. 804, 819, 833, 849, 858
Riddle, ___ 961
Riggs, ___ 840
Ritchey, ___ 825
　J. B. 826, 914
Rivers, Henry 829
Rhea & Tynell 798
Rhea, A. E. 804
　Mrs. A. J. 811
　B. S. 804
　John S. 804
Rhoades, J. E. 841
Rhodes, Mary F. 935
Roach, Charles 829
Roberson, J. H. 818
Roberts, G. W. 829
　I. T. 835
　J. S. 876
　Joseph 799
　Mary 877

Roberts, Cont.
　Sarah 876
　William 828, 876
Robertson, A. B. 840
　Elijah 799
　James 800
　John P. 850
　Joseph W. 804
　Peggy 893
　Sibyl 944
　Titia 869
Robinson, J. B. 961
　J. D. 830
　J. E. 977
　L. M. 840
　W. A. 901, 965
　W. T. 847
　Alexander 976
　Alice 977
　Barbary 952
　Catherine 965
　Charley E. 978
　David 977
　Eliza 977
　Eliza Helen 969
　Harry 977
　Henrietta 978
　John 846, 977
　John B. 849, 976, 983
　John Morgan 978
　Julia 977
　Lillie Dale 978
　Lizzie 978
　Margaret E. 977
　Mary 977
　Matilda 975
　Mattie 978
　Rachel 976
　Sallie E. 978
　Sidney 978
　Stephen 977
　William 952
　William Loyd Garrett 977
　Willie 978
　Zelpha 952
Rodgers, A. C. 798
　John B. 811
　Mary A. 862
Rogers, A. C. 826
　Commodore 819
　David S. 882
　Emeline 882
　John 813
　John B. 820
　Levi 814
　Mary 882
Rollin, Ellen 924
Rollings, John 956
　Julia 956
Rooker, Thomas 856
Rooth, John W. 925
Rosborough, J. E. 842
Rosco, E. R. 937
Rose, J. G. W. 855
Rosecrans, ___ 890
Ross, J. C. M. 825
　R. F. 830, 834
　W. M. 843
Roundtree, Tobitha L. 971
Rough, Philip 854
Roughton, J. M. 944
　Elisha H. 922
　Ellender J. 922
　Ida 944
Rowan, Harriet 888
　Stokley D. 819
Rowland, Wm. 799
Rucker, Gideon 855
　James 855
Rudd, Rebecca 936
Rushing, M. P. 990
　Richmond 859
Russ, John 814

Russ, Cont.
  Thomas 814
Russell, W. E. 843
  W. F. 943
  Emmett 943
  Wm. M. 804
Rust, ___ 893
Rutherford, ___ 840
  E. A. 834
Rutland, ___ 852
Rutledge, ___ 843
  H. M. 829
  R. F. 943
  Arthur 829, 830
  Ida 944
  James H. 943
  John 799
  Samuel 943
Safley, David 814
  Jesse 814
Sain, G. T. 840
St. John, A. J. 859
  A. M. 917
  H. J. 858, 987
  George 854
  M. B. 917
  Fatima 917
  John 917
Sales, Cornelius 852
  William 852
Sapp, Margaret 873
Sanders, C. 800
  Elihu 815
Saunders, David 891
  Delilah 940
  Mary K. 891
Savage, J. H. 889, 981
  L. M. 918
  George 815
  John H. 819, 820, 849,
    870, 877, 885, 918, 920,
    958
  Monroe 849
Sayne, Susan 919
Scarborough, ___ 799
Schrader, John 815
Schroeder, George 831
Schure, ___ 852
Schurer, Charles 851
Scott, T. J. 840
  Ed. 835
  Elizabeth 877
  Francis 877
  Jonathan 877
  Mary 877
  Mary E. 903
  Sam 877
  William 849
Scruggs, Eliza 957
  James A. 957
  Sarah F. 957
Seay, Wm. 836
Sadgly, Blake 857
Seitz, A. P. 825
  A. T. 835
Self, Melchesedec 854
Sellers, Matthew 847
Seratt, John 799
Settle, ___ 962
Sevier, ___ 810
Sevillirant, Caleb 855
  Wm. 855
Sewell, ___ 843
  Fatina 917
Shackleford, ___ 840
  D. P. 883
  H. 834
  J. C. 883
Shake, Louisa 937
Shanks, Hannah 892
Sharon, Isaac 799
Sharp, John 799
Shaw, ___ 842

Sheafe, C. A. 835
Sheckley, J. L. 856
Sheid, H. S. 944
Shield, P. C. 806
Sheid, Cara C. 944
  Ella C. 944
  James 829, 944
  James H. 944
  James M. 944
  Jessie L. 944
  Kittie W. 944
  Mary C. 944
  Mary E. 944
  Sibyl 944
  Will F. 944
Shelly, Margaret 877
Shell, James 815
Sherrill, John 829
  Uriah 834
Shields, T. W. 850
  Alexander 824
  William 824
Shockley, J. 865
Short, A. M. 834
Showers, P. T. 849
Shroder, Dora 946
Shurlock, S. B. 890
Simms, E. P. 806
  F. M. 803
  H. L. 820
  Jane 881
  Samuel V. 830
  Wm. G. 804
Simpson, ___ 810, 842
  Atlanta 978
  Catherine 925
  Charles W. 978
  David 829
  Della B. 978
  Eddie 978
  Eva 883
  Horace L. 978
  James 799
  James L. 978
  Jane S. 870
  Jas. 978
  John 851
  John W. 805, 866, 883
  Joseph 855, 857
  Louis E. 978
  Louisa 988
  Mattie 978
  Nancy J. 978
  Pharaba 925
  Robt. D. 978
  Thomas 799, 847, 849, 978
  William T. 978
  Wm. 810
  Wm. M. 806
Simrell, S. 952
  Mary Viola 952
Sims, ___ 830
  J. M. 834
Sinvil, Amanda 862
  Daniel 862
  Rachel 862
Sloan, ___ 826
  Ellen 932
  John L. 932
  Mary J. 932
Smallman, F. H. 806
  M. B. 833
  M. D. 804, 819, 952, 958, 974
  Cordelia 902
  Margret 880
  Nancy A. 886
Smith, ___ 811, 826, 852, 942
  A. P. 980
  C. C. 819
  F. M. 819
  G. R. 851
  J. C. 843

Smith, Cont.
  J. D. 878
  J. G. 860
  J. H. 834
  J. J. 979
  R. A. 858
  R. G. 810
  W. C. 804
  W. G. 805, 806, 877
  W. R. 979
  W. T. 805, 878
  Alfred 980
  Alice P. 980
  Anna V. 945
  Archibald J. 945
  Archibald Y. 945
  Asa 855
  Aubrey 979
  Baxter 987, 989
  Bettie 945
  Cannie 979
  Catherine 974
  Catherine J. 979
  Charles 803
  Charlotte 944
  Clinton 945
  Daniel 980
  Edith May 980
  Effie 979
  Eliza 973
  Eula Leath 980
  Frank K. 945
  George C. 878
  Joel B. 944
  Joel M. 944, 945
  John 814, 818
  John B. 842
  John Bateman 844
  John J. 828
  John Y. 979
  Henry P. 878
  Lawson M. 945
  Linnie Mason 980
  Lollie 979
  Lotta R. 945
  Margaret E. 977
  Martha 878
  Mary A. 885
  Nicholas 846, 847, 973, 977, 980
  Olive Ione 980
  Penelope 980
  Sarah 973, 977
  Thomas 858
  William 829
  William H. 945
  Wm. 814, 830
  Wm. Nicholas 980
  William S. 979
Smithson, A. J. 858
Smart, O. (Miss) 919
Smartt, ___ 826
  A. P. 820
  F. M. 825
  G. W. 915
  H. F. 834
  W. B. 818
  W. C. 821
  W. H. 915
  Ann 915
  Cornelia 915
  George M. 914, 915
  Mary J. 915
  Peggie 914
  William C. 914
  Wm. 814, 819
  Wm. C. 814
Sneed, T. J. 852
  Cynthia 954
  Martha 965
  Nancy 954
  Thomas J. 954, 965
Snipes, Britain 814

Snodgrass, ___ 877
  D. L. 805
  H. C. 800, 805
  J. H. 806, 811
  J. O. 804
  S. M. 800
  David 806
  Fannie L. 911
  James 810, 811
  Jos. 911
  Lue 911
  Samuel 803
  Thomas 811
Solomon, B. J. 820
Southern, D. M. 806
Sowers, Cicero 858
Spangler, George 814
Sparkman, Caroline 861
  Elizabeth 871
Sparks, ___ 826
Sperry, C. L. 800
  T. L. 810
  Thomas 800, 810
Spicer, Burrel 858
Spurlock, ___ 825
  C. J. 819
  D. C. 820
  G. J. 810
  S. B. 825
  Brown 814
  Cicero 820
  Frank 819
  James 814
  John 814
  John L. 819
Squires, J. G. 982
  Cecil H. 982
  Jonathan G. 982
  John 982
  Maria 982
  Mattie F. 982
  Pearl 982
  Sarah C. 982
Stafford, A. 830
Stainback, Clara B. 916
  George T. 915
  George W. 915
  Lucretia T. 915
  Mary 916
Staley, R. M. 843
Stanton, S. S. 867, 874, 881, 895
Starkley, Isaac 814
  Nathan 810
Starnes, ___ 807
Steagall, George W. 843
Steakley, W. L. 819
Steele, ___ 929
  John P. 804, 819
Stephens, E. 860
  J. T. 860
  Elijah 855, 857
  James W. 830
  John 835
Stephenson, B. S. 829
  P. T. 829
  Volney S. 842
Stevens, John 830
  Michael 830, 834
Stewart, D. M. 855
  J. Y. 850, 851
  T. W. 878
  David S. 878
  Elizabeth F. 879
  Frances 878
  Joseph Wyatt 879
  Leonie 879
  Lillian May 879
  Lizzie Gertrude 879
  Martha M. 879
  Martha Maranda 879
  Mary Lucinda 879
  William A. 879

Stipe, Angeline 916
  Dameris N. 916
  George S. 916
  Glaphrey 916
  Glaphrey O. 916
  Jacob 916
  James P. 916
  John 916
  John M. 916
  Lucy E. 916
  Mary F. 916
  Sarah M. 916
Stockstill, ___ 814
Stokes, ___ 852, 980
  W. B. 849, 850
  Fannie 981
  Hannah L. 981
  Harriet A. 981
  Malissa 980
  Mary 980
  Melissia J. 981
  Munford 981
  Norah 981
  Parilee A. 981
  Sallie 981
  Sylvanus 980
  Thos. 980
  W. Jordan 981
  Wm. B. 980
Stone, C. H. 934
  D. G. 825
  I. C. 835, 945
  Ada Flora 946
  Albert Marks 946
  Archibald 855
  Dora 946
  Ella Jane 946
  Iraby Claiborn 946
  John 855
  Parker F. 859
  Sally 945, 946
  Sarah E. 946
  Thomas 945
  Usibid 854
Story, E. 805
  W. F. 805, 879
  Catherine 879
  Ephraim 879
  Hattie E. 879
  Noah W. 879
  Thomas 879
Street, ___ 842
Strong, ___ 842
  Samuel 849
Stroud, B. S. 834, 946
  Fannie 947
  Horace 947
  Nancy 946
  Wade 829, 833
  Walter 829
Strowd, Pollie 942
Stubblefield, W. J. 814
  George 819, 833
Stump, Frederick 934
Stype, Jacob 816
Sugg, Hard 799
Sullivan, A. J. 971
  Charles 814
  Clement 814
  Mary J. 971
Summers, Penelope 980
Sutton, Edmund 855
  Roxanna P. 919
  Westley 829
Swales, Susannah 896
Swan, W. T. 816
Swann, M. E. (Miss) 961
  W. L. 818
  Mary 961
  William 961
Swift, R. A. 800
Swindler, ___ 800
  Clark, Sr. 800

Swofford, Mrs. T. J. R. 811
Talley, P. C. 856
  W. A. 860
  Araminta 951
  Elizabeth 951
  Spencer 951
Tannatt, Tennie 822
Tate, Robert 814
Tatum, Robert F. 860
Taylor, C. J. 931
  E. W. 850
  F. M. 947
  J. W. 800, 879
  N. M. 991
  W. J. 840
  Albert S. 947
  Amanda M. 931
  Andrew J. 947
  Creed A. 879, 880
  Daniel 947
  David 846
  Durinda 963
  Edna 935
  Edmund 854
  Eliza J. 947
  Elizabeth 991
  Isaac 799, 803
  James 817, 830, 835, 854
  Jane B. 905
  John L. 829
  Josephus Z. 947
  Lucinda J. 947
  Lulu F. 947
  Margret 880
  Mary 913, 947
  Narcissa 925
  Richard 909
  Robert E. L. 947
  Roger S. 947
  Sarah E. 947
  Thomas 803
  Thomas E. 806
  William T. 947
Temple, Newton I. 833
Templeton, Amanda R. 878
Terrell, ___ 840
Terry, Joseph 799, 801, 803, 804
Thacker, E. E. 834
Thomas, ___ 840
  F. H. 834
  J. F. 842
  John F. 947
  Joshua 947
  Mary J. 948
Thomason, Pleasant A. 850
Thompson, J. A. H. 860
  J. F. 819
  J. L. 820, 833, 894
  Burwell 949
  David 799
  George 949
  John T. 851
  Lizzie 920
  Nancy 949
  Virginia 949
Throckmorton, ___ 805, 811
Thrower, J. H. 860
Thurman, O. M. 825
Tillford, ___ 815
Tillman, ___ 929
  B. M. 804, 819, 833
  Mrs. C. J. 937
  J. D. 833
  Eliza N. 937
  Elizabeth 937
  Flurina C. 937
  Joseph 937
  Joseph P. 937
  Marshall 962
  Martha J. 937
  Mary A. 937
Timmons, ___ 840

Timmons, Cont.
　James 829
Timmins, Susan 924
Tippitt, Catherine J. 979
Tipton, Stephen 814
Title, Adam 816
Tobe, Enoch 814
Todd, A. F. 858
　James 855
　Jesse 855
　Mary 937
Toliver, Charles 834
　John 830
Towles, J. H. 880
　S. L. 902
　Baxter Benton 880
　Emma J. 880
　Isabel 902
　John W. 820, 880, 901, 902
　Joseph 880
　Lavenia L. 880
　Lucinda 880, 901
　Mary E. 880
　Oliver 901
　Oliver J. 880
Townsend, C. N. 834
Tracey, ___ 962
Tratt, Henry 858
Travis, J. M. 835
　Barton S. 858
　Daniel 854
Troost, ___ 827
Trott, Henry, Jr. 859
　James J. 859
Troxler, Delilah 924
Tubb, E. 851, 959
　L. 852
　Elial 981
　Fannie 981
　James 847, 975
　Jessie Frances 958
　John B. 958
Tunley, Elliott 855
Turner, ___ 814, 840, 852
　E. 847
　F. L. 857
　G. W. 836
　Ann 880, 881
　Edmund 847
　Edward 852
　Frank 881
　James 880, 881, 973
　John 799
　Mary 881
　Mary E. 973
　Wm. 880
Turney, ___ 810
　P. 919
　Hopkins L. 804, 805
　Joseph 849
　Peter 804, 805
　Samuel 804, 958
Tyra, Mrs. N. G. 851
Tyrell, Wm. 799
Tysee, Martha M. 957
Upton, Elizabeth 957
Usselton, A. J. 834
Vanatta, McAdoo 851
Vance, E. B. 858
　T. J. 860
　Samuel 858
Van Dyke, T. Nixon 804
Vanhooser, Ulysses 819
Vannoy, R. M. 835
　Elizabeth 924
Vantrees, John 847
Vaughn, John 799
Vick, Columbus 853
　Eli 853, 982
　Eliza 982
　Lucinda 961
　Sarah A. 983
　Sarah C. 982

Vick, Cont.
　Will A. 853, 983
　William 853, 969, 983
Vincent, A. F. 841
　B. F. 858
　Richard 854
Vining, Thomas 799
Voss, John 803
Wade, P. M. 851
　T. M. 849
　T. W. 977. 984
　W. W. 804, 849, 850, 851,
　　958, 983
　Bartlett 855
　Burrell 834
　Caroline 983
　Ida Belle 984
　Louella 983
　Mary E. 958, 984
　Memucan 807
　Pleasant M. 849
　Thomas 799
　Timothy W. 983
　Wm. H. 983
　Wm. M. 983, 984
Wafford, Nancy 949
Waggoner, J. A. 948
　J. W. 948
　Addie M. 948
　Alice G. 948
　Eliza 948
　James H. 948
　James N. 948
　Nannie R. 948
　Rebecca 948
　William H. 948
Wagoner, J. W. 834
Wait, W. 842
Wakeman, ___ 800
Walden, Geo. W. 842
Walk, ___ 846, 853
Walker, E. W. 836
　Claude 985
　Hampton 984
　John G. 829, 831, 834
　Laura 985
　Mary 925, 984
　Mary Jane 985
　Nancy 951
　Samuel 984
　Samuel Rosco 985
　Sarah H. 985
Wallace, D. F. 826, 914
　S. D. 800
　Matilda 883
　Perry S. 826
　Rush N. 829
　Wallace 826
Walling, H. L. 822, 825
　J. N. 811
　S. D. 818
　S. J. 818, 843
　C. Jesse 825
　Jesse 820, 825
　Joseph 879
　Katie 879
　Sarah 879
　Smith J. 803
Walt, A. 836
Walters, Mary A. 950
Ward, ___ 842, 843
　H. B. 800, 881
　R. H. 948
　Annie Pearl 882
　Bessie 881
　Christianna 881
　Elam 881
　Ella M. 881
　James 858
　James F. 948
　Jared 881
　Maggie C. 882
　Margaret J. 939

Ward, Cont.
　Milton 846
　Nannie M. 961
　Noah 948
　Norman A. 881
　Sallie 881
　Sallie M. 882
Ware, Helen 986
　Richard 814
　Wylie 814
Warren, ___ 810
　Arthur 854
　Bluford 861
　Elizabeth 991
　John 811
　Sarah 861
Washington, Mary 912
Waterhouse, R. G. 915
　Ann 915
　Elizabeth 915
Waters, L. B. 822
　S. 850
　Lucy 974
Watkins, Alemia A. 908
　Paul J. 908
Watson, Virgie R. 883
Watt, Henry 859
Watterson, William S. 829, 831
Weatherford, John Q. 858
Weaver, Benjamin 799, 801
　Mary 921
Webb, ___ 825
　A. J. 917
　B. M. 849, 952
　D. W. 985
　F. Z. 851
　G. H. 917
　J. K. P. 820
　H. B. 917
　J. Z. 851
　Amanda 864
　Bethel Magness 985
　Biras 815
　Carrie 986
　Chesley 815
　Didama 917
　Hallie 986
　Helen 986
　Isham 917
　James 815, 913, 917
　Jane 917
　Joseph 917
　Julius 985
　Malvina 917
　Martha J. 875
　Mary 894, 913, 917
　Mary E. Dovey 917
　Mattie 986
　Melvina 913
　Nora 986
　Robert Bethel 986
　Robert L. 917
　Sarah 962, 985
　Thomas 917
　Virginia 962
　Watson 962
Webster, Jonathan 829, 830,
　　836
Weedon, Harriett 956
Weel, ___ 961
Wells, Mary J. 942
Wendel, Annie 822
West, E. J. (Miss) 902
　R. B. 851
　John 894
　Julia E. 894
　Martha P. 969
　Samantha 900
　Sarah A. 983
　Thomas 846
Westmoreland, Joseph 817, 818
Whaley, S. B. 851
　Elijah 851

Whaley, Cont.
  Eliza 969
  Isaac 969
  Nancy 969
  Thomas 846, 850
Wheeler, ___ 868
  J. D. 852
  Isabel 902
Wherry, Jackson 854
Whitaker, Martha 939
White, ___ 810
  H. J. 900
  Hugh L. 982
  James 840
  John 799
  Moses F. 830, 833, 834
  Wm. 820
  Woodson P. 883
Whitehead, James 799
Whiteman, W. S. 841
Whitesides, James 833
Whitlock, James 814
Whitman, I. W. 942
Whitrock, James 815
Whitson, W. V. 819, 833
  Elizabeth 971
Whittaker, David 856
Whitworth, E. M. 948
  Benjamin F. 948
  Hattie 949
  Minerva L. 949
  Virginia 949
Whorley, Kittie 959
Whorton, ___ 807
Wiggins, Herald 829
  Hunley 829
Wilcher, Thomas 799
Wildman, Francis E. 924
Wilhite, James 800
  Stephen 800
Wiley, H. A. 987, 989
Wilkerson, ___ 840
Wilkinson, A. L. 918
  B. C. 917
  Bell 918
  Cleveland L. 918
  Elizabeth 918
  Fatima 918
  George L. 918
  George W. 917
  John F. 918
  Mary 917, 918, 943
  Millie 926
  Thomas B. 918
  William D.918
Willey, Caroline 914
Williams, ___ 800, 841, 843, 941
  D. O. 849
  E. H. 918
  E. N. 918
  F. A. 803
  J. J. 833
  N. W. 799, 918
  O. D. 852
  W. E. 919
  Alice 919
  Charley 919
  Chas. 965
  Cleve 816
  Delia 963
  Elijah 799
  Fannie 919
  Frank 919
  James 800
  Janie 919
  John 799
  Josephine 965
  Nancy 951
  Nannie M. 919
  Nathaniel 804
  Thomas 855
  Thomas J. 858

Williams, Cont.
  Tim H. 867
  Wm. 830
  Wm. B.834
Willis, ___ 840
  S. 927
  Cynthia E. 927
  Peter 829
Wilson, ___ 815, 826
  C. T. 834, 841
  L. M. (Miss) 901
  M. L. 851
  R. 842, 843, 943
  T. J. 833, 841, 844
  W. T. 834
  Allen 901
  Charles T. 834
  Elizabeth 901
  Henry 829
  Isaac 814
  James 883
  John 814
  John A. 817, 821, 824
  Lucinda 880, 901
  Mumford 800
  Nancy E. 883
  Rebecca 883
  Thomas 814
  Wisley 816
Winfrey, Nancy 963
  Tabitha 962
Winstead, E. 882
  J. W. 882
  W. J. 862
  W. W. 882
  Emeline 882
  Ephraim 882
  Margaret 882
  Mary M. 882
  Nancy J. 882
  Serener E. 882
Winter, James 799
Winton, ___ 840
  J. C. 949
  P. H. 919
  Blanche 949
  Clark 949
  Edwin 949
  Emma O. 919
  Harris S. 919
  James 829
  John 949
  Lulillian 919
  Martha 949
  McRamsey 919
  Nancy 946
  Stephen 829, 835, 919
  Susan 919
  Wooton 949
Witherby, J. B. 842, 923
  Joel 923
  Mrs. 837
Witherspoon, A. B. 905
  V. J. (Miss) 905
  Jane 905
Witt, Mary Jane 864
Witten, ___ 905
Wolfe, Anne 890
Womack, ___ 811, 814, 825
  F. M. 835
  J. J. 820
  S. L. (Miss) 902
  W. C. (Mrs.) 825, 826
  Abner 815
  Isham 829
  James 851
  Wm. 815
Wood, ___ 852
  J. H. 859
  S. H. 949
  W. J. 858
  Ed. J. 821
  Edmund J. 919, 920

Wood, Cont.
  Elizabeth 949
  Grand 859
  Jales 954
  James 855, 858
  John 854, 855, 949
  John H. 919
  John S. 858
  Lizzie 920
  Lun 954
  Mary F. 949
  Mary J. 949
  Mattie 954
  Rachel A. 956
  Roxanna P. 919
  Sarah C. 949
  Susan 949
  Thomas 949
  Thomas C. 859
  Thomas G. 855, 858
  Walter 855
  William 855
Woodard, A. B. 833
Woodbury, Levi 857
Woodlee, Elijah 888
  James 904
Woodley, John 813, 814, 815, 816
  Milton 825
Woods, A. 842
  James L. 834
  Waymond L. 804
Wooldridge, John 846
Woolsey, Catherine 879
Wooton, ___ 840, 949
  J. D. 841, 950
  Fannie 950
  Jesse 829, 831, 833
  Jonathan 950
  Lillie 950
  Nancy 950
  Wade H. 950
Wright, D. S. 829
  I. N. 810
  R. V. 850
  Allen T. 847
  John 855
  William 847
Wyatt, Hiram 830
Wylie, ___ 860
  H. A. 859
  William A. 840
Yates, J. W. 843, 950
  Ida 950
  James 950
  Lillie May 951
  Mary A. 950
  Sarah 861
  Wilton Earl 951
Yell, Archibald 945
  Bettie 945
York, F. M. 820
  Byron M. 921
  George W. 920
  Josie P. 921
  Martha 920
  Thomas 820
  Thomas W. 921
  William L. 921
  William T. 920
Young, ___ 853
  C. C. 810
  J. S. 886
  O. F. 880
  W. B. 883
  W. M.810, 811
  Bettie C. 883
  Charles C. 883
  Elizabeth 882
  Emma J. 886
  Eva 883
  Frank S.883
  Hayden M. 883

Young, Cont.
  James 810, 882, 955
  James E. 883
  John 882
  John S. 826
  Martha 955, 969
  Mary E. 884
  Matilda 883
  Minnie L. 884
  Nancy 955
  Nancy E. 883
  Nettie C. 884
  Oliver F. 882
  Sallie R. 883
  Samuel 852
  Samuel A. 883
  Sarah 882
  Stephen H. 884
  Virgie R. 883
  William M. 883
  Wm. 810
Youngblood, B. F. 816
  Allen 814
Zachery, Ann 915
Zell, D. D. (Miss) 943
  F. M. 943
  James 829, 932
Zergin, ___ 852
Zollicoffer, ___ 867
Zwingle, Christopher C. 880
  Emma J. 880
  Lavenia 880

www.ingramcontent.com/pod-product-compliance
Lightning Source LLC
Chambersburg PA
CBHW020648300426
44112CB00007B/294